Avengers Infinity Saga and Philosophy

D1226035

Popular Culture and Philosophy® Series Editor: George A. Reisch

For full details of all Popular Culture and Philosophy® books, visit www.opencourtbooks.com.

Popular Culture and Philosophy®

Avengers Infinity Saga and Philosophy

Go for the Head

Edited by
ROBERT ARP AND
HEATHER L. RIVERA

OPEN COURT
Chicago

Volume 131 in the series, Popular Culture and Philosophy®, edited by George A. Reisch

To find out more about Open Court books, visit our website at www.opencourtbooks.com.

Open Court Publishing Company is a division of Carus Publishing Company, dba Cricket Media.

Copyright © 2020 by Carus Publishing Company, dba Cricket Media

First printing 2020

Printed and bound in the United States of America.

Avengers Infinity Saga and Philosophy: Go for the Head

ISBN: 978-0-8126-9485-7

Library of Congress Control Number: 2020933880

This book is also available as an e-book (ISBN 978-0-8126-9487-1).

Contents

A Seriously Mind-Blowing Book about Seriously Mind-Blowing Movies

What do all Bad Guys have in common, whether in the fictional or the real world?

They all treat people like mere objects and use them to get whatever it is they want—and these people at the very least are harmed emotionally or physically, and at the most die horrible deaths.

Serial killers use victims to satisfy the desire for power, or control, or to "stop the voices." Sexual predators who have sex with young women while duping them into thinking they're "connected" to the porn business are not only deceiving them, but they're using them like sexual objects. While staying late at the office one evening, a businessperson bucking for a promotion discovers that the co-worker who's in competition for the same position left his excellent report on his desk, and she decides to copy it and turn it in to corporate as her own report. Not only is it stealing and plagiarizing, but she's effectively using him (his thoughts, experiences, and writing skills) to get the promotion.

Governments, institutions, and corporations will use people too: consider the way Stalin's or Mao Zedong's Communism used people and murdered them; the same with Hitler's Third Reich; or even the number of bastards complicit in the Enron scandal, where innocent people—and their bank accounts—were treated like trash.

Why does using a person bother us so much? Put simply, we think that a human is the most important, respect-worthy, and sacred thing in existence. That's why almost every moral code, whether it's secular or religious, has rules against unjust killing as well as rules in favor of individual rights, the primary one being a right to life.

But there are times when it seems like a person should be used. Consider the soldier who jumps on the grenade, killing himself, but saving ten others nearby. We call that person a hero. Of course, he did it willingly. But, we know it was the right thing to do, or so it seems. There's not much of a stretch, then, from "One person did, in fact, willingly give her/himself to save ten" to "One person SHOULD give her/himself to save ten."

That's Thanos's thinking. It's utilitarian, through and through. A utilitarian thinks that the moral decision is the one that creates the most benefit for the most people involved, even if it means some have to suffer or die in order to achieve that benefit.

In order to save the universe from overpopulation—which, in turn, would cause over-consumption of resources and, ultimately, the DESTRUCTION of the universe—Thanos has to sacrifice half of the consuming universe. In other words, people—and people-like entities—need to be "put to use" by being put to death!

So Thanos is actually a strictly moral being! Can you believe that?!? (At least, from a utilitarian perspective . . .)

That should blow your mind.

In fact, you have to keep reading, because some of these mind-blowing chapters explores Thanos's moral perspective and his mental health. Other chapters look at the mind-blowing implications of time travel. And others . . .

Well, you've seen the movies, and you've already started to think about some of the deep philosophical issues these movies raise. The next step on your path to Enlightenment? Read this book.

I

The Snap

1
Rights and Wrongs of Reversing the Snap

Philip M. Mouch

Imagine your spouse didn't come home one day. In fact, the news is full of reports that lots of people seem to have vanished. Later you discover it has something to do with those superheroes. (You knew the Sokovia Accords were a good idea that didn't go far enough.)

Devastated by the loss of your loved one, you arrange a memorial service. Indeed, you spend the next couple of months attending memorial services for lost loved ones, friends, neighbors, and co-workers. After that, things begin to take on a semblance of normalcy. In some ways, things are even better than before: ample housing and food supply made available due to the reduced population has nearly eliminated homelessness and hunger.

After a year, you still grieve for your spouse, but it has become clear that the surviving heroes aren't going to do anything to bring everyone back. They help in ways that they can, but you know that it's up to you to get your life back on track. However, it's another year before you're able to bring yourself to start going on dates. Many of the early ones involve tears, as nearly everyone lost someone in what some have started calling the Snap. But over time the stories have been told and other topics of conversation come to dominate. After yet another year, you find someone who makes you happy. You date and eventually marry, finally able to move forward with your life.

Undoing the Snap

Two more years into your new life, your missing spouse returns, with no knowledge of the previous five years. They

3

didn't know they were away. For them, it was just this morning that they last saw you. They come back to find out you have remarried and started a brand-new life with someone else. Further, the family that used to live in your apartment (you moved in three years ago to be closer to your job) has suddenly reappeared and wants to know why you are living there.

Laws are quickly passed to protect the property rights of those who survived the Snap, as well as suspending polygamy laws at least temporarily so that relationships may be sorted out. Charitable organizations begin fixing up abandoned homes to provide housing for those who suddenly find themselves displaced. Meanwhile disputes over jobs, assets, and relationships drive wedges between those who had vanished, and those who survived the Snap. The most pressing concern is the rampant food shortages as agriculture had been pared back significantly because of the reduced demand. Political turmoil also erupts as some of the returning politicians expect to still hold office, though they have long since been replaced. Meanwhile, the heroes who had miraculously brought back billions of people seem unable to find solutions to the many problems created by their actions.

Stories like this one must have played out many times in the aftermath of *Avengers: Endgame*. Iron Man, Captain America, and the other Avengers recover the Infinity Stones that Thanos used in *Avengers: Infinity War* to end half of life in the universe in order to bring back all those who vanished. While those who had vanished in the Snap (in *Infinity War*) returned, new problems arose.

Rights and Wrongs of the Return

We know from *Spider-Man: Far from Home* that at least some of the things imagined above did happen. People were displaced from homes. Peter Parker's Aunt May is working with a charity to help those displaced by events during their five-year absence. People who had moved into new housing suddenly found the old occupants returned. One of Peter Parker's classmates returned to discover that her younger brother was now older than she was. Though that movie touches on these issues only briefly, we know that they did come to pass. After five years, the world has changed, and by bringing back those who vanished, problems great and small are created. Are those problems enough to argue against undoing the Snap?

What makes an action wrong? Philosophy has not discovered a single answer that is acceptable to everyone, but it has given us some insights. Consequences for actions are relevant when evaluating different possible actions. "The road to Hell is paved with good intentions," after all. If an action harms people, it should make us reconsider whether we ought to do it. On the other hand, we don't think "The ends justify the means" either, so the consequences are not the only things that matter. The rights of others also are relevant to moral decision-making.

These two sayings are overused, but they still offer important insights. We don't generally think that only intentions matter (since good intentions can still lead to harmful results), and we also don't think that only the consequences matter (since, we can do a lot of wrong in bringing about a good outcome). Often the best we can do is balance out the competing concerns and arrive at a decision that at least acknowledges the complexities of the issue before us.

Hunger and Homelessness

In the matter of relationships, certainly half the world's population suddenly returning would create a lot of confusion and difficulties for many people. With respect to a romantic couple, unless both people disappeared or both remained, there will be issues navigating the five years they were apart, in large measure because one half of the couple will think no time at all has passed. Yet however complicated and uncomfortable these reunions may be, any harms caused by the return of those who disappeared would seem to be heavily outweighed by undoing the harms initially caused to them. After all, just because it may be inconvenient for a missing spouse to return doesn't mean that the spouse shouldn't be saved if possible.

Weighing the inconvenience, and even the likely emotional distress, of a loved one returning unexpectedly against the harm done by cutting that loved one's life short is a very easy calculation. Similar considerations apply to questions of property rights. Difficulties in working out problems for either interpersonal relationships or ownership of property, no matter how serious, don't outweigh the value of people's lives. No doubt these matters will be complicated, but we ought not to make people sacrifice their lives to avoid these difficulties.

The most serious problems seem to be the distribution of power and resources. Unless there is some way to generate food quickly, doubling the population instantaneously will mean that many people are likely to suffer from starvation. Many people, both survivors of the Snap as well as those recently returned, will die from lack of sufficient food, medicine, and other necessities. Further, while sorting out who has rights to a house or an apartment may be thorny, convincing a political leader who returns that they are no longer in power may lead to power struggles that could ultimately end in war. The heroes might be able to help with that second issue, but we have no evidence that they can provide for an additional four billion people.

Here, then, is something that might properly give us pause. In *Avengers: Infinity War*, Thanos explained to Gamora his reason for wiping out half of all life in the universe: "It's a simple calculus. This universe is finite; it's resources, finite. If life is left unchecked, life will cease to exist. It needs correction." While there are many good reasons to question Thanos's justification prior to his action, now that the deed has been done and the world adjusted to the new reality, is it right to bring back 3.5 billion people only to have many of them suffer from starvation and death? What's more, possibly causing the death of at least some of those who survived? No matter who suffers from not enough food, is it really good to bring about a situation where many will? Perhaps it matters how many will survive, but how to draw that line? If we brought back 3.5 billion people, and that led to the death by starvation of 3.5 billion people, was it worth it? Haven't we just caused a lot of unnecessary additional suffering? What if only two billion people die? One billion?

We might wonder whether the Stones themselves could undo the disappearances without at least some of the worst consequences imagined above. It's always a bit odd to try to impose real-world issues on the fantastical worlds inhabited by superheroes. The rules that govern what can happen are always a bit fuzzy. In a world where magic exists, and where technology borders on the magical, exactly what can and cannot be done is often left up to the demands of the story, so we cannot say with much exactness what is possible for the Infinity Stones to accomplish. However, we do know that there are limits to what the Stones can do. Bruce Banner/The Hulk uses the newly recovered Infinity Stones to bring back those destroyed in The Snap. He tells Hawkeye that he tried to bring back Black Widow, who had sacrificed herself to retrieve the Soul Stone. However, he was unable to revive her, so we know the Stones cannot do absolutely everything. But perhaps providing food and such is not beyond the purview of the Stones and the worst situations would not come to pass.

We do know, from *Spider-Man: Far from Home*, that housing problems were not taken care of in the Hulk's use of the Stones.

No mention is made of food shortages, though, so perhaps important resources were accounted for by the Hulk. Without knowing more of how things worked, this is all speculation. For example, we see in *Spider-Man: Far from Home*, people returning to places they were at the time of The Snap. A basketball game at the school was interrupted by people returning to the court. That raises questions about people who disappeared while flying on airplanes or while driving cars. Do they reappear in the vehicles, or in the places they were (on the highway or well into the air)? While genies (and other wish granters) are notoriously picky about wording, perhaps the Infinity Stones aren't and many of these problems never arise.

Gambling with Time

Still, there's no real consideration of any of these concerns by our heroes. The closest we come to seeing such consideration is Tony Stark's insistence that nothing about the last five years is to be changed. Bring people back, but don't undo the time that has passed. His reason for this concern is clear: He doesn't want to lose the daughter that he and Pepper Potts had and raised. He saw the dangers of undoing The Snap, and was careful to avoid them. So perhaps the worst dangers we might imagine were also foreseen and avoided. While those may be interesting stories to tell from one perspective, they don't fit neatly into a superhero action movie, so they weren't given any screen time. Still, if this problem cannot be addressed in some way, it would count as a serious objection to undoing The Snap.

While the problems raised by returning all life that had vanished in The Snap may be troubling but ultimately resolvable, there is another, more serious problem: What if the heroes fail? The ramifications of failure are devastating. When the Avengers go back in time to find the Infinity Stones, Bruce Banner is charged with retrieving the Time Stone. Because Doctor Stephen Strange has not yet had the accident that would lead him to become the Sorcerer Supreme, the Time Stone is still possessed by the Ancient One. She explains to Banner that if he were to take the Time Stone, it would cause a divergence in the timeline. In this new reality, the universe, without the protection offered by the Time Stone, would be imperiled with horrific consequences for the inhabitants of the new timeline. For this reason, she refuses to hand the Stone over to Banner. She only relents upon discovering that Doctor Strange, during the fight with Thanos, handed over the Time Stone. Since she trusts the man Strange would become, she agrees to relinquish the Stone to Banner, who promises to return it so the divergence in the timeline can be collapsed and the past protected.

The Ancient One is not very specific when it comes to the threat the absence of the Time Stone poses: "Remove one of the stones, and that flow of time splits. Now this may benefit your reality, but my new one, not so much. In this new branch reality, without our chief weapon against the forces of darkness, our world would be overrun. Millions will suffer." One such threat we know about is Dormmamu. Doctor Strange used the Time Stone to force Dormmamu's surrender. Presumably, there are other threats as well. If, however, we take the Ancient One literally here, only millions are threatened by the absence of the Time Stone. Compared to the countless lives across the universe lost in The Snap, risking millions of lives may be worth it. Millions of lives is a lot, but compared to even just the 3.5 billion or so lives lost on Earth, it might be worth the risk.

But I don't think we should take the Ancient One's concern that literally. Just before the lines just quoted, she said, "If I give up the Time Stone to help your reality, I'm dooming my own." I'm not arguing that millions of lives lost wouldn't be a tragedy, but that number doesn't sound like the doom of an entire reality. I don't think the Ancient One is trying to express the literal nature of the threat, but merely throwing out a number to help dramatize what is at stake. (Alternatively, the writers weren't being very careful about that particular line.)

We might wonder what the chances are, what the risk really is. After all, if we're almost certain to succeed, such a wager might be acceptable. Usually, we are unaware of what the chances of success are, but not this time. We know that our heroes' odds of success are 1 in 14,000,605. Doctor Strange, in *Avengers: Infinity War*, looked at the possible outcomes in the future, surveying over fourteen million of them, and discovered that the heroes succeed in only one of them. It is that one chance that Banner's promise to return the Time Stone hangs upon. If they fail, they will likely be unable to return the Stone, and the Ancient One's concern for the divergent timeline will become reality.

(One of the things not addressed in the film is what will happen to the universe given that the Infinity Stones were destroyed by Thanos. Captain America returns the Stones to their proper place in history, thus avoiding the split in realities the Ancient One warned against. Her concerns, though, sound general: it's not just that the Time Stone is necessary to protect reality at that moment in history, but it is a general defense against the forces of darkness. Yet, in the heroes' present, Thanos has already destroyed the Stones. Why has that time not descended into darkness? This opens the possibility that the Ancient One was lying about the dangers of handing over the Stone to Banner. That line of inquiry, however, goes beyond the topic of this chapter, so I'll dismiss it as a curious hiccup in the script and proceed as though the Ancient One was telling the truth.)

Consider the risk Banner is asking the Ancient One to take. It's one thing to sacrifice yourself for others, but it's quite another thing to sacrifice someone else. In *Avengers: Endgame*, we see both Hawkeye and Black Widow try to sacrifice themselves so that the other might live and retrieve the Soul Stone. While the sacrifice is tragic, we also admire it; it was a noble sacrifice, giving up oneself for the good of others. Contrast that with Thanos's sacrifice of Gamora in *Avengers: Infinity War*. Even if we thought Thanos's goals were admirable, killing someone else—without their consent—to bring about those goals strikes us as villainous. It is a violation of Gamora's rights. (If she had volunteered, that would have been a different situation.)

Which of these two examples does Banner's request most resemble? He is not wagering his life to retrieve the Time Stone. Rather he is wagering the lives of all of those in the timeline created by removing the Time Stone, and it's a wager for a 1 in 14 million chance. While his goal is easier to defend than Thanos's, it doesn't give him the right to gamble with the lives of others, certainly not with so many lives and on such flimsy chances.

The Downside of Resurrection

Should Banner attempt to retrieve the Time Stone to undo The Snap? Considering the potential consequences, considering that the heroes would be putting countless of innocent lives at risk to return to life those already destroyed, it's hard to see how the answer could be yes. The potential consequences are heavily weighted against the heroes succeeding, and failure in this situation puts the same number at risk that they are trying to save. Further, they would be using lives of others in a gamble to rescue some. (Note, they are not asking those who are alive whether they are willing to take the chance.) This would violate the right to life of those innocents who they would put at risk. So, both the likely consequences and the rights of others would argue against the heroes taking the risk and undoing The Snap.

We might be tempted to say that, since the heroes do succeed, "All's well that ends well." However, the success of the heroes is not the point, especially since Banner cannot know they will succeed when he speaks with the Ancient One. He is pursuing a course which is very likely to fail and will lead to even more death and suffering. Since at the time he asks for the Time Stone, success seems very unlikely, it's still wrong to risk so many lives.

None of this is to argue that Thanos was right to perform The Snap in the first place. Even if Thanos meant well, the means by which he went about achieving his goals violates the rights of all those whose lives were snuffed out. But simply because he acted badly, it does not mean that absolutely anything goes in response. Specifically, if it puts countless more lives in very real jeopardy, we threaten to repeat Thanos's mistake, rather than undo it.

Obviously, we want the heroes to win. Watching Spider-Man dissolve into dust in Tony Stark's arms was heart-wrenching, and it's not difficult to understand the impulse to undo all those deaths if possible. But, as Thanos's own example illustrates, it's not enough to want to achieve some noble end if the means you must take to get there tramples on the rights of countless others.

Thanos ignored the rights of half of the universe in order to bring the balance he thought was needed to preserve life. Our heroes also ignore the rights of countless beings in order to undo the death Thanos has brought about. It may be trite to say, but in this case, two wrongs do not make a right.

2
What Does Life Mean after the Snap?

JOHN ALTMANN AND ANGEL L. G.

You're lying on the couch with this book in your hand when you look up and see your mother and father in the kitchen making dinner. Your sister is in her room and everything seems like a typical Friday night in your household when suddenly your mother is utterly terrified and a scream rises from her throat. You look up and see your Father disintegrating into nothingness and soon your Mother follows suit.

You're confused and scared, you rush out to see your neighbors outside of their homes frightened and wondering aloud in fear what has happened to their family and friends. Days pass and you realize that what had happened to your community, had occurred to half of all life on Earth. Businesses from all over have gone under, entire militaries have collapsed, and the world tentatively hangs in the balance. In the aftermath of such wide-scale death, what has become of life for the living? How will they respond to such an atrocity? Perhaps the bigger question is how will they be *defined* by it?

This is the question Thanos leaves the Avengers with after his fateful Snap with the Infinity Gauntlet in *Endgame*. How do beings with power that defies human imagination including among them Thor who is legitimately a God, live with themselves when their power was meaningless in the face of great evil?

Iron Man, The Incredible Hulk, and Hawkeye all answer this very question throughout the course of *Endgame*. Their answers come from superheroes in philosophy whose powers allowed them to boldly ask such questions and to afford them the best answer such questions and give hope to others. These superheroes were known as Existentialists, who all had to deal with the significant events of their time the same way the

Avengers had to contend with Thanos. Their names are Friedrich Nietzsche, Albert Camus, Jean-Paul Sartre, and Emmanuel Levinas and by the end of this chapter, dear reader, it is our hope that you will discover the superhero in yourself as it relates to philosophy, and ask the most meaningful questions of life itself with absolute courage. Existentialists Engage!

Tony Stark and Human Freedom

Early on in *Avengers: Endgame*, Tony Stark and Nebula are adrift in space as Tony seemingly comes to terms with his impending death. He's exhausted and weak, his eyes have lost all life in them and with his last bit of strength, he grabs his Iron Man helmet and records his final days including saying goodbye and affirming his love to Pepper Potts, whom he hopes recovers the helmet after his death.

Just when death seems to be about to claim Tony, Captain Marvel shows up and returns the ship to the new location of the Avengers back on Earth. Though depleted of most of his strength and will, Tony still has enough to confront Steve Rogers about the issues between them stemming from past movies including *Civil War*, before finally fainting and needing to recover from his whole ordeal.

As Tony heals up, the Avengers led by Captain Marvel, find Thanos and ambush him but discover that the Infinity Stones were destroyed by him so that his mass murder of half the Earth's population could not be undone. After Thor decapitates Thanos and the team comes to terms with this revelation, five years pass and Tony discovers the greatest power he possesses is not his Iron Man suit, but the power of human freedom and self-determination.

In the five years since the Snap wiped out half of the world's population, Tony Stark has created his own sanctuary of peace amidst the wide-scale grief and devastation. He's living in a cabin with Pepper Potts and their daughter Morgan, a life that is the complete opposite of the life he had so long been accustomed to living as a rich playboy and the head of Stark Industries.

Tony feels a sense of peace with this new life so much so that when Steve Rogers, Scott Lang, and Natasha Romanoff propose the idea of going back in time and stealing the Infinity Stones, otherwise known as a time heist, Tony sends them away. But Tony ultimately figures out a way to travel through time successfully so as to defeat Thanos before he can get all of the Infinity Stones together and assemble the Infinity

Gauntlet. The only question that remains for Tony is how he will exercise his freedom. Will he return to the Avengers and bring to them the means of stopping Thanos or will the answer die with him as he instead looks ahead to a tranquil life with Pepper and Morgan?

This problem that Tony wrestles with is one that Jean-Paul Sartre (1905–1980) confronted in his writings. Among them was an essay titled "Existentialism Is a Humanism," which can be boiled down to the phrase "Existence precedes Essence." What Sartre argued was that while many people held the view that God fashioned us to be who we are, that our human freedom is what allows us to essentially define ourselves. Thanos might fancy himself a God, but neither he nor anyone else controls the path either Tony or any of the Avengers take in life. That responsibility of creating his own path rests entirely upon Tony's shoulders and is created through the exercise of his freedom.

In the end, Tony not only chooses to return to the Avengers with the key to successful time travel and thwarting Thanos, but towards the end of the grand battle when Thanos goes to snap his fingers with the Gauntlet, he fails as Tony took it from him and wore it himself. Tony would then snap Thanos and all of the devastation he caused out of existence. His last words before the snap were "I am Iron Man." In the end, that was how Tony defined himself: through his freedom and by choosing to the very end to be Iron Man, he preserved the freedom of billions. It was the Human Freedom of Tony Stark that gave Iron Man the strength to achieve the feats of a God.

To Hulk Smash the Boulder or Not

When we first lay eyes on the jolly green giant in *Avengers: Endgame* we notice that he fits all three of those descriptions but with a shocking new twist. He's wearing shirts now! After spending eighteen months experimenting in the gamma lab and after his embarrassing double defeat at the hands of Thanos, the Hulk and Bruce Banner are now merged as one. Despite his numerous attempts in the past to prevent this very same thing from happening, Bruce seemingly has had a drastic change of heart on how he views his alter ego saying: "For years I've been treating the Hulk like he is some kind of disease, something to get rid of. But then I started looking at him as the cure." Who can dispute that with the unlimited brute strength of the Hulk mixed with the immense intellect of Bruce Banner, you'd have a formidable foe that any team would want on their side?

At the diner we even got to see the Hulk fully embrace his new body and mind combo by taking photos with some of his tiniest fans (thanks to Ant-Man for snapping the photo). What this shows us (and Black Widow who was seemingly impressed) is that much like Tony Stark, Bruce has embraced his life after the Snap mostly by removing the source of his biggest existential angst. And angst is something Albert Camus (1913–1960) has a lot to say about in his book *The Myth of Sisyphus.*

In this book we see the following passage that pretty much sums up as to how we could possibly get to this point where Bruce and Hulk become one:

> All great deeds and all great thoughts have a ridiculous beginning. Great works are often born on a street-corner or in a restaurant's revolving door. So it is with absurdity.

Bruce's idea to merge himself with the green brute must have come during a time he fell into the void of the Absurd and who could blame him (or them)? After all Thanos's Snap wiped out half of the world in a random and unpredictable kind of way. There's no telling how many families were broken up or hospitals left without attending doctors or nurses. It's possible that Banner also reached the same conclusion Camus did with this next passage:

> There is no longer a single idea explaining everything, but an infinite number of essences giving a meaning to an infinite number of objects. The world comes to a stop, but also lights up.

The point behind the story of the myth of Sisyphus is to imagine someone like the Hulk rolling a giant boulder up a hill for an infinite number of years. We all know Hulk has unlimited strength and stamina but how would Bruce's psychological well-being hope to stand up to this over time? The solution is found at the end of the story:

> I leave Sisyphus at the foot of the mountain! One always finds one's burden again. But Sisyphus teaches the higher fidelity that negates the gods and raises rocks. He too concludes that all is well. This universe henceforth without a master seems to him neither sterile nor futile. Each atom of that stone, each mineral flake of that night filled mountain, in itself forms a world. The struggle itself toward the heights is enough to fill a man's heart. One must imagine Sisyphus happy.

Later on in the movie when the Hulk time travels with the rest of his Avenger pals, he sees his past version of himself and is immediately embarrassed. He watches how the Hulk pulverizes parked cars as much as he does any enemy standing in his way. The new Hulk looks on and wonders why he wasn't more passive or at least had more control over his aggression. The new Hulk cannot relate to the rage expressed by the old Hulk because he has finally found his happy place. In the end it does not matter how often the Hulk and others are called to save the world, what matters is that they find joy in it, whether it comes from saving the world or assembling to make fun at Ant-Man's expense.

A Soldier for the Other

From the very beginning of Steve Rogers becoming Captain America, he has been a man dedicated to the safety and well-being of his neighbors both at home and abroad. Now even all this time later in the wake of Thanos wiping out half the human population, that attitude has not changed. After the Avengers' plan to ambush Thanos and to reverse the mass extinction fails, and we fast forward five years, Steve Rogers is running a support group for people trying to find their place in a post-Snap world and on top of that, is still working with what remains of the Avengers as Captain America on a way to reverse the damage done by Thanos. Even though Rogers knows he'll never be able to move on from his grief, a fact that he actually confesses to Romanoff, he's still committed to helping others move on from theirs. So when Scott Lang emerges from the Quantum Realm and explains to Rogers and Romanoff what it was like in the Quantum Realm and how that might be a key to stopping Thanos and undoing his damage, Rogers's sense of purpose as Captain America in the name of protecting and preserving the lives of others is renewed. This idea of finding meaning in your life through the existence of other people may seem strange, but as we'll see, Steve Rogers was in excellent company.

The French philosopher Emmanuel Levinas (1906–1995) had lived through World War II and the Holocaust in his lifetime, with the latter event having a significant impact on his thought. Levinas is most known for his views concerning the ethics of the Other, which to put it simply means how we are to treat other people particularly those that are unlike us. Think back to one of Captain America's biggest arcs throughout the Marvel movies, rescuing a brainwashed Bucky Barnes who used to be his best friend.

Bucky had become the Other to Captain America because Bucky had become a soldier for Hydra, an organization that was an arch-nemesis to Cap and his ideals. Yet Levinas would argue that it's the fragility of the Other, such as the fragility of those in concentration camps or of Bucky Barnes having been brainwashed, that nurtures in us as it did Steve Rogers when confronting his best friend as Captain America, the idea of doing no harm and helping if you're capable. Captain America upholds this idea with such resolve that he even forsakes his friendship with Tony Stark in *Captain America: Civil War* because he knows Tony means Bucky harm due to Bucky having killed Stark's parents while brainwashed.

This idea of living for the Other and doing no harm to them is a defining characteristic of Rogers's personality all the way through to *Avengers: Endgame*. Outside of him being a grief counselor for post-Snap survivors as seen in the five-year flash forward in the movie, during the final climactic battle with Thanos there is a point amidst the mayhem where Thanos is close to killing Thor. But in a stunning feat, Captain America with his selflessness and courageous heart, is able to wield Thor's hammer Mjølnir and save his life.

When you can live your life with the compassion for those around you that Steve Rogers has, you see, much like Tony Stark in affirming his freedom as Iron Man, that strength is granted to them that can save even Gods if used for the right cause. For Steve Rogers the man and Captain America the hero, much like Levinas, meaning in life is found through the hardship and fragility of our neighbors, and the power we find within ourselves to do something about it.

The Blind Leading the Hawkeye

The opening of *Avengers: Endgame* shows us the perfect picture of life that Hawkeye has been fighting to sustain. With just one Snap from Thanos, it all goes away and in Hawkeye's mind the world no longer makes any sense. The next time we lay eyes on Clint he is in Japan slaughtering members of the Yakuza, a Japanese mafia, claiming that he is ridding the Earth of the scumbags that have taken for granted what his family no longer had. Hawkeye (or Ronin) is confronted by Natasha Romanoff and convinced to leave this life of nihilism, as she saw it, for a more meaningful endeavor with the rest of the Avengers.

Nihilism or the belief that life is meaningless is something the philosopher Friedrich Nietzsche (1844–1900) knew all too well. Not because he was suffering from it, but because he wrote extensively of the danger of nihilism which sprouts from the realization that there is no higher being to bestow purpose onto our lives. In his most famous work, *Thus Spoke Zarathrustra,* Nietzsche offers ways to cope with nihilism one of which is to embrace the chaotic nature of the world by famously saying "One must still have chaos in oneself to give birth to a dancing star."

Back at the Avengers HQ, Hawkeye immediately volunteers himself to be the guinea pig of the time travel test runs. Maybe it is because he believed he already has nothing to lose or maybe it is because he hopes to regain that purpose by getting his family back. Either way the process behind getting his family back by any means necessary worries Black Widow who insists on going with him later in the movie to recover the Soul Stone (a decision she will pay the ultimate price for).

Speaking of that fateful scene, Nietzsche would have this to say regarding the life sacrifice that is required as a trade for obtaining the Soul Stone: "You must be ready to burn yourself in your own flame. How could you rise anew if you have not become ashes?" Perhaps this thought crossed the mind of Natasha as she did everything she could to get Clint out of the way. She witnessed his overwhelming transformation as the alley Hawkeye to the rogue Ronin and felt that he needed to change no more. Perhaps she saw this as a pivotal moment where Hawkeye would recognize the sacrifice she made, regain his faith in his fellow man and change back to the loving father he once was. Her sacrifice gave him the vitality he needed as he saw that her death was not meaningless and was the start of him being able to regain meaning in his life.

The Hero Within

The arcs of Iron Man, Captain America, The Hulk, and Hawkeye can be said to represent the existentialist views of Marvel itself. Through its Phase One films and especially with the final crescendo of *Avengers: Endgame*, Marvel's answer to the question of the meaning of life can be summed up in one word: affirmation.

Whether what's being affirmed is the freedom to define yourself, the dignity and humanity of the Other, or the chaos and absurdity of the universe as a whole which we choose to live in spite of, Marvel shows through the threat to life itself that Thanos represents, that we must all have the courage to affirm *something*. That's why even five years after the Snap,

Avengers like Captain America, The Hulk, Hawkeye, and perhaps most of all Iron Man, commit to affirmation in the face of the ultimate danger in Thanos. They all chose in their own ways the path of affirmation and in doing so, showed the true depths of goodness that human beings are capable of. When we look upon these heroes facing the ultimate terror in Thanos, we are reminded of the terrors that we have confronted and must confront.

Thanos is not just a cosmic tyrant who caused the extinction of half the population and whom the Avengers must defeat. Thanos more broadly represents atrocities such as the genocides both historically and today, that are being perpetrated across the globe. Thanos represents climate change that will irreversibly alter our way of life and the life of many generations to come, all while leaving a considerable trail of death in its wake. Thanos represents every war that human beings have waged on each other whether with stones and spears or tanks and bombs.

Thanos is the personification of our most vile capabilities as a species, but we don't have to be Thanos. We can choose the hero within and we can choose to be like Iron Man, Captain America, Hawkeye, The Hulk, and every other Avenger that wouldn't let Thanos wipe meaning itself off of the Earth.

The Marvel Cinematic Universe showed us, on a grand scale, the duality that exists within all of us between exercising our great power for good or ill both for ourselves and our neighbors. For the last ten years of showing us the complexity of the human experience through the eyes of the superhero in all of their power and spandex, all that's left to say in the words of a hero we once knew is: "Marvel for life."[1]

---

[1] Rest in Power Meaghan Lynai Joel. You changed the lives of everyone you crossed paths with and I wish to thank you from the bottom of my heart for crossing paths with me. I will cherish every memory forever. —Angel L. G.

3
Confronting Grief in the Post-Snap World

BENJAMIN J.J. CARPENTER

Endgame starts with a poignant reflection on death and loss, as Tony (Iron Man) and Nebula are suspended in space light years away from those they care about. Tony records a monologue for his wife and teammates reflecting on his own death, a death that is ultimately delayed until the end of the movie.

Despite the film's numerous action scenes and the ultimate triumph of the Avengers over Thanos, *Endgame* is largely a movie about death, grief, and mourning as the characters attempt to grapple with the loss of fifty percent of all living things. What follows the initial rescue of Tony and Nebula is a series of scenes wherein the Avengers commiserate their failure to stop the Snap, arguing amongst themselves about who was right, before facing Thanos and realizing that there is nothing to be done.

Loss and Grief

When faced with a loss, few of us know how to react. Even if a death is expected, even if it was preceded by a long and happy life, loss is always something to be grappled with. Though to die is inseparable from being human, the loss of an individual is enough to leave us 'at a loss'; it takes time to learn to live with that lack. For most of us, death will punctuate our lives, and short of a disaster we'll experience loss gradually.

Mass loss of life has been a common occurrence throughout history—with both manmade and environmental disasters able to take many lives all at once. Such events are traumatic for those who survive them, for they experience grief on an overwhelming scale. In the case of *Endgame*, the scale of death is almost impossible for us to imagine—

requiring the supernatural power of all six Infinity Stones to even be possible.

How, then, do our heroes react to such a loss? Of course, it's not quite appropriate to refer to the dead as lost, in the case of *Endgame*, is it? The Snap was no natural disaster, no accident of nature. It was an intentional act carried out by a single person, the villain of this drama, the Mad Titan Thanos. In acquiring the Infinity Stones and snapping his fingers as he does, Thanos takes away life—just as if he and his servants had invaded planets and butchered half of the population.

When confronting the overwhelming number of deaths, we are confronted not simply with lives "lost," but with lives that have been taken. In this sense, Thanos himself is death—a fitting role for him to play given the similarity between his name the personified Greek God of Death, Thanatos. Thanos fancies himself a God (with this becoming much more explicit towards the end of *Endgame*), and his successful act of murder on a cosmic scale is enough to ensure his place as a terrible villain. But he's more than just any villain. Thanos represents that which cannot be denied, the "inevitable," and despite his ultimate failure, the inability of our heroes to undo what he did forces each of them to confront their own failure. We and our heroes have to accept the lives that have been taken.

Each Avenger handles this in a different way. Tony settles down with his wife and has a child. He tries to put it all behind him, and forget both the Avengers' failings as well as the loss itself. Steve (Captain America) tries to help others accept and work-through their grief—attending support groups where we get a glimpse into just how heavy the burden of Thanos's actions are. Despite this, Steve tries to look on the bright side, coming close at one point to claiming that some good may have come out of the snap. Bruce (the Hulk), too, moves on—reveling in his newfound celebrity status. Thor, of course, kills Thanos—an impulsive act of vengeful violence that comes out of a sense of failure and being responsible for allowing the Snap to happen.

But Thanos's death changes nothing, and Thor sinks into a deep depression (with weight-gain used as a shorthand to convey this in the movie—unfortunately though this fact is used to ridicule his character). Clint (Hawkeye) goes on a murderous rampage, delivering bloody slaughter to anyone he thinks should have died instead of his family, but this doesn't bring them back—only turning him into more of a villain.

Go for the Head

I went for the head.
—THOR

But there is one member of the Avengers who both refuses to move on—like Tony and Steve—or fall into depression or violence—like Thor and Clint—and that's Natasha (Black Widow). With Nick Fury among the taken, Natasha becomes the director of the broken remains of SHIELD, working alongside several other survivors to try and hold together societies across the galaxy. We see Natasha meeting with her new teammates, all of which are busy attending to their own problems, leaving her alone in directing SHIELD.

Whilst we can presume that Natasha is helping to stabilize a world thrown into crisis, she can only treat the symptoms, not the cause. About the Snap itself, there is nothing to be done. Yet whilst her original teammates move on in more or less healthy ways, Natasha remains at her post. She has a duty, a duty that the Avengers failed to uphold, but despite that failure, Natasha refuses to move on. She cannot let go of the desire to do something, even if nothing can be done.

How should we act in the face of unimaginable violence and death? Natasha's ethical problem could be expressed as the question "How do we act in order to ensure that the lives taken from us still matter?" This is a question explored by the philosopher Judith Butler, in her books *Precarious Life* and *Frames of War*, where she explores the value of life in connection with an idea of 'grievability'.

If we are able to grieve and mourn for someone whom we lose, then this indicates that their death means something. But experiencing another's death as a loss, we come to realize the value their life had. When we feel the pain of this loss, part of our grief is to remember the dead, to engage in practices of memorial. Butler explores examples of those people who become ungrievable, whose lives are made not to matter precisely because we cannot mourn for them or who we are made unable to remember.

Examples are those who die in war, fighting on 'the wrong side' (from whatever perspective), or those whose ways of living are so foreign to us that we struggle to recognize them as human just as we are. Butler's work thinks about this us-them divide, pondering the deep ethical concerns of "Who gets to matter?" and "What lives get to be human lives?" For Butler, these are deeply ethical questions, rooted not only in considering 'Who matters and why?' but also in how the situations of our lives make it more or less possible to grieve for certain lost lives. Butler isn't primarily concerned with moral duties or virtues, her project isn't an attempt to work out in advance how we should act, but she instead focuses on our ability to respond to the situations we find ourselves in.

Applying Butler's thoughts on grief, we can think through how *Endgame* explores the collective trauma of Thanos's victory—and how this sense of violation and the pursuit of justice plays a part in ensuring that his victory does not last. In our world, without superpowers and magic, there is a finality to death. So Butler's work is primarily focused on how victims of large-scale violence can be made invisible, particularly when this violence is at the hands of a large political structure. When thinking about *Endgame*, we of course have any number of supernatural (or perhaps pseudoscientific) possibilities for undoing Thanos's victory. But within the movie, it's only through grief that these possibilities are revealed.

Another obstacle to our ability to mourn, and therefore to recognizing the lost live as valuable, is scale. When we think about great disasters, natural or manmade (such as acts of war), that result in a drastic loss of life, it is all too easy for us to become so overwhelmed that we cannot grieve for the individual lives lost, but only for the idea of these lives. In these instances, death can quickly become a numbers game, with individual lives becoming mere statistics.

We have ways of trying to mourn occasions of mass death. We may act to build memorials, to remind ourselves and others that these people once lived. And in *Endgame* memorials are depicted, as Scott (Ant-Man) finds his own name written on one of so many white stone monuments. These monuments mark the names of those Thanos killed, and the work that goes into constructing and maintaining them is clearly one way of trying to mark a loss, honoring and remembering their deaths so that their lives matter. But the list of names is colossal, the grief remains overwhelming and impersonal—a crisis that becomes impossible to work through.

We can contrast this to Tony's funeral at the end of the movie, where we experience a sustained, communal experience in personal grief. We know that Tony mattered, not only because of his actions impacting the plot, but because his death is felt as a loss, and his life is something we want to remember. In taking their lives in the way that he does, Thanos renders those lives ungrievable.

For our heroes, this is precisely the problem. The scale is overwhelming, and they simply cannot comprehend it. The death toll disorientates the Avengers, and dwelling on the

Snap, the deaths, and their own inability to stop it just induces a sense of dread, it makes them feel numb. Being so overwhelmed and confused, most choose to, in one way or another, turn away from it and try to put the Snap behind them. In turning away, most never confront their grief, and are not able to mourn, instead simply refusing to deal with what happened.

For the most part, the Avengers lack the moral strength to face the horror around them. We can say, then, that Natasha stays in her grief and her sense of loss in a way that her teammates refuse. But it is precisely her unwillingness to turn away from her pain, that she is able to retain her belief within her own duty. For most of the Avengers, dwelling on the Snap seems to push them towards a kind of nihilism—a philosophical perspective defined by the nihilist's inability or unwillingness to recognize anything as meaningful. However, Natasha believes that something can be done, even when everyone around her fails to believe that. She alone has the moral strength to face what happened, to confront and feel that pain whilst also holding on to her sense of agency, her sense of 'I can act' even if she doesn't precisely know what there is to be done.

Winning the Right to Die

> Even if there's a small chance we could reverse this, we owe it to everyone who is not in this room to try.
> —NATASHA

Natasha's refusal to leave her post, despite others around her (notably Steve) encouraging her to "get a life," creates the possibility of saving the day. It's precisely because she remains at SHIELD headquarters, ready and willing to act, that Scott is able to find her there. The next few scenes depict the gradual reassembly of the group, with several of them reluctant to return precisely because of the pain involved in confronting the state of the world. Particularly in the attempt to recruit Tony, Natasha is central—with her sense not only of duty but also hope serving as a sharp counterpoint to Tony's cynicism and despair. As the group reforms, Natasha is very much their moral core—overtaking even Steve in that role, as we should be careful not to forget that even Steve was trying to move on and let go.

Natasha does not live to see the Snap reversed. She dies on Vormir, sacrificing her life to obtain the Soul Stone. We knew that someone was going to have to die, having been introduced to the price for the stone in *Infinity War*. We can consider

Natasha's death as part of a commentary on the virtues of self-sacrifice, of how giving your life for a cause greater than yourself can be a supremely virtuous act.

Natasha is one of two characters within the Marvel Cinematic Universe to die in order for the Soul Stone to be obtained, the other being Gamora. Both of these characters are not only women, but both are the only women in the original line-ups of their respective teams (the Avengers and the Guardians of the Galaxy). Gamora was thrown to her death by the hands of an abusive father (an act that the movie seems to partially suggest is rooted in love). Natasha, however, arrives on Vormir with Clint, and the two fight with one another over who should die to obtain the stone.

Ultimately, Natasha 'wins' the right to die, with the implicit justification of the narrative being that Clint needed to live to be reunited with his family (a reunion which is then barely depicted within the movie). Many of us will remember the uncomfortable scene from *Age of Ultron* where Natasha tells Bruce that she is a monster for being infertile. If the question is 'whose life matters more, Clint's or Natasha's?'—the film answers with Clint's. Natasha's only family is the Avengers itself, and therefore within the logic of the movie, she has to die.

The Moral Opposite of Thanos

> For the last five years, I've been trying to do one thing . . .
> —NATASHA, before offering her life

Both Natasha and Tony die to save the world, but only one of them is given a long funeral sequence, where the majority of the cast gather around to mourn the death of this 'great man'. Whilst I think we could argue that Natasha's death forms a guiding thrust for the subsequent plot of *Endgame*—particularly when a distraught Bruce says "We have to make it mean something", before using the stones to reverse the Snap—she seems to be mostly forgotten by the end of the movie. Both Natasha and Tony knowingly give their lives—though perhaps in Natasha's case there's more certainty that she will definitely die—not because they want to die, but because they want to stand on the side of life.

We can read both of them as sacrificial heroes, dying in the line of duty to save those of us incapable of defending ourselves. But if we consider how the film 'acts' to memorialize those who die, *Endgame* certainly seems to put more weight and significance on Tony's death than Natasha's. I'm not suggesting that Tony's death shouldn't have been given the significance that it did, but different levels of significance are assigned to the loss of each of these two characters.

Natasha's sacrifice, a sacrifice made for the lives Thanos took, serves to make her the moral opposite of Thanos in a way that no other character quite achieves. Sure enough, all the Avengers oppose Thanos's goals, and of course Tony dies using the Gauntlet to stop the Mad Titan but he does so through violence. He does to Thanos what Thanos would have done to everyone else. Though it may have been necessary (and the film certainly seems to present it as such), Tony's use of the stones—with which he could have done anything—is an act of 'pre-vengeance'.

Thanos the Egoist

We're the Avengers, not the pre-vengers, right?
    —TONY, in his argument with Steve

So, though his death can certainly be read as a heroic sacrifice, Tony dies supporting his world view that remains rooted in conflict and violence. When given near-omnipotence, all Tony can think to do is destroy his enemy, and there's very little moral consideration as to the weight of their lives. Sure enough, they serve Thanos, and they look like monsters, but they are never given a chance to redeem themselves and are instead simply blinked out of existence by precisely the same means that the movie presents as being so unjust in the first place. We should, of course, remember that Tony himself was much like those he kills (think back to the original *Iron Man* and how complicit Tony was in the deaths of innocents), and though he has developed as a character, he was only able to do so because he was given a chance. In this sense, Tony and Thanos represent nearly identical perspectives of control and dominance—it just so happens that Tony is on 'our' side, the side of the human. Again, we can ask: who counts? Who is grievable?

Natasha, however, does not perpetuate this violence with her death. Instead, she gives herself and only herself. We can view her as a noble martyr—placing her in a very long line of those who thought it ethically right to give their lives for others. But more than this, we can say that Natasha is willing to become Thanos's ultimate victim. In giving her life for the Soul Stone, Natasha is able to say, with her death, "You get only me," rather than the millions who died in the Snap.

We see Natasha choose to act to give herself for the sake of life itself. It's precisely this act of self-sacrifice in the name of life that so securely makes her the opposite of Thanos. Whereas Natasha gives all she has in the hope of saving others, sacrificing her health and ultimately her life, Thanos is the ultimate egoist. He wraps his goals and ambitions up in noble language, claiming that he wants to bring about some kind of cosmic balance but only Thanos is able to see the imbalance. He and he alone is mighty enough to be the judge, jury, and executioner. The continual way that Thanos's project is tied to him as an individual—such as his talk of "I am inevitable"—clearly demonstrates that it is his project, that it is about him. The lives lost cannot be grieved because they don't matter—only Thanos's legacy is important.

Not only that, but Thanos considers himself above those he kills; he imagines himself an impersonal cosmic force; and for all his claims that the deaths will be perfectly random, there's no sense that Thanos himself might die in the Snap. When he realizes that his work could always be undone, even if it succeeds, Thanos doesn't abandon the project. Instead, he decides to use the stones to become a God—remaking the world in his image, effectively killing everyone except himself to ensure his dream comes true.

Nobody else ever mattered to Thanos; they were always beneath him. Conversely, everyone mattered to Natasha, and she would rather die than live in a world without them. Just as Thanos is death, Natasha is life.

The Value of Grief

Thanos has a retirement plan.
—ROCKET

Endgame illustrates the depth of grief, depicting how difficult it can be to confront loss both personally and collectively. It helps us to reflect on how loss and the pain that comes with it can be ethically instructive, which is to say that it helps us meditate on how we value our lives in connection with others. Despite the suffering that comes with grief, perhaps *Endgame* provides us with a reason to sit with our sense of loss, however we experience it, learning from it rather than running from it. And perhaps through sitting with that grief, it may be possible for us to recognize that whatever we've lost mattered.

Through experiencing grief, we give value to those who are no longer here, and that this will help us to better reflect on the question "who matters?" Perhaps in our sense of loss, we can find some aspect of our shared humanity, something that binds us together, and that could serve as an ethical guide to help us navigate our lives and our deaths.

4
Why Does Grief Hurt So Much?

J. KEEPING

At the climax of *Avengers: Infinity War,* Thanos succeeds in collecting the six Infinity Stones and, with a snap of his fingers, destroys half of all life in the universe. Sobs and shocked gasps came from the audience as we watched these characters that we had come to know and love over the past decade—Spider-Man, Black Panther, Nick Fury, and so many others—crumble into dust.

When the film ended a few minutes later, I looked over at the friend I came with. She looked stunned, bewildered, and mortified—as if she had momentarily forgotten that these were fictional characters in a made-up story. I recognized that look: it was the look of someone whose world had been shattered by some terrible loss, and they didn't know how to go on. It was grief.

My friend recovered from her shock fairly quickly, but a year would pass before we got to see how the survivors of the Snap coped with their loss. *Avengers: Endgame* is a movie about grief. Not just insofar as the film, especially in its first act, depicts in stark detail the grief experienced by the main cast. The entire story, including *Infinity War,* can be seen as a philosophical exploration of grief: what it is, what it means, how to deal with it. Grief, you see, is more than a mere emotion such as fear or anger. Grief is a complex, multilevel phenomenon that cuts to the heart of what it means to be human. In order to understand grief, and in order to understand *Endgame,* we must see that both are fundamentally about *time.*

Grief is what we experience, and what we must go through, when someone close to us dies. There are other ways to lose a loved one—through a breakup or other permanent estrangement—but the *core* meaning of grief involves the death of a loved one. And the theme of death can be found everywhere in *Avengers: Endgame* and the movie that preceded it. Thanos has made his whole existence about bringing death, as symbolized by his name, derived from *thanatos*, the personification of death in Greek mythology. Yet he imagines himself to be *preventing* death (and suffering) by stopping overpopulation. The Soul Stone cannot be obtained without the sacrifice of a loved one. And the Avengers' journey into the past brings them face to face with their lost loved ones: Tony encounters his father, and Thor his mother.

The Pain of Grief

Although grief is normally thought of as an emotion, it's quite different from everyday emotions such as fear or anger. The latter are episodic, meaning that they arise, last for anything from a few seconds to a few hours, and then pass. Grief lasts for months or even years, it can wax and wane in intensity, and often incorporates other emotions into its course. If a "regular" emotion such as fear or joy is an episode, then grief is more like a season of a Netflix series such as *Daredevil* or *Jessica Jones*, where each individual episode forms a chapter in a larger narrative, and by the end of the season things may be very different from how they were at the start.

Although grieving is normally associated with sadness, it may involve other emotions as well. For example, we learn at the beginning of *Captain America: Civil War* that Tony Stark still carries guilt over a fight he had with his father the day his parents died in a car accident. Later, when Tony learns that his parents were in fact assassinated by the Winter Soldier, he is overcome with violent rage. Although the grief and the rage are emotions in their own right, they are also part of the overall "story" of Tony's grief.

Grief superficially resembles sadness. They have a similar physiognomy: our face is downcast, our posture sagging as if we were bearing a heavy weight. The two most salient characteristics of grief, however, are not shared by sadness, and it is through a consideration of these that deeper meaning of grief is revealed. The first of these is acute affective pain. Grief *hurts*.

This pain is sometimes located inside the chest or abdomen, either in the form of a cold, dark weight or an emptiness—as if something inside had been torn out. Or it may be diffused through the body, an insistent ache in the muscles or the skin. Consider Tony at the beginning of the movie, when he and Nebula are adrift onboard Peter Quill's ship *The Milano*. His eyes are haunted, his face haggard, his posture drained. He looks *broken.* Consider Clint's tears after he watches Natasha die. There's something much more significant than sadness going on here.

Loss of Meaning

Grief is profoundly *disorienting.* In grief, we don't know what to do, what to think, what to feel. Our words are halting, our actions hesitant. Our surroundings take on an unreal or dreamlike quality. We may have difficulty concentrating or maintaining interest in things. There is a peculiar "stunned" look characteristic of grief that we see in the eyes of the characters throughout the first act of the movie. In grief we're adrift without bearings, not unlike Tony and Nebula floating powerless in the void of space. Or consider the images of New York City after the five-year time lapse: drained of color, empty and lifeless. The harbor is full of abandoned ships; Yankee Stadium is silent and empty.

What's missing here is not just people; we see a world drained of *meaning.* This is how the world appears in grief: all the pieces are there, but they no longer seem to fit together. What was taken for granted now seems alien. Ordinary tasks become daunting: a member of Cap's encounter group describes how difficult it is just to make it through a dinner date with his partner. Why is grief like this?

The key to this riddle, along with the plan the heroes concoct to undo what Thanos has done, has to do with *time.* In grief, the world seems meaningless to us because, in a sense, we do not inhabit it. Not as it exists now. Instead, we inhabit the world of the past, the world in which our loved one was still alive. Our thoughts and feelings, our habits and beliefs, remain attuned to that world. Perhaps we had breakfast with them every day; perhaps we only spoke on the phone once a week. Either way, they were integral to the shape of our lives. If we did not rely upon their presence, we at least relied on the *potential* of their presence; if they were not always in our thoughts, they were part of the background of our thoughts which made them fit together and make sense. Without them, our life is like a table missing a leg, unbalanced and constantly in danger of toppling over.

As we learned in the second *Avengers* film, Hawkeye's central pillar of meaning was his family. When they crumble into dust, so does his life. He's simply unable to go on as before, and we see the tragic result. Thanos, the driver of the action in both *Infinity War* and *Endgame,* presents an extreme example of this same phenomenon. Although apparently quite rational and intelligent, Thanos remains committed to a plan that makes no sense. Intending to "save" the universe from overpopulation, he wipes out half the life on every inhabited planet. There are many flaws to this approach, not the least of which is that not every planet is overpopulated!

Stuck in the Past

Thanos is unable to see this because he is emotionally "stuck" in the past. Long ago his planet Titan was at the brink of disaster because of overpopulation, and his proposed "solution" was to murder half the populace, chosen at random. His plan was rejected, and his planet became devastated, apparently leaving him as the only survivor. Unable or unwilling to move on, he remains trapped in that moment when he failed to "save" his world. Because he is in a sense "still there" (in his feelings if not his thoughts) he sees everything through the distorting lens of this situation. So, to him his "solution" *seems* to apply to *every* planet, even planets that are not overpopulated, even when it's obvious to everyone else that what he is doing is objectively, monstrously wrong. As much as he is the bringer of death, Thanos is himself motivated by grief.

Thanos does not *believe* that every populated planet he encounters is, or is the same as, his homeworld Titan. He is not, strictly speaking, deluded or confused. But human (and giant purple alien) subjects do not live in a world of objective facts, but rather a world of *meaning* that determines what these facts *count as* for us and how they *fit together*. This world of meaning is not made out of objective facts that can be separated from one another, but is primarily *relational*. German philosopher Martin Heidegger speaks of this in terms of what he calls "the referential totality of significance." Not being German philosophers, we will refer to this as the "for-structure of meaning" instead.

Heidegger uses the example of a hammer: a hammer is *for* hammering nails, which is *for* building a bookshelf, which is *for* holding books, which are *for* studying, which is *for* getting your philosophy degree, which is *for* going to law school, which is *for* getting a job as a lawyer. We don't *think* of all this when we think of a hammer, but it is there in the "background," so to speak, and without it a hammer would just be an oddly-shaped chunk of metal. What this tells us is that we will never to be able to get to a meaningful world by adding up objective facts.

Moreover, so much of what we know is not *factual* knowledge at all. Hammering is a skill, and being able to use a hammer effectively involves being able to grip it, to gauge the amount of force necessary, and other things that cannot be conveyed in words. British philosopher Gilbert Ryle, following Heidegger, expressed this distinction in terms of "knowledge-how" versus "knowledge-that." We know *that* a hammer is used to hammer nails, but knowing *how* to use a hammer to hammer nails is a different matter entirely. The most obvious example of knowledge-how is skills such as hammering, typing, riding a bicycle, and so on. But existentialist thinkers such as Heidegger and Maurice Merleau-Ponty argue that knowledge-how is fundamental to everything we do. Speaking is a skill, and consequently our ability to articulate any fact rests upon knowledge-how. Most importantly for our purposes, our *emotional* lives are of the knowledge-how variety. We learn to feel as we learn to speak, and like a skill we learn it by *doing*.

This unspoken world of our affects takes shape over time. Therefore, when there is a sudden shift in our life-circumstances, we can find ourselves inhabiting a world of the past that no longer maps onto the facts of the present. This is what happens in grief—this is, more than anything else, what grief *is*. Readjusting our affects can be as slow and painstaking as learning a new language. We have a word for it, and that word is *grieving*. Some, like Thanos, do not go through the work of adjusting their affects at all, and continue to live in a past that does not conform to the present. But most of us—hopefully—do go through the work of rebuilding our lives to fit the changed world we find ourselves in.

Steve Rogers alludes to this after the man in his therapy group tells the story of reconnecting with his partner:

> That's great. You did the hardest part; you took the jump, you didn't know where you were going to come down. And that's it, that's those little brave baby steps we gotta take. Try . . . to become whole again, try to find purpose. . . . You gotta move on. The world is in our hands. It's left to us, guys. And we gotta do something with it. Otherwise, Thanos shoulda killed all of us.

This is a wonderful speech, and a succinct description of both the challenge and the necessity of grieving. However, Cap later confesses to Natasha that he finds himself unable to move on. *Endgame* does present us with a counterpoint to Thanos: it's not Captain America but Iron Man. After he and Nebula are rescued by Captain Marvel, Tony returns to Earth a broken man. Starving and dehydrated, he rises from his wheelchair to vent his rage and despair at Steve, then rips off the chest unit that contains his nanotech Iron Man armor and collapses to the floor. Tony rejects his previous identity and refuses to keep on going as before.

Something to Live For

The next time we see him, Tony is a very different man. Gone are the trappings of wealth and technology; he now lives in a country house with his wife Pepper and their daughter Morgan, who was evidently born not long after the Snap. In the shorthand language of film, these scenes tell us good deal about how to deal with grief. Our emotions are not within our direct control; we cannot simply choose to feel a different way. What we can do is create the *conditions* for our feelings to change on their own, to readjust.

Tony has traded the life of a superhero for that of a father. He has left his old life behind in the literal sense that he has relocated to a very different setting. His daily habits have changed too; we see him playing with his daughter and doing dishes. What this shows us is that if we wish to successfully grieve, we cannot continue living the same life as we did before our bereavement— we must build for ourselves a *different* life. Cap alludes to this in the advice he gives to his therapy group: "You took the jump; you didn't know where you were going to come down."

Grieving involves taking a leap into a different life, and we can't know in advance what that life will look like. Grieving involves risk, and that is perhaps why so many of the characters are unwilling to do it. Out of all the surviving Avengers, Tony is the only one who gives up his old life after the Snap, and consequently he's the only one who becomes whole again. Tony is at peace, but the others retain that broken, staring look in their eyes, even after five years have passed. Like Thanos, they continue to live in the past.

When his former teammates attempt to recruit Tony for their "time heist," he reveals the third key to successfully grieving: finding something to live *for*. "I have to tell you my priorities: Bring back what we lost, I hope yes. Keep what I found, I have to, at all costs." Cap tells his therapy group that in order to become whole again, we must find purpose. Tony makes it clear that his purpose is now his family, and especially his daughter Morgan.

Tony's daughter invites another powerful contrast with Thanos. Both love their daughters, but Thanos murders

Gamora in the pursuit of his obsession, while Tony does the opposite: he sacrifices his life to save Morgan—along with the rest of the universe. This returns us to the theme of time: Our children represent the future, so symbolically Thanos sacrifices the future for the sake of the past, whereas Tony sacrifices himself for the sake of the future. It fits the movie's themes that, despite the role that time travel plays in the plot, the heroes do not attempt to reverse time or change the past. In fact, Bruce tells us that you *can't* change the past using time travel. This is thematically relevant because successfully grieving involves leaving the past alone and being open to the uncertainties of the future.

Analyzing grief through a consideration of how we relate to time explains the profoundly disorienting nature of grief, and why it takes so much time and work to recover. What it does not account for is the *pain* that distinguishes grief from other emotional phenomena. Why does grief hurt so much? We have already touched on the answer to this question. Grieving is a matter of reconfiguring our network of subjective meanings to fit the world as it now exists, in the wake of our loss. We learned that in order to change the way we relate to the world, we must change ourselves. Another lesson of existentialist philosophy is that *we are what we do.*

Our identity is constituted by our actions, our subjective meanings, and our relationships with others. We literally *cannot be what we are* without other people, especially the people with whom we have close relationships. In the wake of the Snap, Natasha continues her role as an Avenger, protecting the world. She also appears to take on the task of co-ordinating the surviving heroes spread across the Earth and in space. In so doing, she is strengthening her ties with other people. Natasha makes a big deal out of "having red in her ledger" and how Clint, and later the rest of the team, "saved" her. Natasha cannot be the person she is without the other Avengers. Clint cannot be the person he was after he loses his family in the Snap, and instead degrades into a sick parody of himself, hunting and murdering those whom he deems unworthy of living. Thor loses his identity when his family and his homeworld perish, as symbolized by the loss of both his hammer and his eye. Just as the meanings that constitute our world can only be what they are by being interconnected in a network of other meanings, *we ourselves* can only be what we are through our interconnections with other people. Cap says that we must find a way to "become whole" after bereavement, because the people whom we have lost are literally a part of ourselves. Grief hurts so much because we have lost a part of ourselves. It is the affective equivalent of amputation.

Again and again, *Avengers: Endgame* reminds us that it's only through others that we are made whole. Natasha finds Clint and saves him from his bloody, tortured existence, just as he once did the same for her. When Thor is at his lowest point, wallowing in alcohol and self-pity, Bruce reminds him that when he had lost himself on the planet Sakaar, it was Thor who helped him out of it.

One of the functions of mourning rituals such as funerals is to bring people together so that they can support one another, even if it is only by standing in respectful silence, as the surviving cast does at Tony's funeral. This is the second time we see all the heroes assembled together, and this time it's not for some spectacular superhero battle, but a uniquely *human* kind of heroism, one of which all of us are capable. Each one of us is capable of the quiet heroism of bravely moving on in the wake of terrible loss, and of helping others to do so.

II

Time Travel

5
Getting Time Travel Right

Duncan Gale

> We're talking about time travel here. Either it's all a joke, or none of
> it is.
> —Dr. Bruce Banner, holder of seven PhDs

I think I speak for many Marvel fans when I say that walking into *Avengers: Endgame* on opening night was an intensely emotional experience in many ways, but topmost among them was the fact that we were finally going to get closure on a year-long cliffhanger.

When we last saw our heroes in *Avengers: Infinity War*, they were at their lowest possible moment. While wielding all six of the Infinity Stones, Thanos had snapped his fingers, resulting in the unimaginable trauma of half the population of the universe eerily fading into dust in the wind. We were all confident that *Endgame* would offer a resolution of this act of mass genocide, but how exactly?

If you were familiar with the comic-book source material, namely the 1991 six-issue mini-series *The Infinity Gauntlet* written by Jim Starlin (who has a star-making turn in *Endgame* as "Support Group Man #1"), then you might have speculated that the solution would have something to do with Thanos's long-suffering daughter, Nebula, wresting the Gauntlet from him and simply undoing all of the atrocities he performed with her own snap of the fingers. But such a solution, while compelling within the context of the comics, would be far too facile for the Marvel Cinematic Universe. In the comics, the Infinity Gauntlet is a device that can effectively make someone God by giving the one who wields it omnipotence, period. But in the Marvel Cinematic Universe, the Gauntlet is more like a wearable nuclear bomb, capable of great destruction but at the price of potentially doing profound harm to the user as well. Consequently, the prospect of undoing its effects would also be considerably more difficult.

Such difficulties become even more evident when we are treated to a diabolical fake-out at the beginning of *Endgame* in the form of the Avengers tracking down Thanos only to discover that he has used the power of the stones to make them self-destruct, leaving absolutely no recourse for the destruction he has caused. Thor's subsequent decapitation of the Mad Titan feels like the quintessential act of impotent rage. Five somber years pass, and we finally begin to see a glimmer of hope only when that most unlikely of Avengers, Scott Lang's Ant-Man, resurfaces and tells the rest of the team about the possibility of time travel. With the introduction of this trope, *Endgame* enters that fabled pantheon of Time Travel Movies, but with a twist—the characters in this movie have seen all of those other movies:

> SCOTT LANG: Look, we go back, we get the stones before Thanos gets them, Thanos doesn't have the stones. Problem solved.

> CLINT BARTON: Bingo.

> NEBULA: That's not how it works.

> CLINT BARTON: Well, that's what I heard.

> BRUCE BANNER: Wait, but who? Who told you that?

> JIM RHODES: *Star Trek, Terminator, Timecop, Time After Time.*

> SCOTT LANG: *Quantum Leap.*

> JIM RHODES: *Wrinkle in Time, Somewhere in Time.*

> SCOTT LANG: *Hot Tub Time Machine.*

> JIM RHODES: *Hot Tub Time Machine, Bill and Ted's Excellent Adventure.* Basically, any movie that deals with time travel.

Screenwriters Christopher Markus and Stephen McFeely have seen all of those movies and go out of their way to handle the issue differently this time. One unique feature of *Endgame* as a movie is that it's so self-consciously determined to get time travel *right*.

Time Travel and Philosophy

STEVE ROGERS: Tony, after everything you've seen, is anything really impossible?

TONY STARK: Quantum fluctuation messes with the Planck scale, which then triggers the Deutsch Proposition. Can we agree on that?

But does *Endgame* actually get time travel right? What does it even mean to "get time travel right"? These are difficult questions to answer since time travel is, as far as we know, not yet a scientific reality and may never be. One reason why it may never be is because there's considerable debate among philosophers as to whether time travel is even *logically* possible.

One of the standard discussions of this topic is David Lewis's "The Paradoxes of Time Travel." Lewis says that he believes time travel is possible but also results in paradoxes which he regards as "oddities, not impossibilities." One such oddity is that a time traveler will have a separation between external time and his or her own personal time. For instance, if I go back in time to the year 1990, I am now out of sync with external time, but if I remain in the past then I will continue to experience my own personal time as I always have. If I stay in the past until 1992, I will age two years and experience it as two years just the same as if I had remained in the present.

I can even interact with my past self. Lewis sees no earth-shattering consequences arising from such a scenario. As he describes it, "an event in a time traveler's life may have more than one location in his personal time. If he doubles back toward the past, but not too far, he may be able to talk to himself. The conversation involves two of his stages, separated in his personal time but simultaneous in external time" (p. 147). This situation occurs a couple of times in *Endgame*. Two of the most notable instances are when present-day Steve Rogers encounters his younger, slightly more energetic self, and when present-day Nebula encounters her younger, far more sadistic self.

This all seems clear enough so far. But now consider that the reason why I'm such a fan of the Avengers today is that when I was a child, I met a strangely familiar man one day who told me about all of these fascinating characters. Unbeknownst to me, he had just seen a movie about them, but I had no access to such a movie so I instead sought out the Avengers in comic-book form. I became a lifelong fan and years later I went to see *Endgame* on opening night. As I left the theater, I fell through a time warp into the past. While in the past, I sought out my younger self and told him about all of these fascinating characters from this movie I just saw. Give yourself a pat on the back for correctly deducing that I am that very same strangely familiar man whom I had encountered when I was a child. So, the reason I'm so interested in the Avengers is because my older self told my younger self about them. Huh? This is an example of what Lewis refers to as a causal loop, a circular chain of events in which each event is explained by the one that came before it but nothing can explain the chain itself:

> The parts of the loop are explicable, the whole of it is not. Strange! But not impossible, and not too different from inexplicabilities we are already inured to. Almost everyone agrees that God, or the Big Bang, or the entire infinite past of the universe, or the decay of a tritium atom, is uncaused and inexplicable. Then if these are possible, why not also the inexplicable causal loops that arise in time travel? ("The Paradoxes of Time Travel," p. 149)

A possible example of this occurs in *Endgame* when Tony Stark interacts with his father, Howard, during a pivotal scene at Camp Lehigh Army Base:

> TONY STARK: I thought my dad was tough on me. And now, looking back on it, I just remember the good stuff, you know? He did drop the odd pearl.
>
> HOWARD STARK: Yeah? Like what?
>
> TONY STARK: No amount of money ever bought a second of time.
>
> HOWARD STARK: Smart guy.

While it's not laid out explicitly, Howard appears to be hearing this for the first time, even though Tony is supposedly quoting his father's own words back to him. But if Tony first heard this expression from his father who first heard it from adult Tony, then where did it come from in the first place?

One more case Lewis covers that is important for our purposes is what is often referred to as the "Grandfather Paradox." Something like this is touched upon at one point in *Endgame*:

> JIM RHODES: If we can do this, you know, why don't we just find baby Thanos, you know, and . . . [*pantomimes choking baby Thanos to death*]
>
> BRUCE BANNER: First of all, that's horrible.

JIM RHODES: It's Thanos.

BRUCE BANNER: And secondly, time doesn't work that way. Changing the past doesn't change the future.

Setting aside the issue of whether or not Dr. Banner should be horrified by Rhodey's suggestion, he would seem to be correct in asserting that killing baby Thanos would not solve their problem, especially if one of their allies in the fight is Thanos's daughter, Nebula. (Before going any further I should note that Nebula was most likely adopted by Thanos just like his other daughter Gamora, but for the purposes of this example let's assume she is his biological offspring.)

If the Avengers, including Nebula, go back in time to try and kill baby Thanos, Nebula's very existence actually demonstrates that they *cannot* do so. Lewis reflects on the strange meaning of this "cannot" in relation to his own hypothetical time traveler: "His failure by no means proves that he was not really able to kill Grandfather. We often try and fail to do what we are able to do. Success at some tasks requires not only ability but also luck, and lack of luck is not a temporary lack of ability" (p. 150). So, if the Avengers went back in time and tried to kill baby Thanos, they would presumably fail, not because they were constrained by the laws of logic but simply because, however many attempts they have made or will make, they always do happen to fail. The very existence of Thanos's offspring is definitive proof of their failure.

How to Time Travel the Marvel Way

BRUCE BANNER: Think about it. If you travel to the past, that past becomes your future, and your former present becomes the past which can't now be changed by your new future.

NEBULA: Exactly.

SCOTT LANG: So *Back to the Future* is a bunch of bullshit?

One of the climactic moments of *Endgame* involves Nebula killing a younger version of herself, which would certainly seem to create just as extreme of a paradox as killing one's own father or grandfather. So clearly, time travel in the Marvel universe works a little bit differently than in some of its more conventional treatments. At this point it's worth taking a brief detour into the comic books of the Marvel universe, many of which feature stories that offer some especially radical interpretations of the logistics of time travel.

One such example can be found in issue 50 of *Marvel Two-In-One*, a series which features the solo adventures of Ben Grimm, the orange rock–like member of the Fantastic Four also known as the Thing. In this issue, Ben tries to go back in time to prevent the accident that created the Fantastic Four in the first place and thereby also prevent his mutation into what he regards as a grotesque monster. He is seemingly successful in doing so, but when he returns to the present nothing has changed. Ben's friend Reed Richards, the brilliant scientist and leader of the Fantastic Four, explains, "Your past is immutable, Ben. You are what you are! Any change you make in the past results in another reality—a new one caused by your presence. I'm sorry, Ben . . . I thought you knew . . . " (I've slightly changed the story here to keep it simple.) With this statement, the rules of time travel are effectively established for the Marvel Comic Book Universe. The past of your own timeline cannot be changed, but if you go back in time and seemingly change the past, that will create an alternate branching timeline from that point forward. This means that Marvel comics can tell stories within not just a universe but a multiverse.

This alternate timeline model allows for the creation of many popular storylines in the Marvel comics, but since *Endgame* is the first Marvel Cinematic Universe film to incorporate time travel as a major plot point, it's still unclear the extent to which such a model might be used in the Cinematic Universe—although the upcoming movie title, *Doctor Strange in the Multiverse of Madness*, suggests that these elements will be utilized in a more extensive way.

The incident in which Nebula kills her past self and the case of two different Thanoses (dare I try to pluralize Thanos?) being killed on two separate occasions (decapitated by Thor and snapped away by Tony Stark) seem to implicitly assume such a model, but one of the only direct references to these ideas is made by the Ancient One during her rooftop conversation with Bruce Banner as he attempts to convince her to relinquish the Time Infinity Stone:

THE ANCIENT ONE: The Infinity Stones create what you experience as the flow of time. Remove one of the stones and that flow splits. Now, this may benefit your reality, but my new one, not so much. In this new branch reality, without our chief weapon against the forces of darkness, our world would be overrun. Millions will suffer. So tell me, Doctor, can your science prevent all that?

BRUCE BANNER: No, but we can erase it. Because once we're done with the stones, we can return each one to its own timeline at the moment it was taken. So, chronologically, in that reality it never left.

This exchange is especially fascinating because it is between two highly intelligent people from two completely different realms, the mystical and the scientific. The Ancient One is concerned that removing the Infinity Stones will throw off the fundamental balance of reality. Dr. Banner, evincing the pragmatic problem-solving ethos of the scientist, responds that such worries are irrelevant if the logic of time travel is strictly followed. The Ancient One remains unconvinced, and only gives up the stone when Banner reveals that her star pupil, Stephen Strange, had earlier given up the stone to Thanos himself. But her suggestion of the potential dangers of creating alternate realities and her skepticism about being able to simply "erase" events through time travel are important themes that echo throughout *Endgame*'s treatment of the subject.

These themes come up again during a pivotal scene where Tony Stark finally agrees to help with the Time Heist. He clearly lays out his terms to Steve Rogers, "We got a shot at getting these stones, but I gotta tell you my priorities. Bring back what we lost, I hope, yes. Keep what I found, I have to, at all costs." What Tony has finally found is the happiness of family life with his wife Pepper Potts and his daughter Morgan. His aversion to erasing the last five years is therefore motivated by purely selfish concerns, though we can hardly blame him for having these. Still, independent of this case it is worth asking: if the Avengers could use the miracle of time travel to simply erase the last five years of suffering humanity, should they?

Such a solution looks easier, but these kinds of quick and clean answers tend to be most tempting to those of an absolutist frame of mind. And there is no one who more exemplifies such a frame of mind than Thanos, as evidenced in this exchange during his encounter with the head trio of Avengers towards the end of *Endgame*:

THANOS: You could not live with your own failure. Where did that bring you? Back to me. I thought by eliminating half of life, the other half would thrive. But you've shown me that's impossible. And as long as there as those who remember what was, there will always be those that are unable to accept what can be. They will resist.

TONY STARK: Yep, we're all kinds of stubborn.

THANOS: I'm thankful. Because now I know what I must do. I will shred this universe down to its last atom. And then, with the stones you've collected for me, create a new one, teeming with life, that knows not what it has lost, but only what it has been given. A grateful universe.

STEVE ROGERS: Born out of blood.

THANOS: They'll never know it. Because you won't be alive to tell them.

What separates the Avengers from Thanos is their resistance to easy solutions. Yes, they use time travel, but only to collect the stones to bring everyone back, after which they will of course dutifully go back in time to return the stones to their proper time and place so as to avoid chaotic branching alternate timelines. They could easily just erase Thanos and all of his actions out of the timeline entirely, but it is important for people to remember these events so that they never happen again. Thanos's solution is to hit the reset button on the universe and start over. For all we know, the new universe Thanos creates might be a veritable utopia, but it would always be tainted. Such a scenario recalls the musings of the character of Ivan in Fyodor Dostoevsky's *The Brothers Karamazov*. At one point Ivan poses the following thought experiment:

> Tell me straight out, I call on you—answer me: imagine that yourself are building the edifice of human destiny with the object of making people happy in the finale, of giving them peace and rest at last, but for that you must inevitably and unavoidably torture just one tiny creature, that same child who was beating her chest with her little fist, and raise your edifice on the foundation of her unrequited tears— would you agree to be the architect on such conditions? Tell me the truth. (*The Brothers Karamazov*, p. 245)

Thanos would agree to such terms without hesitation, which is what ultimately makes him a villain despite his seemingly "good intentions." But the Avengers are all too aware that a paradise built on human suffering is no paradise at all.

Time travel has been used in all sorts of ways in movies and literature—as a metaphor, as a way for unlikely people to connect, as an avenue for exploring mind-bending paradoxes. In *Avengers: Endgame* it is the light at the end of a very long tunnel. For some that light is so blinding that they recoil from it, like Clint Barton who, when first hearing of this new chance from his old comrade Natasha Romanoff, simply responds, "Don't give me hope."

In the face of the mind-boggling act of mass genocide committed by Thanos, time travel gives the Avengers the opportunity to respond with an equally powerful and purely constructive act of mass restoration. Such an act is not without its sacrifices, most notably Natasha and Tony. But what ultimately makes the treatment of time travel in *Endgame* so satisfying is that it refuses to cut corners or simply hand-wave away any complex paradoxes. It confronts the complexities of the subject head-on and demonstrates the power of a truly cathartic narrative experience.

6
Nebula's Time Travel Paradox

CHARLENE ELSBY

It's a well-known fact that time travel and, in particular, travel to the past, must be exercised with extreme caution. Altering the past, we imagine, could change the present and the future, according to some chain of cause and effect that, given how complicated it is, seems almost completely unpredictable.

Some smart people have pointed out that whenever time travel to the past comes up, we all seem very concerned about altering the future through tiny and seemingly inconsequential actions—and yet no one in the present seems concerned about changing our future with those same tiny and inconsequential actions. Maybe we're not so concerned about ensuring a good future for ourselves as we are concerned about making sure that *my* future still exists—that the world in which I live remains, even if it means that I have to let all those past atrocities happen as they did.

The question arose for science fiction author Nathaniel Schachner in the story "Ancestral Voices", the original source of the Grandfather Paradox (the time travel trope in which someone goes back in time, kills their own grandfather, and then disappears). Schachner's main character, Dr. Pennypacker, travels back in time only to kill one of his great ancestors, which results in his own demise as well as the demise of many other people, whose existence all depended on that ancestor surviving and continuing to do things.

The situation brings up the general question—Does what happened in the past stay in the past? The problem arises in the history of philosophy only when we come to think of time as the fourth dimension, in addition to the three dimensions of space.

Avengers: Endgame alters our conception of this time travel problem. When the Avengers travel back in time to collect the infinity stones, the Hulk assures them that it isn't possible to change the present by altering the past, because once you travel back into the past, it becomes your present. He says, "I don't know why everyone believes that, but that isn't true. Think about it: If you travel to the past, that past becomes your future, and your former present becomes the past! Which can't now be changed by your new future!"

The usual problems result. For example, if you travel back in time to a point at which you already existed, does that mean there are two of you? The notion of self-identity over time is an interesting question and often comes up when we question whether we can go back in time and catch ourselves doing something we did in the past—perhaps even stop ourselves. The idea that there could be *two* of me seems like a paradox in itself, like the very existence of two of the same thing should lead to their mutual destruction. (There's an episode of *Doctor Who* where The Doctor and Rose Tyler travel back in time to her infancy, and he warns her, "Don't touch the baby," but of course she does and all Hell breaks loose.) This is an interesting question for someone else to solve.

The Grandfather Paradox

Depending on your concept of what time is, it'll be possible to travel in it or not, travel backwards or forwards or forwards and backwards, and it may be possible to change the place to which you're traveling—or it might not. If backwards time travel is possible, it seems that our present and future realities depend at least in part on the whims of time travelers, the most minute actions of whom could change our reality beyond recognition, even to the point of our own non-existence.

A more exact formulation of the problem locates the backwards time travel paradox more acutely—is it possible to travel back in time and change the past in such a way as to negate one's own existence? If I exist and travel back in time to kill myself, then I will not exist to travel back in time. But if I do not kill my past self, I will exist, and thereby it would be possible to travel back in time to kill my past self. (If I exist, I can negate my own existence; if I don't, then I can't—and I therefore exist.)

When Nat Schachner's character Dr. Pennypacker travels back to the past, he finds himself in the middle of an altercation featuring Attila's Huns. There is a girl who seems to be in danger, and Pennypacker saves her from one of the Huns. Then he recognizes his own features in the Hun's face—that particular Hun, he infers, was fully intending on making babies with the woman whom Pennypacker had just saved, and from those babies Pennypacker himself would eventually come into existence. Pennypacker shoots the Hun, and returns from the past to find a lot of people have disappeared in what *used* to be the present.

While Nebula's subplot in *Endgame* has been identified on various websites as a plot hole, it is, in fact, less dubious than the traditional formulation of time travel paradoxes. It makes more logical sense for a past self to kill a present one, than it does for a present self to kill a past one. In the years since Nebula was traveling the galaxy with Thanos to collect the Infinity Stones, she's made a lot of progress. She has a fancy shiny headpiece now, and not only does she look cool, she's *become good*.

That takes a lot of personal development—loyalties are built over time and are broken over time. The Nebula that exists today who hangs around with the Guardians of the Galaxy has been through some shit that the past Nebula has not. It seems that there almost *are* two people. But they are the same consciousness hooked up to the same neural networks, and that gives past Nebula access to present Nebula's memory banks. (This aspect of the plot depends entirely on our accepting the computer model of consciousness.) Past Nebula isn't interested in the personal growth of the present Nebula. All she's interested in is using the factual information to which she now has access through their shared consciousness; she will use it to anticipate and foil the Avengers' schemes.

This brings to light an aspect of backwards time travel that gets a lot of attention, but isn't often spelled out in any great detail—that a future person has an epistemological privilege that a past person does not. "Epistemology" is a word for the study of knowledge, and in general we accept that in the future, you'll know more than you do now—over time, we experience things, and we know more. That's just how stuff works (in general, of course, excepting cases of memory loss for any number of reasons).

It's in every time travel story—the advantage of the future individual is that they know how the past is going to unfold. It's in *Back to the Future* (which the Hulk claims that the Avengers' method of time travel is definitely *not*.) Wouldn't it be great to travel back to the past with a sports almanac detailing the losses and victories for the past several decades and make some bets? We'd have to assume that those bets wouldn't constitute the small change necessary to alter the future, of course, but what's one inexplicably lucky person among many?

In Nat Schachner's grandfather paradox, Dr. Pennypacker travels to the past knowing what had happened. We assume this is generally true of all time travelers—because we have records of the past, we think we know what happened, and we think we know what not to change. An extreme example would be *Don't kill your own grandfather* (or great-great-great-great and so on grandfather, as in Schachner's story). The moral of that story is clear—when Pennypacker returns to the present, thousands upon thousands of people just fade out of existence.

We know what happened in the past. The Avengers travel to the past to locate the Infinity Stones, which they could not do if they didn't know that the past had happened—where the stones would be. We don't know what happens in the future. Is that because we as human beings are limited in our knowledge, or is it because the future hasn't happened yet? The epistemological privilege that future people have over present people depends on our concept of the future—and whether it already exists to know or doesn't.

Time as a Dimension Similar to Space

The idea of time travel is relatively recent to philosophy. And that's because the idea that time is something that might be traveled in is itself relatively recent to physics. Traditionally, we have thought that it's possible to travel in space, and that traveling in space takes time.

Aristotle's book *Physics* discusses how time is the number of movement—it's the way we quantify movement of all sorts (movement in space, growth, decay, or really any kind of change). Time seems inseparable from change, and we talk about whether or not in the absence of change we would even notice time passing, or if time passes at all if nothing is changing. Aristotle thinks that time is the number of change, but also the number of rest. That is to say, if something doesn't change at all, we can still use time to measure *for how long* it hasn't changed. But others equate time and change in such a way that we conceive of *stopping time* just as a possible universe in which *nothing changes*. What I'm saying is, the concepts go together.

Until now—now that there's such a thing as "space-time" and we conceive of time as the fourth dimension. We used to have only three dimensions to move around in, those being the three dimensions of space (think forward-backward, left-right, and up-down). We say our world is three-dimensional, because everything in it takes up space. Everything that exists in space was supposed to be three-dimensional (though some subatomic particles would beg to differ). Now, we have a fourth dimension, and we have to conceive of things not as just taking up space, but taking up time as well. And if time is a dimension like the three dimensions of space, it's possible to move around in it.

This one realization brings up so many conceptual difficulties—if time is the measure of change, how much time does it take to travel in time? Are we time traveling right now just by moving forward in space? Is time, unlike space, privileged in one direction? Because it seems as if I can move forward and backward in space all I like, but like when I try to move in time, it's always going toward. Or I'm going forward in it—maybe time doesn't move at all, but I move *in* time, like I move along a road. And if time is laid out like a road on which I'm traveling, does that mean the future *already exists?*

It seems as if, should I want to travel to the future, the future would have to already exist. Maybe this is why we can conceive of traveling backward in time so easily, but forward seems more difficult. I know that the past existed, so I think there's somewhere to travel to. But the future is *indeterminate*, so maybe I can't travel there—because it doesn't exist yet. The *Avengers* concept of time assumes many possible worlds could come to be, which makes the future indeterminate; the Avengers will only win the battle against Thanos in one of how ever many possible futures, and *the actual future depends on their choices*.

This is the key difference about how we conceive of the future. In the traditional philosophy of Aristotle, the past is *necessary*, while the future is *contingent*. You can say true things about the past, because it happened—now the past is necessary. But the future isn't—it depends on the choices made by individuals. His example in *De Interpretatione* is whether or not there will be a sea battle tomorrow. Whether or not the sea battle will happen depends on the choices made by sea captains. And it seems this part of the traditional philosophy is retained for the *Avengers*. While there aren't an infinite number of possible futures, the future is still contingent on the choices made *now*.

When the Ancient One at first refuses to give Bruce Banner the Time Stone, it is because the future is contingent. He'll only be able to return the stones to their original places in their original timelines *if he succeeds*, and at this point, that is by no means certain. The Ancient One has to predict the future based on the choice that they make now—that is to say, they recognize that the future is contingent on the deliberate choices we freely make.

And is it possible to travel to somewhere that's only *contingent*? Before the choices have been made that will make the future what it is? If not, then it seems we can only travel back in time and not forward. But the *Avengers* complicate things by specifying a subjective view of time. It's part of the Hulk's reasoning for why you can't go back in the past and kill yourself— once you travel there, it's *your present*. Couldn't we make the same argument that when we travel to the future, it becomes the present?

The Nebula Solution and Subjective Timelines

What if there is no one *objective* time in which we all subsist? And by "objective time", I mean the one overarching timeline in which we're all taking part, popping in and out as we see fit, but always assured that the one master timeline will be there for us—and everyone in it. It seems that there is one overall timeline in the *Avengers* universe; we have to save Spider-Man in this one, and then he will *be saved*. It's not satisfactory to us that he's saved only in one of many possible universes—it's *this one* we're worried about.

We could interpret the Hulk's statement about the subjective nature of time as an indication that there is no such overarching timeline. There would instead be many timelines— your timeline, Tony's timeline, Captain America's timeline, Scarlet Witch's timeline, and so on. But I think that solution is generally unsatisfying, because we like to believe that there is one unified world that we all share. We like to think that there's *the* past and *the* future and *the* present, not just my past, my future and my present. And Spider-Man is alive—not just to you and not just to me, but *alive*.

There's another way out—with some finagling, we can make sense of the claim that when I travel to the past, that past becomes my present. By traveling through the quantum realm, the *Avengers* alter both what time they exist in, and *how long* it takes for that time to pass. Unlike space, time moves, *and* we move in it. We can't conceive of time travel as being exactly analogous to space travel, because space itself doesn't move— or else what would it move in? (To be fair, there are philosophers who claim that time doesn't move, we move in it, for example D.C. Williams's "The Myth of Passage.")

But if there is a contingent future, then time does move, and it moves forward—but that doesn't mean we have to move forward in it. So time travel is going to be different from traveling in space, because the thing in which we're moving is moving too. If we had to have an example of a similar kind of space travel, we might picture it as taking a run and then jumping onto a moving train—but even then, we'd have to specify that the train on which we're jumping may or may not exist (because the future is contingent, as least as far as *Avengers*-themed philosophy is concerned). So maybe our comparison between our concept of space and our concept of time *just isn't helpful*. Time is a dimension, and that makes it possible to move around in it, but the *way* in which we move around in time can't be compared to the way we move around in space, because they're very different kinds of dimension.

When Nebula kills her past self, she's not subject to the same concepts of time that informed the grandfather paradox. When we think that traveling back to the past to kill our grandparents would negate our own existence, we're using an old concept of time. We might ask how 2014 Nebula was able to travel *forward* to 2023 when for her the future doesn't yet exist, but *it does*, because the one actual timeline has in fact advanced to that point. That doesn't mean that *the entire* future already exists. We might be better off describing the "past" and "future" in terms of "stuff that has happened" and "stuff that has not happened yet." The difference between the past and the future is still as Aristotle thought—the past is over and done, while the future is yet to come.

Present Nebula can kill past Nebula in the present, because past Nebula exists in the present, and now the present is, for past Nebula, also the present—not the future. And that's all there is to it. It's the same principle according to which Thanos comes back from the past to the present, although he died at the beginning of the movie. The only difference is that we never see two Thanoses together and he doesn't kill himself.

7
Something Strange about Time Travel

RHYS WOODWARDS

One of the many philosophical puzzles we take away from the Marvel Cinematic Universe is the question: Is time travel possible? And if so, what would it look like?

The nature of time travel hasn't just grabbed the attention of sci-fi fans; it has intrigued philosophers for decades and it's fair to say that such questions were motivated by the increasing interest in science fiction.

Does future Nebula killing past Nebula mean that future Nebula ceases to exist? If not, why not? What makes time travel in the Marvel Cinematic Universe "strange"? Get it? Strange . . . Hopefully, in showing that time travel in *Endgame* is a little more complex than we might originally have thought, we should be able to see that the Nebula situation, future Nebula killing past Nebula, is *not* a huge mess.

What Is Time Travel?

Much of *Endgame* is spent traveling into the past. Of course, travel into the future can also count as time travel. However, the interesting problems, such as future Nebula killing past Nebula, arise from travel into the past.

Without giving a precise definition of time travel, it seems easy enough to pick out genuine and non-genuine cases. Tony Stark in 2023 travelling backwards in time to visit his father Howard is no doubt a genuine case of time travel. It's more difficult to give an example of non-genuine backwards time travel since most cases are science fiction.

Maybe the best example is of a fortune teller who somehow 'sees' a past scene in a crystal ball. It might seem or feel to the fortune teller as if they are really there in that past scene, but they are not, they are just imagining it, and so this does not count as genuine time travel. Unfortunately, neither does the freezing of our beloved Captain America. It might feel to Steve Rogers as though he has time-traveled; after all he was frozen for nearly seventy years, but it's at best a stretch to claim that this is genuine time travel.

So, what makes examples of time travel genuine? Time travel necessarily involves a discrepancy between the time elapsed from your departure to your arrival. Normally, when we travel, we travel into the future. The duration of the journey is the time that has passed between our departure and our arrival. If I set off toward London at 1:00 P.M. and arrive at 2:30, then the duration of the journey has been an hour and a half, and this is the amount of time that I have traveled toward the future. However, this is not the case for a time traveler. It is possible for the time traveler to set off toward London at 1:00 P.M., the duration of his journey be an hour and a half, yet his arrival be three years prior to his departure! A case of genuine time travel must involve this strange discrepancy.

This might seem confusing. However, applied to a frozen Captain America it makes more sense. Steve being frozen does not count as time travel because the duration of his journey, if you can call it that, matches the amount of time elapsed between him being frozen and being awoken. He traveled seventy years into the future and was frozen for seventy years. Tony traveling to meet his father counts as time travel because the time elapsed between his departure in 2023 and his arrival in approximately 1970 was not a total of fifty-three years. Anyone who has seen the film can tell you it was much quicker than that!

At the very least, genuine cases involve embarking on a journey of which the time at departure and arrival does not match the length of time passed to embark on that journey. This is the reason why, when we think of time travel, we more than likely think of traveling back to the past. All travel into the past counts as time travel since we are normally traveling into the future. If it takes a time traveler any time to travel into the past, then they have time traveled—no matter how little time it took.

The Grandfather Paradox

It is not uncommon for philosophers to think that there is something inherently "Strange" about time travel, "Strange," get it? This strangeness is shown by time travel paradoxes. Use of the word "paradox" suggests that there is some underlying contradiction in our commonplace conception of time travel. The most famous, and often mentioned in criticisms of *Endgame*, is the Grandfather Paradox.

To get to the bottom of this apparent contradiction, first consider the possibility that you travel backwards in time to kill your grandfather at a time when your parents were not yet conceived. If time travel is at the very least possible, then there is nothing to rule out the time traveler putting themselves in this tricky situation.

Some philosophers argue that backwards time travel, without limitations, must be impossible. They do so because such an impossibility means that you cannot get yourself into the kind of situation that gives rise to these paradoxes and contradictions. Claiming that backwards time travel allows for the messy situations and arguing that it is impossible prevents these paradoxes and contradictions from arising.

David Lewis simply denies that it is possible to travel backwards in time and kill your grandfather because if you did, it would result in a logical contradiction. According to Lewis ("The Paradoxes of Time Travel"), if an action brings about a logical contradiction then it can't be possible to act in this way. "It is logically impossible that Tim should change the past by killing his Grandfather in 1921. So, Tim cannot kill his Grandfather."

Lewis does think that time travel is possible, just that it has limitations. Lewis sets out the limitations to time travel so as to make it more coherent. These limitations are dictated by logical contradictions such that Tim, on his time traveling adventures, would be unable to act in any way that would bring about a logical contradiction. The contradiction is present in the conflict between there being a Tim related to his grandfather in this way, and Tim killing his grandfather before the time that Tim's father was conceived.

Such theorizing is about time travel in the actual world, and this might not look like much help when we discuss time travel in *Endgame*. Time travel in the Marvel Cinematic Universe is more permissive than Lewis's conception; it seems that, at least in *Endgame*, logical contradictions arise even in less drastic cases than time traveling murderers.

Consider that great scene in which future Captain America fights past Captain America. It cannot be the case that past Captain America both fights and does not fight future Captain America, however, at least in the Marvel Cinematic Universe taken as a whole, this seems to be the case. There are loads of further scenarios in *Endgame* that have the same result. In order to make proper sense of time travel in *Endgame*, we need to find a conception of time travel that explains and accounts for these strange contradictions.

Even if we had a "contradiction-free" conception of time travel in the Marvel Cinematic Universe, one that admits these contradictions, we're still left with the question of how it all fits together. I could never forget those awesome suits and I am sure you have not too! We can do much better than a notion of time-travel fraught with contradictions. Furthermore, I think I can identify clues in *Endgame* that point to a more satisfying account of time travel.

To help gain a better understanding of time travel in *Endgame*, we should discuss what I think is the most troubling scene when it comes to time travel, future Nebula killing past Nebula. The Grandfather Paradox is just as well illustrated by this Nebula problem. We can ask the question of how, if future Nebula kills past Nebula at a time before the future Nebula decides to travel backwards in time, it is possible for Nebula to exist at such a future point? Surely this future Nebula should cease to exist at the same time that past Nebula ceases to exist? The problem is that past Nebula has been murdered before she ever had access to time travel. This should mean that there was never a future Nebula to travel back in time in the first place. How then is it possible for there to be a future Nebula? This question haunted me as soon as I left the theater.

If the rules of time travel in the Marvel Cinematic Universe were as Lewis describes then there really is no way in which future Nebula could kill past Nebula, since this would result in a logical contradiction. We need to find a more permissive conception of time travel that helps explain these cases. Without any further explanation of the nature of Marvel Cinematic Universe time travel we seem to be left with a nonsensical conception, one fraught with contradiction and absurd consequences. But I think there is an answer to this.

A Better Conception of Time Travel

Time travel may look "Strange" to the ever-questioning philosopher; however, I think Marvel Cinematic Universe time travel is distinctive. Future Nebula killing past Nebula can be resolved with reference to the convoluted explanation of Marvel Cinematic Universe time travel given by Professor Hulk.

Multiverse theories should be no stranger to the committed sci-fi fan. Such theories have also captured the interest of many philosophers. Opinion amongst philosophers varies greatly in this respect too! Multiverse theories hold that there are multiple universes. If it helps, we can think of them as different worlds.

For some Philosophers each "world" contains different objects and what goes on in one world does not and cannot affect what goes on in another. A multiverse theory states there are multiple possible universes. Some philosophers argue that what goes on in one universe does not and cannot affect what goes on in another distinct universe.

I won't go into lengthy detail about quantum mechanics, I don't think I could even if I wanted to! However, the "many worlds" interpretation of quantum mechanics could be crucial to understanding time travel in the Marvel Cinematic Universe, After all, it is no accident that we're introduced to the quantum realm in the Ant-Man movies.

Think back to your high-school physics teacher's classes on electrons; these electrons are extremely complex quantum particles. A Quantum Particle is the smallest physical quantity and cannot be divided any further. Before we measure or observe any given property of an electron it is in a superposition. When something is in a superposition it means that it possesses two conflicting properties at the same time. Don't worry, this should feel strange! An electron before it is measured is actually both hard and soft, but then, once measured, it is either hard or soft but not both. Quantum particles don't actually possess the properties "hard" and "soft" but this is a simple way to illustrate the point. It goes from having indeterminate value (being both hard and soft) to a determinate value (being either hard or soft but not both). When a particle is in a superposition, it isn't merely that we do not know whether it hard or soft. According to the interpretation we're pursuing here, the particle actually possesses these two conflicting properties.

The many worlds interpretation helps us to understand how a particle goes from being in a superposition to possessing one determinate property. This interpretation is one of many and is by no means the standard view in the philosophy of quantum mechanics. However, I think it is of great significance to understanding what is going on in *Avengers: Endgame*. The many-worlds interpretation understands the pre-measurement state of the electron as representing two distinct worlds, the electron is hard in one world (A) and soft in a different world (B). When we measure the particle's spin it only represents the value in this world, be that (A) or (B).

Don't worry if you don't follow; this should feel extremely peculiar. To simplify, before measurement the particle possesses two conflicting properties, after measurement it possesses only one of these properties. How do we get from indeterminate to determinate properties? The many-worlds interpretation claims that the superposition represents distinct worlds and when the electron has a determinate value it represents the property of that electron in this world. The many-worlds theorist claims that there is also another separate world in which the electron is the opposite of what it is in this world.

How is this of help to *Endgame* and Marvel Cinematic Universe time travel? Good question! First, it fits extremely nicely with Ant-Man's quantum adventures, the fact that the quantum realm is even mentioned in the Marvel Cinematic Universe is no accident. Second, it allows for the possibility of a more complex explanation of time travel. This explanation enables us to understand how it looks as if time travel in *Endgame* gives rise to so many apparent contradictions.

The suggestion is that when the Avengers time travel, they not only travel backwards in time but also travel to an alternate universe, another "world."

What evidence do I have to believe that Marvel Cinematic Universe time travel works in this way? When the Hulk approaches the Sorcerer Supreme and attempts to acquire the time stone, she tells him that when the Infinity Stones are taken from their rightful place in the timeline, a branching occurs. The way that this branching is described sounds awfully like the kind of branching that, according to the many-worlds interpretation, occurs when we measure an electron.

This, paired with the direct mention of the quantum world throughout Ant-Man's adventures and *Endgame*, suggest that when the Avengers time travel in *Endgame*, they do not travel through time in the ordinary sense. Instead they travel to a distinct alternate universe. Of course, these universes must bear some causal relation to one another, in order for our heroes to make a difference in their own timeline. Given both points, I think it is fair to say that Marvel Cinematic Universe time travel is more distinctive than we might have initially thought.

This is also where the Nebula problem can be explained. Future Nebula doesn't just travel backwards in her own timeline but rather travels backwards in time and also, more importantly, in a different timeline. This would mean that future Nebula's murder of past Nebula does not result in future Nebula ceasing to exist. Past Nebula is not identical to future Nebula. They do not belong to the same timeline, the same world history, and so the death of one does not result in the death of the other.

We can easily explain the other apparent contradictions. The Captain America I previously called "past" Captain America, does not both fight and not fight "future" Captain America. Rather, we can think of two distinct versions of "past" Captain America. These belong to different universes or time-lines. One fights future Captain America—this is the one we see in *Endgame*—and one does not fight future Captain America—this is the one we see in *The Avengers* (2012). An appeal to multiverse theory, grounded in the explicit mention of quantum mechanics, helps us to rid our beloved story of the apparent contradictions that time travel seems to bring.

These superficial contradictions are not plot holes or a mess up in the movie but rather a subtle hint to a more complex notion of time travel. If we think of time travel in *Endgame* not as involving the traveling backwards in time inside of our own histories in this world, but as involving the traveling backwards in time to a history of some other world, then we get a better picture of what is going on.

This helps us grasp more clearly what it is that the Hulk tells a hopelessly confused Scott Lang, and also helps us make sense of why the quantum realm is mentioned at all. The quantum realm doesn't have to be a hopeless appeal to a complex science to help explain time travel. A good understanding of the many-worlds interpretation can actually help us understand just how time travel works in *Endgame*.

8
Time Travel and the Problem of Evil

RAY BOSSERT

Why would a superhero allow innocent people to suffer? It's a question to consider when Doctor Strange and Tony Stark decide they will not use their powers to prevent or erase Thanos's fatal Snap.

We expect a superhero to take up the suffering of others, to rescue those in peril at the hero's own expense. Consider Hawkeye and the Black Widow in *Endgame* when they are seeking the Soul Stone. According to the movie, whoever seeks the Soul Stone must sacrifice something they love in order to acquire the stone. Confronted with this dilemma, the two heroes literally race against each other to see who can sacrifice themselves for the other's sake. When Hawkeye grasps Black Widow to stop her from falling to her death, she kicks herself out of his grip. They behave how we expect heroes to behave, sparing others and taking suffering upon themselves.

When confronted with the same dilemma, Thanos sends his daughter Gamora to her death against her will. He does mourn her death, with a humanizing tear shed for her, but I suspect that it is the person lying dead at the bottom of the chasm who experiences the greater loss in both cases where we see the Soul Stone acquired. Thanos and Hawkeye are compensated with one of the mystical MacGuffins needed to power the Infinity Gauntlet. Gamora and Black Widow, not so much.

Thanos decides for Gamora that she will suffer for his advantage—and, as he sees it, for the greater good of the cosmos. Thanos's plan might be perverse, but he claims to be well-intended. This version of Thanos believes overpopulation is dooming life in the universe to misery and self-annihilation, so he snaps half of it out of existence to improve the quality of life—if not chances of survival—for the remaining beings. As the villain, Thanos treats the suffering of his daughter and the rest of the universe as necessary evils to achieve his ends.

The movies suggest he is wrong, of course, but his approach ends up running uncannily parallel to two other Avengers: Doctor Strange and Tony Stark, both of whom decide to let the universe suffer for the sake of a grander plan.

Doctor Strange and Tony Stark dominate the Avengers team in terms of strategic planning. They typically have privileged knowledge, due either to Strange's ability to time travel or to Stark's technological supergenius. Both characters make the decision that it's better to allow half of all life in the universe to be eliminated—and to permit the suffering of the survivors—in order to achieve a greater good. Doctor Strange enables the Snap to happen in the first place, and Tony Stark decides they must not use time travel to undo it directly. In this regard, Doctor Strange and Tony Stark also make a choice that is uncannily close to Thanos's. They decide—on behalf of the entire universe—that the suffering of countless others is acceptable when weighed against their ultimate victory.

To better understand how Doctor Strange and Tony Stark justify their decisions, it helps to view *Endgame* through the philosophy (or pseudo-philosophy as some label it) of Boethius, a sixth-century Roman. Despite a prestigious political career, Boethius was ultimately executed on charges of conspiracy against Theoderic the Ostrogoth (whom Boethius had been advising despite sounding like the kind of guy who might himself be hunting for Infinity Stones). Granted, such an interpretation of *Endgame* comes with some caveats. Boethius wasn't imagining a fictional universe where humans were capable of time travel, nor any kind of theories of a "multiverse"— whether based in advanced physics or corporate marketing strategies.

Boethius's most famous work is *The Consolation of Philosophy*, a treatise written while Boethius was in prison awaiting execution. In the text, a fictionalized Boethius converses with the personification of Philosophy, cast as a Lady— who uses reason (and reason alone) to console Boethius. Like *Endgame* today, *The Consolation of Philosophy* was hugely popular in medieval and Renaissance times, repeatedly translated by such outstanding figures as Alfred the Great, Geoffrey Chaucer, and Queen Elizabeth I.

Boethius was especially popular with Christian humanists since, despite his Christianity, he builds his argument without ever turning to Church doctrines or Scripture. He used Greco-Roman philosophical approaches to tackle two significant questions: 1. why would a benevolent and omnipotent deity permit evil to exist, and 2. does God's foreknowledge eliminate human free will? In other words, why doesn't God just snap evil out of existence, and does God's very knowledge of what you will choose force you to make that choice so as not to contradict what God knows?

This question of foreknowledge ties closely with plots of time travel. The fictionalized Boethius, apparently having too much time on his hands while awaiting death, can't help but try to find a paradox between foreknowledge and free will. He ponders that if God knows all things—including things to come—then God already knows what you're going to do. And if God knows it, then it must be true. And if it must be true, then it seems all of your choices are predestined. You can't choose otherwise, because then that would mean God didn't actually know what you were going to do—which would eliminate God's omniscience (p. 120). It's the chronological equivalent of asking God to build a stone heavier than God could lift.

Boethius's Lady Philosophy isn't having any of that. To simplify the argument a bit, Philosophy leads Boethius to conclude that God knows what God knows only because it was a choice—you still chose it. God sees the choices without compelling them (p. 125). He says you have to imagine God sitting outside of time and space, seeing it all unfold at once.

This question of foreknowledge and free will might seem like a fairly abstruse philosophical riddle, but the Avengers movies are heavily invested in the issue. Towards the end of *Avengers: Infinity War*, Doctor Strange and Tony Stark have an exchange about their possibility of success:

> STRANGE: I went forward in time to view alternate futures. To see all the possible outcomes of the coming conflict.
>
> STARK: How many did you see?
>
> STRANGE: 14,000,605.
>
> STARK: How many did we win?
>
> STRANGE: One.

Strange now has foreknowledge of the future—gained by witnessing its various iterations through the cosmic power of the Time Stone.

Boethius thinks we have to understand God as eternal rather than infinite, and by that he means something that doesn't simply continue existing without end but rather something that exists outside time itself. An "infinite" being still rides along the timeline of physical existence. But an eternal being "embraces all the infinite recesses of past and future and views them in the immediacy of its knowing as though they are happening in the present . . . it will be more correct to think of it not as a kind of foreknowledge of the future, but as the knowledge of a never ending presence" (p. 134).

With this distinction between the infinite and eternal in mind, we can categorize how Doctor Strange's Time Stone works. Doctor Strange is only really conscious of one moment at a time: when we see him viewing other futures, he seems to move in fast-forward, then rewind, then fast-forward, then rewind—he isn't really present in the same present as the other characters, and his consciousness isn't coexisting in multiple times simultaneously. Doctor Strange binge-watches the future at high speed: he possesses an Infinity Stone, not an eternity stone. For Boethius, it's as if God sees every frame of every episode of all of history simultaneously. Another important difference is that Doctor Strange watches different timelines. Whereas God simultaneously sees all points along a linear timeline of events, Doctor Strange is actually seeing some kind of interactive, branching-narrative like *Black Mirror*, and replaying it until he has clicked on every possible path.

The knowledge that Doctor Strange gains is supposed to offer the audience some consolation later in the movie when Strange shockingly surrenders the Time Stone to Thanos— appearing on the surface to have betrayed his teammates and given the villain what he wanted.

STARK: Why did you do that?

STRANGE: We're in the endgame now . . . there was no other way.

Strange is playing a very, very long game of chess, and (it turns out) sacrifices many, many pieces in order to set up the conditions for the ultimate victory. This is all fairly obvious to the audience, but the characters are still a bit wary. He seems to have made a horrible choice.

In *Endgame*, Doctor Strange indicates that he can't let Stark know whether they're in the one successful scenario. Doctor Strange obviously thinks that giving Stark a glimpse of his own future decisions will paradoxically prevent them from happening. Apparently, Tony's choice only happens in a narrative vacuum—knowledge of the choice would somehow influence his choice and make him not choose what he needed to choose when he needed to choose it. Phew.

Why wouldn't Stark make the choice if he knew? The movie itself conveniently skirts around the issue, and we are left mainly with conjecture. Maybe it's simply because Tony Stark can't refuse an opportunity to be rebellious and would do the opposite of what someone said he should do just to reassert his free will. Regardless, we are told that Stark's choice has to be unencumbered—even by knowledge of the choice itself. His choice must be free. And this, as you might suspect, relates directly to Boethius's explanation of the problem of evil. Boethius argues that an omnipotent, omniscient, and all-loving deity allows evil to persist because it is the consequence of giving free will to creatures. For Boethius, to do otherwise deprives humanity of one of the key aspects of its nature.

And yet neither Boethius's God nor Doctor Strange are completely passive. Doctor Strange uses his knowledge of the future—of all possible futures—to make conscious choices on his own that veer history towards a particular path. Boethius's Philosophy goes on to reason out the concept of divine providence—the idea that God has a supreme plan and can steer human history towards its goal through miraculous or invisible means. Boethius writes that God anticipates each human choice, and our inevitable flaws are "visible to the eye of Providence as it looks out at all things from eternity and arranges predestined rewards according to each man's merit." Even if God doesn't have a Time Stone, God has all of eternity to sort out just the right ways to maneuver human behavior to get the intended results.

Boethius thus explains his own suffering in prison as well as the rest of humanity's. God tolerates it because it does not prevent the greater good that is to come. In fact, God's ability to play the ultimate script doctor enables him to transform the suffering into events that actually advance the plot. Likewise, when *Avengers: Endgame* establishes some ground rules of time travel, they accept that some bad must be permitted to achieve the preferred ending . . . such as when the team decides not to stop the Snap from ever happening.

Ignoring plot holes for a second, there are reasons for this decision, both in terms of plot and audience investment. In terms of plot, the movie at least pays lip service to avoiding time travel paradoxes—what would happen to their universe if they erased the conditions that required them to travel back in time in the first place? This is vitally important to Tony Stark, who does not want to risk erasing the birth of his daughter. (Whereas Thanos will kill his daughter in order to kill half the universe, Stark will let others experience death and suffering to save his daughter's life.) Additionally, the choice not to stop the first Snap from happening also bolsters audience investment. Preserving the Snap "honors" whatever emotional investment the audience had watching their heroes evaporate (remember when Joss Whedon refused to bring back Agent Coulson despite the *Agents of SHIELD* television series?).

This means that both Doctor Strange and Tony Stark are willing to accept the Snap and the five years of suffering that follow. Both heroes are willing to allow the death, the grief, the enormously negative impact on quality of life and living conditions that will be experienced across the entire universe. They do this because of a vision of a future where the dead are resurrected, life is restored, and justice prevails.

We have seen the importance that Boethius places on free will as a divine gift, but Boethius also argues that there are occasions where human beings are paradoxically free to willingly reject that gift. This occurs when we surrender ourselves to our emotions and desires. Boethius writes: "Destructive passions torment them, and by yielding and giving in to them, they only aid the slavery they have brought upon themselves and become in a manner prisoners of their own freedom" (p. 119). Think about how many opportunities the Avengers squandered to prevent the Snap in *Infinity War*. Each time the Avengers came closest to victory, they blew it because a character let their passions drive them to seek personal revenge instead. Ironically, the Avengers fail to prevent destruction precisely because some of them are so busy avenging fallen lovers, brothers, or friends. (I'm looking at you, Star Lord and Thor.) Bound by their emotions, these characters did not rise to their full potential as heroes.

Did Tony Stark Aim Small?

When Stark finally acquires the Infinity Gauntlet, he becomes a god. He can will anything into or out of existence.

And what does he do with it?

He reverses (but does not erase) Thanos's Snap—a restoration. And he wishes Thanos and his minions out of existence—a form of destruction. But, as far as we know, that's it.

It doesn't seem as though he used his power to end world hunger or poverty. Nor did he wish a clean, renewable, affordable fuel source into being. He doesn't erase cancer or AIDS. He didn't even stop *X-Men: The Dark Phoenix* from being released. And he certainly doesn't use a Snap to give himself a body capable of surviving a Snap. Perhaps more troubling, he doesn't really seem to think about the consequences of unsnapping people. What if spouses had remarried? What if people's homes had been sold, and their jobs given away? Where are the infrastructure and resources to suddenly support an instantaneously doubling of the world population? Tony Stark doesn't seem to have had a plan to eliminate suffering—even though he was, for the moment, omnipotent.

In his 1972 review essay, "The Myth of Superman," Umberto Eco (also the author of *The Name of the Rose* and other extremely smart novels) observes that superheroes are notoriously limited in their world-saving imaginations. Eco points out that the capitalist demands for book sales limit Superman from using his superpowers to make real change in the world—instead, he uses them to preserve the status quo. Saving the world from bank robbers and mad scientists does not change the world—if anything it stops change from occurring.

Superhero stories have changed a lot since 1972. *Endgame*, after all, starts with the world in a kind of post-apocalyptic setting. But is the movie's world really all that different from the one we know? Even after ten years of public awareness of space aliens, superheroes, and supernatural beings, characters go to group therapy to talk about their love life, and kids still excitedly snap selfies with celebrities in diners. The world of the Marvel Cinematic Universe doesn't feel as though it has evolved all that differently from our own.

Nor is the world after Stark's Snap really any different. Stark's Snap seems to say: Yeah, the real world is okay enough just the way it is, I'll just reverse this one fantastical element of intergalactic eco-terrorism.

Justice and Philosophy's Consolation

"If we can't protect the Earth, you can be damn well sure we'll avenge it."

Tony Stark says this to Loki in the first *Avengers* movie. (Perhaps because someone decided we needed a reason for them to be called Avengers?) Thor makes good on this promise when he beheads Thanos in the beginning of *Endgame*. Early in the film, the Avengers track down Thanos in an attempt to reverse the Snap. The moment when it becomes clear their plan has failed, Thor metes out vengeance—swiftly and with very little thought (to say nothing of jurisprudence or due process). Is this justice?

One of the consolations that Philosophy offers Boethius is the ability to reason out the ultimate victory of justice in any scenario. Justice is, as Thanos says of himself, inevitable. Obviously, justice prevails if the powers that be capture and punish the evildoer. But what if the evildoer escapes direct punishment? Boethius says that escape without punishment is an even more severe punishment. If justice is a good, and punishment for wickedness is a good, then the evildoer who escapes justice has been deprived of a good. The evildoer might not see it that way, but Boethius uses such a perspective to push the point further: the evildoer who does not see the goodness in paying for their crimes is sacrificing his dignity, honor, and humanity. He becomes something less than he should be.

How does post-Snap Thanos come off to you? Does he seem to be living up to his utmost potential? He went from being a powerful, intergalactic warlord and nothing short of a god, to chilling in a hut and unable to defend himself in the least. But even worse, from Boethius's point of view, is what wickedness has done to Thanos's honor and value.

When War Machine suggests that Thanos must be lying about destroying the stones, Nebula responds "My father is many things, but a liar is not one of them." So Thanos is not completely shameful—he tells the truth, but the implication of Nebula's statement is that Thanos has many less than noble traits. As Boethius's philosophy predicts, we can see that Thanos is a wretched creature. His inability to recognize his own wretchedness only makes him more wretched. (And even his plan is futile, since populations will most likely double again without the Gauntlet to control them.) Thanos's evil is self-destructive—literally. He's barely even worth decapitating—and part of the shock of Thor's action is that it is so unnecessary.

The audience gets to see Thanos die a second time when he disappears after Iron Man's Snap. Justice seems poetic this time because Thanos meets the same end as the innocents he erased at the end of *Infinity War*. Whatever way you spin it, punishment for wickedness is so inevitable that the villain dies twice in one movie.

In Boethius's Philosophical Universe, God allows suffering because it is a consequence of freedom, but providence weaves human choices into a pattern that always produces justice. In the Marvel Cinematic Universe, Tony Stark allows the world to suffer because it is the only path by which to achieve all of his goals: life for his daughter, justice for Thanos's victims, and the resurrection of those who disappeared.

To conclude, let's return for a moment to our first example of self-sacrifice for the sake of another. Hawkeye would rather lose his life than see Black Widow die, and he technically never actually sacrifices her. But Black Widow's choice still depends on harming her friend—albeit a lesser harm than death. Hawkeye now has to carry her loss with him.

Perhaps it's merely pain that acquires the Soul Stone, rather than sacrifice, since in *Endgame*, Hawkeye is the unwilling participant in the bargain. He doesn't make the sacrifice, but still feels its effects. The pain of loss proves one has a soul. Indeed, that pain gives us the most human glimpse we ever get of Thanos. It might be a lesser loss than death, but it still means that one superhero, Black Widow, permitted the suffering of another to achieve a greater good. The consolation Philosophy offers at such moments is that suffering will always be paid for by justice—and the film shows this to be true. However, the degree to which an individual *feels* consoled by such a philosophy is another question.

III

Ethics

9

With Infinite Power Comes No Responsibility?

JAMES HART

> Give me a break! I'm doing what has to be done. To stave off something worse.
>
> —IRON MAN, *Captain America: Civil War*

When Iron Man and Captain America clash in *Civil War*, it's not just over the specific approach to the Sokovia Accords, or even a personality clash. A deeper philosophical issue divides them.

Tony Stark is a consequentialist—he cares about the consequences of his actions on the world, above and beyond any other moral factor. He wants to maximize the amount of happy, good lives in the multiverse and minimize the number of painful and bad lives, and the ends justify the means in this pursuit.

This means that Stark is happy to hurt one person if it were to save the lives of many. Steve Rogers on the other hand believes there are certain moral principles that are so fundamental they cannot be broken, even if they were to lead to better consequences. This makes Rogers a deontologist—someone who follows moral rules regardless of the consequences.

This is not a new observation, or even a particularly interesting one. What is interesting, however, is that the problems our heroes face in *Endgame* might finally settle the moral debate in Captain America's favor. With an infinite number of lives on the line, making the right decision has never been so important, but Iron Man faces an extra threat: infinitarian paralysis.

For Rogers, decision-making is usually fairly easy, he only needs to look at the situation in front of him, work out which actions are morally permitted and which are not, and punch the closest bad guy. Stark however cannot do this. Instead, he must work out which series of actions will most increase the balance of good lives compared to bad lives, and only after that can he punch the bad guy. Sometimes this might mean he won't punch the bad guy at all, and sometimes it means he might even punch a good guy.

Naturally, it is very complicated figuring out how one's actions might affect the total value of all lives. An act that at first glance might seem good, when considered in light of all the consequences might be bad. For instance giving up your seat for the old lady on the bus might have the unintended consequence of reducing her fitness, and so she becomes more prone to illness.

We are all aware of situations like these in our lives. How many times have we naively attempted to help and only made the situation worse? Thankfully, for most of us these cases, whilst they might occur regularly, do not have horrific consequences. However, for Iron Man, the consequences of getting things wrong can be pretty large.

Nothing demonstrates this better than when Iron Man almost destroyed the Earth in *Avengers: Age of Ultron*. In creating an AI to protect the Earth from extra-terrestrial threats, he accidentally created a genocidal maniac. So Stark is more aware than most how important and difficult it is to calculate the consequences of your actions, and pick the right response.

But Stark is not one to hide away from difficult calculations, even if he does occasionally get them wrong, and with the supercomputers JARVIS and FRIDAY on his side, he has had some pretty overpowered calculators to back him up. The moral calculations were hard, but at least pre–*Infinity War* the numbers were finite.

However, come Thanos and Tony's introduction to the rest of the Multiverse, these calculations are suddenly going to involve numbers orders of magnitude larger. To complete an infinite number of calculations in a finite time might be a supertask too far, even for Ironman.

Infinitarian Paralysis

Suppose however that he can get past the practical difficulties in calculating the consequences of his actions, Tony will soon realize deeper issues underpin his moral philosophy.

Nick Bostrom identifies the issue, which he calls *infinitarian paralysis*. The idea is that if the universe is infinitely large, then there will be an infinite number of good and happy lives and an infinite number of bad and sad lives. In Tony's case, Marvel's multiverse has an equal number of blissful Asgards and despotic Sakaars. Because of this any action, whether it would seem to produce good or bad consequences would in fact, make no difference to the total number of happy or sad lives in the multiverse.

Stark's super-computers will spit out the same answers to every action: 'the moral value of the multiverse is unchanged, sir'; he cannot tip the cosmic balance in favor of the light! Doing any 'good' in this world would make less difference than adding a single atom to the world would increase the mass of our solar system.

Bostrom argues that as soon as we recognize this, we're effectively morally paralysed; we become incapable of acting morally or immorally. As such, as soon as Tony Stark realizes that he lives in an infinite multiverse, he will become incapable of acting heroically, a pretty bad fate for a superhero.

To illustrate this, let us imagine that Tony Stark has created an infinite orphanage to house all those orphaned by the Snap. Call this Stark's Orphanage, it's a version of Hilbert's Hotel. The orphanage comes with all the trappings of a Stark mansion and there are an infinite number of rooms in the orphanage. Orphans flock from every corner of the multiverse, from St. Petersburg to Pasadena and from Titan to the Astral Plane. As such, the orphanage soon has an orphan in every room. Despite this, there are still an infinite number of orphans living on the streets. The balance of happy to sad orphans is infinite to infinite.

But then Tony has a smart idea, if he moves all the orphans along by one room, so that the orphan in room one moves to room two, and the orphan in room two moves to room three etc., he can fit another orphan in his orphanage, without kicking anyone out. This seemingly good act however, has no effect on the balance of happy to sad orphans. When Tony plugs the numbers into FRIDAY, he receives the same answer as before: the balance of happy to sad orphans is infinite-infinite. He has not even dented the problem.

Similarly, he could kick out hundreds of orphans back onto the street, and the cosmic balance would remain unchanged. No action is better than any other. By his own standard, he can never do any good; he has been infected with infinitarian paralysis.

Even the Snap itself seems to have no effect on the cosmic balance of light versus darkness. Thanos, in killing half the people in the multiverse, might have killed an infinite number of people, but he has also left an infinite number of people alive. It seems that not only does infinitarian paralysis prevent you from doing anything good, it might also justify actions previously thought immoral. Genocide becomes permissible so long as an infinite number of people are still left alive. This disease then is quite dangerous.

The Causal Approach and Butterfly Effects

But Tony might think he has a cure to his paralysis. He might say something along the lines of 'I can't affect what happens on Asgard or Sakaar, but I can affect what happens on Earth, it is the consequences of *my* actions I should care about'.

Nick Bostrom calls this approach the causal approach; 'Instead of maximizing the expected goodness of the world, we could aim to maximize the expected goodness of the causal consequences of our acts.'

It does mean that Stark has to abandon the cosmic scale, but he is willing to bite the bullet. As such, he reprograms FRIDAY, not to calculate the total value in the multiverse and what effect his actions have on the total balance of good and bad lives, but instead to simply calculate the consequences of his actions.

For a while this works, and allows Tony to make moral decisions, it seems his actions only have finite consequences after all. As such, he can see whether they have overall good or bad consequences and he determines how to act as such.

However, the choices Stark has to make in *Endgame* are not the same choices you or I, or even he, makes every day. Whether he chooses to try to reverse the Snap or stay at home and enjoy his life with his family, Stark is making a choice that affects an infinite number of people. As such, the consequences of his actions are not going to be finite in scope.

Whilst reversing the Snap will bring back millions of people to their families and happy lives, countless others will be brought back into lives of slavery or torture, lives that might not be worth living. There will be an infinite number of good and bad consequences of each of his actions and so, once again, he cannot determine the best course of action from its good and bad consequences.

Once Tony realizes this, he might also realize that this case is not the only one where his choices will have infinite effects. Tony would be aware of the Butterfly Effect, that incredibly minute changes can have incredibly large effects, and that in an infinite multiverse these incredibly large effects could be infinite in size. Tony's short exchange with Doctor Strange at the end of *Avengers: Infinity War*, where Doctor Strange looks at 14,000,605 alternative futures, would have confirmed this to him. As such even simple-seeming choices will have infinite effects, and Tony will be morally paralyzed once again.

Expected Value and Difficult Choices

Tony, however, will not take this problem lying down; if there is a way he can fight the paralysis he will. He's going to argue that, as he cannot possibly know what's going to happen in the future, it would be completely unfair for him to be held responsible for every single potential consequence of his actions. Especially when those actions might affect the choices other people make. Tony's actions have unknowingly helped create many of his enemies, but surely he cannot be blamed for their numerous crimes, even if it would have been better had he not accidentally created them.

Tony might have an out. The consequentialist philosopher Frank Jackson argues that because we cannot know all of the many consequences of our actions we should not judge them on their total consequences. He argues that instead we should judge what to do through *expected value*. This is a concept that is widely used in economics, but has also started to gain traction in philosophy.

The idea is that we should consider the likely consequences of our actions and how good those consequences would be. Once we have done this we can provide rough probabilities for each consequence occurring. We should then perform the action that has the best chance of creating the most amount of good. The formula for this can be given as:

Expected Value = Value of Outcome × Probability of Outcome Occurring

If Tony follows Jackson then this means his decisions will be based on what he can expect to effect, and he can make his decision this way. He cannot predict or expect the butterfly effects, either good or bad, and so they should not affect him in his decision-making. He can ignore them.

Instead, he only works with the information he has available to him. He can work out the various probabilities of the predictable consequences of his actions and calculate from this what course of action is most beneficial. For instance, if Iron

Man can attempt to save 1 person with a 50 percent chance of success or try to save 3 people with a 25 percent chance of success, he should attempt to save the 3 people. The expected value of the first option is 0.5 lives saved, whereas the second option has an expected value of 0.75 lives saved. He has escaped the infinitarian paralysis once again.

Tony is moving further and further away from pure consequentialism, but he considers it a small price to pay to escape paralysis. He still gets to keep the (reactor) core of his morality.

Pascal's Mugging and the Infinitarian Trance

However, even this reduced version of consequentialism is going to create new problems for Tony. In cases where there is a miniscule, but predictable, chance to create an infinite amount of value, Tony will be threatened by an infinitarian trance. The chance to create an infinite amount of value will dwarf all other concerns, and Stark will find himself pushed towards taking potentially suicidal risks.

This is a case of what philosopher's call Pascal's Mugging, a form of Pascal's Wager. In the original example, you are approached in the street by a hooded figure who demands you hand over your wallet. You do not hand it over. However, he then claims to have magical powers and threatens to kill an infinite number of people with those powers if you do not hand over the wallet.

You still don't believe he has these powers, but the risk is too great. Even if there is only a one in a quadrillion chance that his threat is real, the expected value of not handing over your wallet is an infinite loss of value in the universe. Therefore, as the rational altruist that you are, you hand over your wallet.

In *Endgame*, this would mean that Stark is morally required to travel back in time to bring back the infinite number of people lost in the Snap. This would be true whether or not Stark could work out a safe way for the Avengers to navigate the quantum realm. Even if the chance is less than one in a trillion that he will succeed he still must take the risk, the expected value is infinite.

In fact, the infinitarian trance is so strong that even if the impact of failing would wipe out the rest of Earth, Tony would still take the gamble. Whatever the cost, the expected value of the planetary gamble is infinite, and therefore outweighs any other consideration.

This fairly obviously seems wrong. Stark should not be gambling with the lives of the remaining four billion people. Something is still very wrong with Stark's philosophy.

Maybe there is one last thing that Stark can try. He might attempt to avoid the infinitarian trance by developing a filter to all minuscule probabilities. Bostrom calls this the *infinity shades* approach. We can imagine Stark building these infinity shades into the Ironman suit. The shades allow him to ignore all actions that have very low probabilities.

This would help Stark in our above case; he is not going to risk the whole Earth to go on a suicide mission. In fact, even if the Earth were not to be in danger of destruction, and it was only his life in the balance, Stark would still not risk it in pursuit of the almost impossible. This all seems perfectly sensible. Maybe Stark has finally overcome his demons and has found a way to make his morality work in the multiverse he finds himself in.

Yet even now, his principles will fail him. It seems that there are cases where he should truly take into consideration minuscule probabilities. For instance, when Ant-Man, Black Widow, and Captain America visit his cabin to persuade him to, at least, try to make time travel possible. At first, Tony rejects their request for help because the probabilities of success are so low. Thankfully, in *Endgame*, he eventually does make the decision to give it a go.

However, if Stark were to ignore all minuscule probabilities he would end up ignoring his responsibilities in cases like this. There is only a small amount of risk to Stark, the emotional difficulty of getting his hopes up and the practical cost of wasting a couple of days working on the issue. These costs would, surely, be outweighed by the chance of saving an infinite number of people, even if that chance is one in a trillion. Stark, in trying to avoid the infinitarian trance, has made himself slightly morally blind.

A common-sense solution might say that in this case he should take off his infinity shades because the risk is so small. But how are we to understand the risk if not by reference to the potential consequences of his actions? Common sense dictates that the size of a risk is partially determined by the size of the values at stake.

For instance, going to the bank without checking the closing time is a small risk if you only have £100 to deposit, but if you have your entire life savings it is a big risk. The expected value in Tony's case is infinite. This is true whether Tony is risking the death of the entire planet or an afternoon with his family. So how can the risk be smaller in one case than the other?

Maybe, when dealing with infinities, there is some limit to the wager that we can make for minuscule probabilities. This would provide a limit on when Tony can use expected value calculations to make decisions, and let him know when he needs to put on his infinity shades. This could be formulated such that the smaller the wager the bigger gambles Stark can take, or that a wager of a certain size, rules out certain minuscule probabilities from Stark's decision-making process.

But of course, this raises the question of where this limit is. If the limit is set too low Tony risks failing to take the chance to save an infinite number of people. If it is set too high, he risks sacrificing too much in its pursuit.

His last chance then might be to try to appeal to moral principles. One such principle might be that we should not wager lives on such minuscule probabilities. But how small do the probabilities have to be for it to be worth waging a life for the chance of bringing an infinite number of people back? Stark would surely take the gamble at fifty-fifty or ninety-ten in favor of success, but he has no way to show why these gambles are ethical.

Most problematically, any appeal to these sorts of principles moves him away from the core of his consequentialist ideals. Saying that there is a rule, or series of rules, that determines how he should act in these cases, is to hold to a deontological principle. There just is no consequentialist way of determining when the risk is worth it.

It really does seem that the events of *Infinity War* and *Endgame* have irreparably damaged Iron Man's ethics. Whatever Tony tries, he cannot escape the infinitarian grip; there is no stopping the rust. He has tried to patch up his ethics, like a Mark 1 Iron Suit, but to no avail.

Whether faced with infinitarian paralysis or the infinitarian trance, there just does not seem any way that consequentialism can work in a multiverse of infinite consequences. Iron Man would be best off, if he set down his calculator and let Captain America take the lead.

10
Natasha, Gamora, and the Soul Stone

T.J. McSherry

One life is not always equal to another, and the value of that life changes when weighed against the greater good. Natasha and Gamora's deaths for the Soul Stone are set up as a futuristic, utilitarian, trolley problem: is the willful death of one individual worth saving the universe?

John Stuart Mill, along with many of us, would certainly agree with the end goal, even though the idea of universal salvation is different for each character. The Soul Stone itself is amoral, even though it is the object of moral choices. The Russo Brothers wanted the audience to see Thanos's act of murdering Gamora as 'bad', and Natasha's martyrdom as 'good', even though both deaths achieved the same result: receiving the Soul Stone.

The fight for the Soul Stone also provides a case study for the ethics of love and friendship. It examines the relationship of Thanos and Gamora in contrast to the friendship of Natasha and Clint, both of which culminate on the peaks of Vormir. When measured against the Platonic and Aristotelian ethics of friendly love, and Mill's utilitarianism, the characters' relationships, and deaths, are reconciled as worthy of the Soul Stone. Gamora's death legitimizes Thanos's commitment to such an extreme end. Likewise, despite her wallowing in self-pity and peanut butter sandwiches throughout the movie, Natasha's martyrdom is the ethical choice over Clint's.

A Galactic Trolley Problem

The difference between moral dilemmas and ethical ones, philosophers say, is that in moral issues, the choice is between right and wrong. In ethics, the choice is between two rights.

—Pamela Warrick

The most famous of thought experiments in moral philosophy is the Trolley Problem. This will sound familiar. Imagine a trolley car careening down a track. If it continues on its current course it will run over, and kill, five people who are tied to the rails farther ahead. Conveniently, you are standing near a switch that, if flipped, would divert the trolley onto a different track and avoid the five captives. The catch is that on this other track is tied one other person. The question, then, is which course of action is ethically correct: passively allowing the trolley to kill the five, or actively saving the five by sacrificing one other who was initially in no danger.

A variation of this exercise replaces the switch with a different complication. In this case, you're standing on a bridge over a single track with no switches or opportunities to divert the car. There's a man of generous body weight on the ledge in front of you. The only way to stop the death of five, in this case, is to physically push the fat man off the overpass and into the path of the trolley. Generally, people are more averse to taking action in this second scenario because of the direct and physical connection with the victim individual. The dilemma becomes even more complex if you know, or love, the person being pushed or any of the people on the track. This didn't stop Thanos when he tossed Gamora off Vormir's peak to her doom (though it might raise the question of how the Trolley Problem might be affected by the addition of a positive incentive). In Thanos's defense, he was not choosing between a 'bad' and a 'worse' choice. He was choosing to sacrifice one person to achieve what he saw as the greater good—Salvation of the universe at the cost uf half of all life (plus one—Gamora).

The Utilitarian Value of Life

John Stuart Mill describes his utilitarianism as the "greatest happiness principle." In other words, the more happiness and pleasure that results from an act, the more moral and good that act is. If that act creates pain and suffering, or simply does not produce pleasure, then the act is wrong, or at least less moral. Mill uses algebra as an example of how results can be derived from known and unknown elements. Like algebra, Mill's utilitarianism relies upon a premise that there are certain defined units that are equal to each other. For our purposes they could be units of happiness or value. In this scenario they may be units of life, of happiness, or both.

The *Infinity Saga* offers several examples and iterations of the Trolley Problem and Utilitarian dilemmas. Most obvious is the through-line of Thanos's willingness to sacrifice half of all living beings to ensure that the remaining populations have the opportunity to thrive.

Thanos's intent was, at face value, a utilitarian effort. By eliminating fifty percent of all living things he would ensure the survival of Earth (and what applies to the Earth applies to the whole inhabited universe), and its remaining inhabitants, in a healthier and more fruitful habitat. He assumed that this would provide net positive pleasure for Earth. Thanos neglected to take into account the suffering of the remaining fifty percent as they mourned their loved ones who disappeared in the Snap. In his defense, that suffering would have been offset by the long-term flourishing of Earth, assuming that mere population control was the sole factor holding the humans back. Utility seeks to maximize pleasure or minimize suffering. Half of all living things suffer briefly in the Snap (as they die). The remainder of humans suffer less, but for longer, in their grief. The question may be raised as to how suffering is experienced throughout all of life on Earth. Plants do not have nervous systems and thus do not experience pain. Animals would immediately suffer similar to humans. Some animals may or may not experience grief, but would probably recover more quickly based on their lives in a more hostile predator-prey environment. For those creatures who experience grief, the suffering would be reduced with each subsequent generation.

Other utilitarian dilemmas are seen in *Age of Ultron*, *Captain America: Civil War*, and, to some extent, *Avengers: Infinity War*, where the team must grapple with the cost of damage to their surroundings (such as Sokovia and nearly all of Manhattan) in exchange for defeating the villain. In *Endgame*, however, the team has to make a more personal sacrifice to stop Thanos's trolley of genocide—who will be pushed off the ledge? When measured by the Soul Stone, both lives (Natasha's and Gamora's) are equally valuable and worthy as trade for the stone.

At risk of sounding insensitive, Natasha's death was more utilitarian than Clint's would have been. The only ones left to mourn her death were the Avengers—a team who knew that death was an option and an acceptable risk for saving the world. With the Snap reversed, Natasha would not have a family relying upon her to provide food and shelter. She would likely have adopted Clint's family as her own, but would never have been able to fill the fatherly gap in their lives.

Love, Death, and Red Skull

What is love, baby don't hurt me, don't hurt me, no more.

—HADDAWAY

Once Clint and Natasha understand the nature of the dilemma, they attempt to circumvent the rules of Red Skull as they vie for position. Rather than sacrifice someone *else* that they love, they each attempt to martyr themselves to allow the other to gain control of the Soul Stone. The Russo brothers would have the audience see Thanos's act of murdering Gamora as 'bad', and Natasha's martyrdom as 'good', even though both deaths achieved the same result: receiving the Soul Stone. Thanos pushed Gamora to "save" half the universe (by destroying the other half) and Clint and Natasha fought for the same object to *re*-save that half again. Thanos, as the 'bad guy' *must* have loved Gamora, otherwise he would not have earned the stone.

Gamora's death legitimizes Thanos's commitment to such an extreme end in that this is the most love he's capable of. Admittedly, we do not know whether the Soul Stone has a threshold that must be met to get the stone. For example, if little Timmy found his way to the mountain and threw his pet goldfish, whom he truly loved, into the abyss we can assume that he would wake up moments later, stone in hand. Looking at the numbers and utility of his choice, Thanos's actions seem ethical. So, too, with the Avengers' objective. So then where can we turn to weigh the moral value of each plot against the other? When good and evil have the same result we can look to philosophy to help us place value on the sacrifice, in this case, by measuring the love. We examine the sacrifice and attempt to appraise the value of each type of love: Thanos's love for Gamora, Clint's love for Natasha, and Natasha's love for Clint.

But did Clint or Natasha really love either of themselves enough for their self-sacrifice to count? The irony and paradox of the Soul Stone is that the assumption of love is only proven true if the conclusion is true (the acquisition of the stone). We might *think* that they love the person about to be sacrificed, but what if they didn't, really? Would Vormir reject the offering and deny access to the Soul Stone? We all know that the Soul Stone accepted both sacrifices, so there was love. But there are different types of love, and two very different kinds were demonstrated on Vormir. For insight on different kinds of love, and how they manifested in the film, we turn to Plato.

Diotima's Ladder

In Plato's *Symposium* the character Socrates relays the tale of a discussion he had with Diotima about the nature of Love. Diotima begins by explaining that, contrary to popular belief at the time, Love is not in fact a god. She describes Love as more of a spirit who acts as an intermediary or mediator between humans and both the things they desire and their gods. The parallel here is too good to be true. Love as a spirit to help humans get something they desire? Perhaps Red Skull is that spirit on Vormir, "guiding others to a treasure he cannot possess", or perhaps it's the stone itself—both the object of desire *and* the spirit, working through Red Skull.

Diotima explains that love between two people can exist on one of several levels, frequently visualized as rungs on a ladder. The steps are as follows, and must be achieved in order:

1. ***Beauty of one form.*** This initial level is merely based upon the attraction of one person.

2. ***Beauty of other forms.*** Diotima's equivalent of "There are other fish in the sea". The realization that the object of attraction shares attributes with many others.

3. ***Beauty of the soul.*** It's what's on the inside that counts; are they a good person?

4. ***Beauty of what makes that person unique.*** They would not be who they are without the upbringing by their parents, teachers, the institutions, and social environment that makes their individuality real.

5. ***Beauty in all.*** All beings are beautiful forms in their own right.

6. ***The true 'Form' of Beauty.*** This level is only achievable and knowable in Plato's Realm of Forms. Everything knowable on Earth is a reflection or shadow of that object's true Form on a higher plane of existence.

In Diotima's words:

> And the true order of going or being led by another to the things of love, is to use the beauties of Earth as steps along which he mounts upwards for the sake of that other beauty, going from one to two, and from two to all fair forms, and from fair forms to fair actions, and from fair actions to fair notions, until from fair notions he arrives at the notion of absolute beauty, and at last knows what the essence of beauty is.

Where on the ladder do the relationships of Thanos/Gamora and Clint/Natasha stand? Thanos has two adopted daughters, Nebula and Gamora, of whom he clearly favors the latter. When Thanos finally reaches Vormir, Nebula has turned against him and has even tried to kill him. He now keeps her restrained and is analyzing her memories to keep an edge against his foes. Clearly, there is no love between the two. Gamora has also been fighting against Thanos, but he seems to know that she will be useful to him in a different way. On Vormir, Red Skull explains that the Soul Stone requires a sacrifice of "that which you love—a soul for a soul." Thanos is stuck at level one in his stunted love for Gamora. In some ways he may admire her tenacity, and certainly is proud of her fierceness as a warrior, but the only reason he has not killed her yet is that he somehow knew he would have to exchange her life for the stone. It's the closest thing to real love that Thanos has experienced and thus qualifies as a worthy sacrifice.

Clint and Natasha have a much deeper and more dimensional relationship than that of Thanos and Gamora, and the moment of sacrifice is also proportionally more complex. Clint and Natasha have more history in their relationship than any two of their other teammates. A villain in her own story, Natasha was raised as a master spy and assassin. By her own admission, she did some terrible things for which she cannot forgive herself. As an Avenger, she tries to do enough good to outweigh the bad in her past. To the contrary, Clint's moments of regret come only after he loses his family in the Snap. He has nothing more to lose, so loosens his moral code on proportional violence and essentially becomes a vigilante. By the time the Avengers are able to travel back in time to retrieve the Infinity Stones for themselves, both characters see the opportunity to sacrifice themselves as a way to make up for the dark moments in their own pasts.

Clint and Natasha have love for each other that makes it to at least level four on Diotima's scale. They have come to a (non-romantic) love despite, and somehow because of, their troubled moments and the institutions and events that made them do certain things. It is these shared experiences and their empathy for each other that allows them to reach such a high mark.

At no point in the movie do either Natasha or Clint consider sacrificing the other for the Soul Stone. Both have achieved a selfless love for their friend. Clint was instrumental in giving Natasha hope for the future and was the only friend or family she had for a long time. Because of this, Natasha never lost hope in Clint even when he went rogue in the beginning of

Endgame. Clint tries to throw himself from the ledge, regretting who he has become over the past five years. He believes he has had his chance at being happy. He relished his time with his family and, not knowing whether the plan will work, wants Natasha to have a chance at fulfillment as well. Clint sees this as his chance to let Natasha have a life with her friends and perhaps a family with Bruce Banner.

From Natasha's perspective, she should be the one to jump. Assuming that all of the Avengers are able to accomplish their part of the plan, and undo the Snap, Natasha wants Clint's happiness to be restored and his family returned to him. She sees that the life of Clint, as a father, has more value to his family than her own. She is their adopted Aunt. Family in name only. This is her chance to remove the 'red from her ledger' and repay not only a debt to society, but to Clint who rescued her from her past.

Perhaps Natasha's physical sacrifice is more of her moral sacrifice of Clint. She acts knowing that she will lose him forever. Natasha has seen his virtue and beauty, and perceives the continuance of his life as her only chance at immortality through *his* memories of *her* legacy. Clint will undoubtedly blame himself forever for not being able to overpower and outsmart Natasha as they fought for the privilege of martyrdom on Vormir. She felt useless trying to manage and coordinate the efforts of inter-galactic superheroes who knew what they were doing. Compound this with the disappearance of her oldest friend and the continued guilt of her past, Natasha was filled with self-loathing. She found meaning on Vormir. She could be useful again. Natasha may not have actually loved herself, but found love for herself by being the best choice (or, the least-bad choice) for death.

What We Have Learned

Avengers: Endgame pits good against evil in many ways, but often in a complicated sense. Thanos, the villain, does bad things but with some noble intent. The Avengers, too, have noble intent yet leave a swath of destruction and calamity behind them. Both Gamora's and Natasha's deaths result in the same thing: acquisition of the Soul Stone.

Sometimes good actions and bad actions have the same result, which blurs the lines of whether that action was good or bad to begin with. The relationships, too, are complex: an adopted daughter kept around for her useful death, and two antiheroes competing for death.

These elements in themselves may or may not have the answers to deep ethical questions, but sometimes it's not what the characters can teach us about philosophy. It's what philosophy can teach us about the characters!

11
Population Ethics for Mad Gods

LEONARD KAHN

Perhaps the most compelling feature of both *Infinity War* and *Endgame* is their main antagonist, Thanos. While Thanos is called "the Mad Titan," he is not irrational, unhinged, or senseless. On the contrary, Thanos has an altruistic goal and a willingness to ask and answer a thorny philosophical question, one with great practical importance. Let me explain.

Thanos's goal is to bring about the conditions under which all people of the universe will flourish. For example, he brags to his adopted daughter, Gamora, that as a result of his actions, the children of her homeworld "have known nothing but full bellies and clear skies. It's a paradise." Yet bringing about and maintaining a paradise is not easy. Thanos's own world, Titan, was "beautiful," but its beauty could not last.

"Titan was like most planets," Thanos tells Stephen Strange, "too many mouths, not enough to go around." The result is the uninhabitable wasteland that we see in *Infinity War*. But unlike the other inhabitants of Titan, Thanos foresaw this catastrophic outcome, and his foresight led him to the central question in the field that philosophers call "population ethics": How many people should there be? Call this the "Population Question."

Thanos first attempted to answer the Population Question with respect to Titan. His answer was that there should be half as many people as then existed. Hence, Thanos concluded that half of the residents of Titan should be killed so that the other half could thrive. Moreover, Thanos believed that the killings of his fellow Titans should be "random, dispassionate, fair to rich and poor alike." Perhaps it is not surprising that the other residents of Titan rejected Thanos's answer and "called him a madman."

Their rejection and the subsequent extinction of the rest of his species shaped the rest of his life. As he tells Thor, "I know what it's like to lose, to feel so desperately that you're right yet to fail nonetheless." Thanos made it his life's work never to fail again. Therefore, he set out to prevent similar outcomes anywhere else—and to do so by killing half of the people everywhere in the universe. Initially, he did this by moving from world to world. But near the end of *Infinity War*, Thanos has assembled all of the Infinity Stones and is able to do this to the entire universe with a single snap of his fingers. He then does exactly what he told Stephen Strange he would do; he watches the sun rise on what he takes to be "a grateful universe."

But how grateful should the universe and its remaining people be? Though Thanos is convinced that his answer to the Population Question is correct, we can be forgiven for harboring doubts.

The Power of the Infinity Stones

Just before Thanos killed him, Loki told the Titan that "You will never be a god." But whether Loki was right depends on what it means to ascend to godhood. In *Infinity Gauntlet*, the comic on which both *Infinity War* and *Endgame* are based, it's clear that, when Thanos wields all six Infinity Stones, his power is limitless. As Mephisto says to Thanos,

> Anything you wish to be, you are. Anything you wish, is. Nothing in the universe dares challenge this claim. There be only one word to describe you . . . *God.*

However, in *Infinity War* and *Endgame* there are limits on what even someone as powerful as Thanos can accomplish with all six stones. He cannot, for example, overcome Thor's use of the hammer, Stormbreaker. And each use of all six stones weakens Thanos. (Likewise, in *Endgame*, using the stones maims the Hulk, and it mortally wounds Tony Stark.)

Here it's worth recalling the distinction made by Peter Quill's father, Ego, in *Guardians of the Galaxy: Volume 2*. Ego distinguished between a small "g" god and a capital "G" God. Small "g" gods such as the Celestials—including Ego himself—are capable of creating, transforming, and destroying life on a grand scale. Ego himself created a living planet as his body (though it took him millions of years of practice to do so). Thanos with all of the Infinity Stones certainly has power on this level, even if his abilities fall far short of those of an unlimited capital 'G' God as in *Infinity Gauntlet*. Perhaps it is no accident that the first word in *Infinity War* that is spoken by a major character is "I," and the last is "god."

ABC's of Population Ethics

One school of thought in population ethics is called "totalism." According to totalism, we should maximize the total amount of happiness in the universe. So totalism's answer to the Population Question is that there should be as many people as brings about the greatest amount of total happiness.

Suppose that we could add a person—call him "Adam"—to the universe and that Adam would live, on balance, a happy life. Somewhat arbitrarily, I'll say that Adam will have 5 net units of happiness over the course of his life. Suppose further that adding Adam to the universe would not reduce the total happiness among other persons by more than 5 net units. Totalism tells us, therefore, that Adam ought to exist. More generally, it tells us that we should add people to the universe as long as the result is more total net happiness. Likewise, we should subtract them from the universe just in case the result is more total net happiness.

Totalism would not look kindly on Thanos's actions. By randomly killing half of the people in the universe, Thanos reduces the total amount of happiness by fifty percent. Worse still, Thanos's action also seems to make the lives of many of the survivors wretched. For instance, we see from Steve Rogers's support group that, even five years after Thanos snapped away half of the humans on Earth, many people remain traumatized, miserable, and unable to adjust. So according to totalism, Thanos's answer to the Population Question is wrong.

Yet Thanos is not the type to take criticism lying down. How might he reply? I will consider two possibilities, focusing on Earth's population since it is the only one we know much about. First, Thanos might argue that by killing half of all humans, he has prevented a future disaster as a result of exhausting the planet's natural resources and bringing about our own extinction. And it *is* true that we face serious environmental and resource problems and will do so for decades—if not centuries—to come. Over the last several hundred years, the world's population has grown at the very same time that measures of individual and total happiness such as income per head, health, and lifespan have increased, yet there is no guarantee that this will continue indefinitely into the future.

But even if we grant Thanos his point, killing half of the world's population will not solve the problem. There are more than seven billion humans on Earth. If half of us were suddenly to turn to dust, it would not take long for us to return to our current levels of population. The last time world population was below four billion was only forty-five years ago in 1974. Even if it took us twice as long to repopulate the world as it did over the late twentieth and early twenty-first centuries, it would be less than a hundred years before we were in the same situation. Thanos likes to say that he is "inevitable," but if he is right that population size will drive us to extinction, then the end of our species is just as inevitable, and murdering billions of humans will only have been a delaying action.

While Thanos's first line of reply fails, he does have a second line of argument that is more promising. He might try to show that totalism itself is problematic. To that end, imagine that he were to offer a totalist a choice between the following two outcomes: Option A is that Thanos would make each of the current inhabitants of the universe ecstatic for its entire life, resulting, let us say, in ten trillion units of happiness. Option B is that Thanos would make the life of each person in the universe just barely better than no life at all, but he would also increase the total number of persons to so great a number that there would be eleven trillion units of happiness. Most of us, if faced with this choice, would strongly prefer Option A since a universe where the life of each person is barely better than not having existed at all is deeply unattractive. But a totalist cannot agree. According to totalism we should maximize the total amount of happiness in the universe, and it is Option B, not Option A, that does this. Hence, totalism leads to what Derek Parfit called the "Repugnant Conclusion," and this fact casts a long shadow over totalism.

Can we find a better theory than totalism to evaluate Thanos's action? There is a school of thought within population ethics called "averagism." According to averagism, we should maximize the average, rather than the total, amount of happiness in the universe. So averagism's answer to the Population Question is that there should be as many people in the universe as would maximize its average amount of happiness.

Averagism holds that if Adam will experience more than the average amount of happiness, then he should be added to the universe but not otherwise. Suppose that the average amount of happiness over a lifetime is 4 units. Since Adam will experience 5 units, his existence will increase the average, so he should be brought into existence, according to averagism.

Despite its differences with totalism, averagism also disapproves of Thanos's murder of half the people in the universe. Recall that when Thanos kills, the deaths are "random." As a result, the effect on the average amount of happiness will be zero. In order to see why this is so, think about the expected effect of Thanos's Snap on the average height of American men, which is about 5 feet and 10 inches. We arrive at that number by adding into a single sum the height of each American man (the numerator) and then dividing that sum by the number of American men (the denominator). If we were to remove at random half of the values in the numerator and then reduce the denominator by half as well, the expected result would be the same: about 5 feet and 10 inches. This is also true if we consider happiness. We arrive at the average amount of happiness for people in the universe by adding into a single sum the happiness of each person (the numerator) and then dividing that sum by the number of people (the denominator). Just as with heights, if we randomly remove half of the values from the numerator and also reduce the denominator by half, then the expected result is the same.

Yet a moment's reflection reveals that the situation is even worse than this. The deaths of half of the people in the universe leave many who remain dolorous, pathetic, or worse, as we have already seen. Steve Rogers tells Natasha Romanoff, "You know, I keep telling everybody they should move on and . . . grow. Some do." But many of us—perhaps even most of us—do not. We see this fact through the eyes of Scott Lang as he wanders among abandoned neighborhoods that have been desolated because of Thanos's action. And we also see this through the eyes of Clint Barton who, after the loss of his entire family, is driven to become a murderous vigilante. Hence, averagism, like Totalism, condemns Thanos's action.

As before, Thanos's best defense is a good offense. Just as Thanos offered the totalist a revealing choice, he can do the same with the averagist. Though he cannot tempt the averagist into the trap of the Repugnant Conclusion, imagine that Thanos were to offer the averagist a choice between these two outcomes: Option A is that Thanos would simply do nothing, leaving all the people in the universe to live out their natural lives. Option B is that Thanos would snap his fingers and kill half of the people in the universe—but not in the way this occurs at the end of *Infinity War*. Recall that these deaths were random. In contrast, the option that Thanos is offering the Averagist is one in which only the least happy half of the people in the universe die. Almost everyone would be quick to choose Option A, but an averagist is forced by her principle to choose Option B, despite the fact that this means countless murders. That is because Option B would increase the average level of happiness in the universe. Indeed, an averagist would seem to be required to ask Thanos to kill even more people if that would increase the average level of happiness. Just as Thanos was able to cast doubt on totalism, so too he is able to cast doubt on averagism.

Yet another school of thought within population ethics is the Person-Affecting View. Though there are several variants of the Person-Affecting View, let's just look at a simplified version of the idea in which outcomes are good or bad only if they affect people who exist. Merely potential people do not make claims on us. Unlike its rivals, the Person-Affecting View does not seek to finetune the number of people in order to bring about the great total amount of happiness (totalism) or the greatest average amount of happiness (averagism). According to the Person-Affecting View, the mere fact that bringing Adam into existence will increase the total amount of happiness in the universe does not mean that we must do so, and the mere fact that Adam's life will be happier than average does not mean this either.

It is not hard to see that the Person-Affecting View also condemns Thanos's Snap. By killing four billion people on Earth alone, he instantly reduces their level of happiness to zero. This was a very bad result for Sam Wilson, for Bucky Barnes, for Wanda Maximoff, to name but three! Moreover, by doing so Thanos also reduced the level of happiness for survivors like Tony Stark, Okoye, and James Rhodes, and countless others.

But, by now, we have come to expect that Thanos has an answer for everything. Just as Thanos's quest throughout *Infinity War* is to end the lives of half of the universe's people, the Avengers' quest in *Endgame* is to bring them back. But Thanos would be quick to point out that the Person-Affecting View gives the Avengers no reason to do so. The nearly four billion humans (as well as the countless quadrillions of extraterrestrial people) whom Thanos killed during the events leading up to the climax of *Endgame* no longer exist and are, at best, merely potential. The Person-Affecting View does not recognize any demands that they place on us. According to the Person-Affecting View, we have no more reason to bring them back than we have to bring back Attila the Hun or Jack the Ripper. If the Person-Affecting View condemns Thanos's mass murder at the end of *Infinity War*, it undermines the motivation for the courageous actions of the heroes in *Endgame*, and Natasha Romanoff's sacrifice was for nought.

What have we learned? Even though every major school of thought in population ethics agrees that Thanos's answer to the Population Question is wrong and his actions tragic, each of these schools suffers from serious problems of its own, problems that are nicely illustrated by thought experiments involving Thanos's use of the Infinity Stones.

Though it might seem as if we have reached a dead end, that is far from the case. In order to see why, let me make a suggestion about what Thanos should have done once he had collected all six Infinity Stones. Philosophical inquiry is difficult, and the Population Question is no exception, as we have seen throughout this chapter. But who would be in a better position to answer the Population Question than one with the power of the Infinity Stones? If Thanos had been willing to reconsider his own answer before acting, he would have been much more likely to do the right thing—whatever that might be—and the rest of us would be much more likely to accept it.

Sadly, we cannot use the Infinity Stones to help us answer the Population Question. Yet wrong answers to it can be catastrophic, and Thanos is right to see the possibility of extinction—such as the one that occurred on his home world—looming for those who make mistakes or who simply fail to try to get the answer right. Though it might seem like something out of a comic book, the fact of the matter is that humanity could develop into a stellar or galactic civilization, which could flourish for hundreds of millions, if not billions, of years. If so we would know far more than "full bellies and clear skies"; we would know the almost limitless potential of our cosmic endowment. Or we could disappear in a few generations. All of this depends in large part on getting the Population Question right.

Endgame concludes with Sam Wilson's meditation on taking up the responsibilities that come with Captain America's shield. He promises a now-elderly Steve Rogers, "I'll do my best." Our responsibilities are even more momentous: the survival and prosperity of humankind. So we too must do our best. And there could be no better start than answering the Population Question.

12
Why Blood Sacrifice?

PHILIP WILSON

Sacrifice has been of immense significance throughout human history. Homer's *Iliad* tells of Achilles sacrificing Trojan captives. Aztec priests performed the mass killing of prisoners of war to ensure that the sun continued to rise. The Temple in Jerusalem in the time of Jesus was not only a house of prayer but a huge butchery, where animals were slaughtered for a 'holocaust' meaning a burnt offering.

That the word 'holocaust' is now used to denote the genocidal practices of the modern world indicates that sacrifice is not only an esoteric practice from the past but continues to flourish throughout the world. Animals are sacrificed in great numbers in the name of religion, while in twenty-first-century Western societies many people work long hours, giving up on leisure and time with their families in order to win the rat-race in a way of living that can be described as self-sacrifice.

At least they harm nobody but themselves, but more extreme acts of self-sacrifice take place: for example, in 2017 a suicide bomber killed twenty-three people at a concert in Manchester, injuring many more.

What Is Sacrifice?

Sacrifice can be defined as a form of gift-giving with the intention of getting something in return. In *Creation of the Sacred*, Walter Burkert tells the story of a politician in Africa throwing dollar bills into raging waters during a boat trip in the hope that his offering would calm the storm. This action typifies the logic of sacrifice: 'I give x in order to get y'.

If Vildan devotes long hours to her job, then she will hope for something in return, such as a high salary, esteem from her peers, or emotional satisfaction. If she gives up smoking, then she will hope to be able to breathe better and to be able to compete at last in that marathon. Even the suicide-bomber hopes for payback, in the form of a privileged place in paradise for eternity. Burkert notes that fatal self-sacrifice has the paradoxical result of prolonging individual religions because of the propaganda effect on those left behind, because some greater cause is at stake.

Sacrifice is found in the natural world, too. Bees routinely work themselves to death and some male spiders lose their lives when they mate, but the respective genetic pools flourish. These animals give x in order to get y, even if they are not around to see y. In the religious sphere, the gift is ritualized. The Aztec priests slaughtered prisoners ceremoniously. Catholics burn candles in front of the images of saints, praying for help with their problems, while the Mass itself is viewed as a spiritual sacrifice.

Many moral philosophers would have a problem with sacrifice when it has bad consequences for others. Whilst we might admire Vildan for working hard or for giving up smoking, or for taking the bullet for her daughter, she would face trial in today's West if she were to sacrifice her daughter, even if she claimed that a supernatural power had told her that it was the only way of preventing ecological collapse. And so, suicide-bombers are generally (but far from universally) condemned for the harm that they bring to others, both the innocent bystanders whom they kill and maim, and to the families of these bystanders.

Two Classic Sacrifices

Let's look at two examples from the world of myth, relating each in turn to the saga of the Avengers. (The word 'myth' should not be taken to imply that a story is false but that it "eternalizes its object, lifting it out of its finite, purely earthly reality, and endows it with epic, larger-than-life characteristics" (Bennett, *Sacred Languages of the World*, p. 83). The Marvel stories are myths by this definition.)

Greek legend tells how Agamemnon accidentally killed a deer sacred to the goddess Artemis, so that she denied a wind to the fleet he commanded. The Greeks were therefore unable to set sail for Troy. To pacify Artemis, Agamemnon was forced to sacrifice his beloved daughter Iphigenia, placing her on the altar and slaughtering her like a sacrificial beast. (In some versions of the myth she is secretly rescued at the last second by Artemis.)

Agamemnon is caught in a dilemma between his duties as a father and his duties as a general. According to the Greek mind, he will be condemned no matter which decision he makes, and he will on his return from Troy be murdered by his wife Clytemnestra for what he has done. The sacrifice of his daughter, however, is successful. A wind arises, and the Greeks depart. There is an analogy with the episode in *Avengers: Infinity War* where Thanos kills his adopted daughter Gamora by throwing her over a cliff on Vormir to gain the Soul Stone. We have the familiar pattern of sacrifice: 'I give x in order to get y'.

Thanos has been instructed by the Red Skull that he can only gain the Stone if he is willing to lose what he loves, and Gamora fits the bill. His sacrifice is efficacious, because he does love Gamora. He gains the Stone and goes on to use it to fulfil his plan. Like Agamemnon, he is caught in a dilemma: he needs to do something immoral in order to achieve what he considers to be a moral end, the saving of the universe from the threat of overpopulation. The movie's poetics leave no doubt about where we should stand, however, because Gamora is a character we have known and loved since she first appeared in *Guardians of the Galaxy*. We are on her side and are horrified at what has happened.

To turn to a second example, Christianity tells of the death of Jesus at the start of the common era. Humankind (according to later theological reflection by such philosophers as Augustine, Anselm, and Aquinas) had fallen from grace because of the original sin of disobedience committed by Adam and Eve, and only the self-sacrifice of Jesus (in his role as God's son) could restore the moral order of the universe in an act of atonement. (The form of the word 'atonement' in English spells out what is going on: things are made 'at one' again.)

There is an analogy here with the way that Black Widow sacrifices herself in *Avengers: Endgame* by leaping off the same cliff on Vormir from which Gamora is thrown, because she wants to undo Thanos's plan now it has succeeded. Again, we have the pattern: 'I give x in order to get y'. However, like a worker bee the self-sacrificer will not see the benefits, and the Widow dies as a result of her leap. Her death is part of the bargain. It is Hawkeye who retrieves the Soul Stone, which he will use alongside the other Avengers to defeat Thanos and bring the movie to a triumphant (if muted) conclusion.

Again, the sacrifice—this time, the self-sacrifice—is efficacious. The place and manner of Black Widow's death are the same as Gamora's, but whereas Gamora is an unwilling victim (who would rather kill herself in an act of defiance than become instrumental to Thanos's genocidal scheme), Black Widow dies of her own volition, and the movie's poetics establishes this much-loved character's death sacrifice as heroic.

Not only have we followed Natasha Romanoff's story from *Iron Man 2*, but we witness a ferocious struggle between Black Widow and Hawkeye in which it seems that first one and then the other of these two heroes will fall to certain death and thus liberate the Soul Stone. Both heroes are willing to sacrifice themselves. Neither is willing for the other to be sacrificed. If Gamora is like Iphigenia, sacrificed against her will for what Thanos sees as the common good, then Natasha is like Jesus, sacrificing herself in order to redeem the world. It should come as no surprise that the stakes are high on Vormir, just as Artemis is not going to be placated with an offering of wine, just as God the Father will only accept the sacrifice of his son.

In 1843, the Danish philosopher Søren Kierkegaard published *Fear and Trembling* under the pseudonym Johannes de silentio (John of Silence). Kierkegaard is somewhat of an outsider figure in philosophy, a Christian who was critical of the Christianity of his day, a profound thinker who refused to follow an academic career, an observer of the radical choices that alone can make us live authentically. He is frequently described as the 'Father of Existentialism'. The title of his work picks up on Saint Paul's injunction to the Philippians to "work out your own salvation in fear and trembling," and the book forms a set of meditations on the Old Testament story of Abraham and Isaac:

> And it came to pass after these things, that God did tempt Abraham, and said unto him, Abraham: and he said, Behold, here I am.
> And he said, Take now thy son, thine only son Isaac, whom thou lovest, and get thee into the land of Moriah; and offer him there for a burnt offering upon one of the mountains which I will tell thee. (Genesis 22: 1–2, King James Bible)

I said that Vildan would today be sent for trial for sacrificing her daughter. Abraham, however, is praised and rewarded by God for being ready to sacrifice Isaac, even though the entire future of Abraham's race depends on this son. They reach the land of Moriah, and Abraham gets the altar ready for the sacrifice, like Agamemnon or God the Father. At the last second, however, an angel appears to stay Abraham's hand even as he is about to plunge in the knife, and a ram is sacrificed instead.

It is possible to read the story positively as being against human (but not animal) sacrifice, yet *Fear and Trembling* picks up on the disquiet that many readers feel at Abraham's readiness to commit holy murder. (Some scholars believe that Abraham does kill Isaac in pre-Genesis versions of the story.) Genesis offers a story of faith, which religions hold up as the highest ideal of all, but there is a lot about the story that might make us hesitate, because faith can make people do terrible things. Even Agamemnon hesitates before killing his daughter. As Immanuel Kant argues, Abraham should have replied "to this supposedly divine voice" that it was certain that he should not kill his son, but that it was not certain and never could be certain that the voice was from God. Abraham's faith, however, is blind. He will not even get anything in return according to the initial bargain. The pattern of 'I give *x* in order to get *y*' has been broken. As Johannes de silentio puts it:

> The ethical expression for what Abraham did is that he was willing to murder Isaac; the religious expression is that he was willing to sacrifice Isaac but in this contradiction lies the very anguish that can indeed make one sleepless . . . (*Fear and Trembling*, p. 60)

It is a deed that is great, but also appalling. The insight applies to religious phenomena in general. Religion has given the world many beautiful things, such as the King James Bible, the Blue Mosque of Istanbul and the soup kitchens run by religious believers in the city where I live. Yet it has also given the world the Inquisition, the Crusades, and suicide bombers.

Similarly, there is a great dignity to Thanos, and many viewers will sympathize with his recognition that overpopulation is leading to ecological disaster, but we are horrified at the way that he throws the hero Gamora over the cliff. Black Widow's death is noble and selfless, but many viewers will remember her lying broken and bleeding at the foot of the cliff, in an act that amounts to suicide, and wonder if it had to be so. Do we have in these cases what John of Silence calls a "teleological suspension of the ethical"?

Ethics Suspended

The teleological suspension of the ethical describes a situation where what is usually regarded as immoral is allowed for the sake of a greater purpose. The law in Western societies, for example, forbids murder but in emergencies police officers are allowed to shoot dead anybody who threatens lives. The ethical is suspended for the sake of a *telos*, a purpose, a greater good. *Fear and Trembling* suggests that in the story of Abraham the ethical is suspended because obeying God's command takes precedence no matter what the circumstances. Nothing is to be gained by Abraham's act beyond proving his faith.

No wonder that such a situation can make us sleepless. It seems to license any evil religious practice you care to name. Johannes *de silentio* even imagines four ways of elaborating the story of this homicidal father/model of faith, in what we might describe as thought experiments (Kierkegaard, pp. 44–48).

In the first thought experiment, Abraham prefers to be thought a monster rather than for Isaac to lose faith. In the second, he loses any joy in life. In the third, he is shocked at the sin he committed by being willing to sacrifice his only son. In the fourth, Isaac loses his faith as a result of what has happened. Which, if any, is the correct reading? Johannes simultaneously puts forward solutions and undermines the possibility of knowing whether any one view can be the right one to take. We can never be sure that we have the right answer.

Perhaps it all comes back to faith, to a leap in the dark. But in that case, into which dark should we leap? Kierkegaard is rightly called the father of Existentialism. The title *Fear and Trembling* is well chosen.

For Thanos, the ethical is suspended for sound utilitarian reasons. Ultimately the universe will be better off if half of its inhabitants cease to exist. Yet the movie's poetics resist Thanos's intent. The death of Gamora becomes too high a price to pay. The ethical should not be suspended. And what of Black Widow? Why does Natasha have to die? Truly for the greater good, the film suggests. We mourn her as she lies bleeding, just as we mourned Gamora, but we also admire her for what she has done. And we mourn alongside Hawkeye the survivor, who will bring back the news of her death to the grieving Avengers.

In Natasha's case the ethical is not teleologically suspended. Her action is instrumental in restoring life to those destroyed by Thanos, no innocent bystanders are destroyed by what she does, and her fall is willed by the agent—a point emphasised in *Endgame* by the determination shown by Black Widow in overpowering the formidable Hawkeye in the fight to see who will die. Similarly, the death of Jesus will save the world, and is agreed to by Jesus himself, who reluctantly submits to crucifixion (for example, Luke 22: 42).

Ethics Restored

We can therefore look back at Thanos's actions in the light of the second sacrifice, of Natasha by Natasha, and conclude that he murdered rather than sacrificed his daughter Gamora. A tyrant has taken innocent life in order to have his way with the universe, which is why it is aesthetically satisfying to see him crumble into nothingness in the final battle of *Endgame*, his plans thwarted, just as it is aesthetically satisfying that Agamemnon should pay for the death of his daughter.

Self-sacrifice, in contrast, can, in the right context, be an example of heroism, of a new identity, assuming that it is done for the right reasons and without collateral damage. Black Widow's death meets these criteria. Ethics is *restored*, not suspended. The ending of the movie confirms this reading in its depiction of the death of Tony Stark, who manages to gain the Infinity Stones in order to defeat Thanos. In using them, however, he loses his own life in what amounts to an act of self-sacrifice. His last words are: "I am Iron Man." He dies not as Tony Stark, "genius, billionaire, playboy, philanthropist," as he puts it in *The Avengers*, but as the Golden Avenger, the hero in the suit of armour. He becomes what he always was, or at least what he has been since *Iron Man*.

Sometimes the nature of the universe is such that the good person must move into nothingness. We are forced to attend to the tragic side of life. (*Avengers: Endgame* emphasizes the tragic nature of Stark's fate by showing him after his rescue by Captain Marvel in a situation of domestic harmony with his wife Pepper and their daughter. The playboy has finally grown up, so that when he loses, he loses a lot.) The Avengers can now gather at Stark's house to grieve for him and Black Widow and to celebrate their lives and their deaths. (Gamora's fate remains uncertain, just as Iphigenia may or may not be alive.)

It's worth recalling that *Fear and Trembling* was written not by Søren Kierkegaard but by his character, "John of Silence." The views expressed in the book should not be ascribed to Kierkegaard, just as the reader of *The Republic* should be wary of ascribing to Plato what is said by Socrates. Kierkegaard is using a persona, in order to make his readers think, and he leaves the answers up to his readers when it comes to existential enquiry. Here he explains his method:

> But above all it must not be done in a dogmatising manner, for then the misunderstanding would instantly take the explanatory effort to itself in a new misunderstanding, as if existing consisted in getting to

know something about this or that. (*Concluding Unscientific Post-script*, p. 223)

Fear and Trembling forces us as readers to keep asking questions, whilst refusing to give answers, as befits a work of philosophy; it is a sign of the philosophy inherent in the Avengers movies that they make their viewers ask the same questions as those who engage with Kierkegaard's troubled vision, whilst refusing any easy answers.

Do we want a moral order where sacrifice is necessary? Is it not time to look for a better way of managing our affairs? Do we want a religion that asks for blood sacrifice, whether in the form of Iphigenia, Isaac, or Jesus, or in the form of the countless wars that have been fought in its name? Do we want a moral universe where the daughter and Black Widow have to die?

Perhaps we can start at last to move beyond 'I give x in order to get y' to a world where we can get y and yet remain who we are. Tony Stark becomes who he always was. It is his tragedy that to do so costs him his life. There is still something here that can make us sleepless.[1]

---

[1] Thanks to the following for their support: Alexa Batterham, Lauren Biermann, Tom Greaves, Kate Lawton, Addya Panayiotou, Davide Rizza, and Jayde Thorpe.

13
Jumping to Conclusions

Tuomas Manninen

In his post-Snap debriefing with the other surviving Avengers, Tony Stark reasons that he and the others lost to Thanos in Titan because Doctor Strange quit the fight: "That Bleecker Street magician gave up the store." When the Avengers ambush Thanos and find the gauntlet without the Infinity Stones, War Machine reasons that Thanos has actually hidden the Stones instead of destroying them, because he thinks Thanos is lying. Steve Rogers concludes that the reason he saw a pod of whales in the Hudson River in 2023 is because there is less pollution and fewer boats traveling that waterway. And after speaking with Red Skull in Vormir, Natasha and Clint conclude that Thanos must have murdered Gamora in order to get the Soul Stone.

What's common to all these inferences is that they employ abductive reasoning. Sometimes called inference to the best explanation, abductive reasoning starts with some observed evidence, and infers what hypothesis, if true, would best explain that evidence.

Although ubiquitous in its use, abductive reasoning is not certain: the conclusion reached via abduction may be false, even when the premises are true; this is especially a problem when dealing with limited amounts of evidence. In the examples above, both Tony and War Machine make incorrect inferences—which are later corrected after new evidence is introduced.

What Is Abduction?

Reasoning can be divided into three main types of inferences: deduction, induction, and abduction. Of these, deductive inferences are necessary and conclusive, while neither inductive nor abductive inferences are necessary, and the latter two are often probabilistic. Let's consider a well-worn example of a deductive argument:

All humans are mortal.

Tony Stark is a human.

Therefore, Tony Stark is mortal.

This inference is said to be necessary, because if the premises are true (All humans are mortal, and Tony Stark is a human), then the conclusion must be true (Tony Stark is mortal). But the same doesn't hold for the non-necessary inferences like induction or abduction, which are more probabilistic in nature.

First, take induction. There are many different types of inductive arguments, but generalization is a common one:

Captain America is worthy to lift Thor's hammer, Mjolnir.

Thor has another weapon, the axe Stormbreaker.

Therefore, Captain America can probably lift Stormbreaker, too.

Although here the conclusion turned out to be true, it did not have to be, on the basis of the premises. Finally, consider abduction. Revisiting one of the examples from above, we get the following:

Gamora died on Vormir.

If Thanos needed a to make sacrifice in order to get the Soul Stone, Gamora would have died on Vormir.

Thanos needed a to make a sacrifice in order to get the Soul Stone.

This particular conclusion turns out to be true, but prior to learning about the price that the Soul Stone commands from Red Skull, neither Clint nor Natasha knew its truth. In fact, they probably didn't even consider this scenario, given how they were operating only with the information that Nebula had—and not even she was privy to the events surrounding Gamora's death.

What's more, while deduction is truth-preserving, induction and abduction are ampliative: they add to our knowledge in ways in which deductions do not. The conclusion of a deduction is said to be contained in the premises, but the same does not hold for abduction or induction. Philosophers still disagree on some of these classifications, like whether abduction is a type of induction, or if induction is a type of abduction—and if inference to the best explanation is abductive or inductive. I will not enter into these discussions; I'm just going to say that induction and abduction are distinct types of inferences and that inference to the best explanation is abductive.

Although philosophers have known about deduction and induction ever since the works of Aristotle (384–322 B.C.E.), abduction is a relative newcomer. Abduction were first introduced by the American philosopher Charles S. Peirce (1838–1914). Peirce considered "abduction to be at the heart not only of scientific research, but of all ordinary human activities." Moreover, "Not only are detective stories full of abductive reasoning, but our everyday lives contain many examples of its effective use."

Different Forms of Abduction

Abductive reasoning takes different forms. Still, according to Peirce, "hypotheses may be very diverse, but all of them have in common that they are formulated to explain an observed phenomenon." (Peirce used the term 'hypothesis' for abductions early on in his writings.) The general pattern typically runs like this:

We observe some phenomenon P.

If hypothesis H were true, then P would follow.

Therefore, observing P gives us a reason to accept H as true.

If this argument were judged from the perspective of deductive reasoning, it would amount to the fallacy of *affirming the consequent*, which is an invalid inference. However, with abductions, we are playing by somewhat different rules.

Selective Abductions

Many abductions are selective in that they aim to choose the best explanation from a multitude of possible ones—hence the term 'inference to the best explanation'. These kinds of abductions include Captain America's in 2012: When Cap-2012 sees Steve Rogers-2023, he infers that he is looking at Loki who has escaped. Given how Cap-2012 knows about Loki's powers, and Loki's penchant to take the appearance of others, it seems warranted for him to conclude that he is seeing Loki masquerading as him. So, we could say that in light of Cap-2012's knowledge, the hypothesis that he is looking at Loki who has escaped is the likeliest explanation. However, due to facts that Cap-2012 doesn't even pause to consider, it turns out that he is wrong. From a more objective standpoint (like, that of the audience's), we know that Cap-2012 is facing not Loki but Cap-2023. If we reconstruct Cap-2012's thinking, we can represent it as follows:

> **Observation:** I see someone who looks like me right in front of me.
>
> **Hypothesis:** If Loki (who is a shapeshifter) has assumed my appearance after he escaped, I would see someone who looks like me in front of me.
>
> **Explanation:** Loki, the shapeshifter, has assumed my appearance after he escaped.

Cap-2012 goes with the hypothesis that looks most likely to him. But in this instance, we (the audience) see that the most likely sounding hypothesis that Cap-2012 considers is not true. As the philosopher Peter Lipton puts it, there is a difference between the best *actual* explanation and the best *possible* explanation; for Cap-2012, the possibilities he considers fail to extend to the actual explanation. In Lipton's words:

> Inference to the Best Explanation cannot then be understood as inference to the best of the actual explanations. Such a model would make us too good at inference, since it would make all our inferences true. Our [inferential] practice is fallible: we sometimes reasonably infer falsehoods. . . . The obvious solution, then, is to distinguish actual from potential explanations, and to construe Inference to the Best Explanation as Inference to the Best Potential Explanation. We have to produce a pool of potential explanations, from which we infer the best one. (p. 59)

The contents of the pool of potential explanation can easily extend as far as the imagination of the person looking for explanations. Granted, not just any potential explanation that we can think of will do—there are certain limitations which preclude some alternatives.

First, explanations (or hypotheses) that are internally inconsistent can be ruled out as potential explanations, for accepting such a hypothesis would commit us to believing in a contradiction.

Second, hypotheses that are externally inconsistent—when they conflict with the observable evidence, or they leave out some of the evidence—ought to be treated with suspicion. However, this is not to say that externally inconsistent hypotheses need to be outright excluded. After all, it could be that the observed evidence is misleading, and the correct explanation would rectify this.

Another example of selective abductions occurs when The Ancient One encounters the Hulk/Bruce Banner at the roof of the New York Sanctum in 2012. The Ancient One is reluctant to hand over the Time Stone to Bruce, despite understanding his predicament. But when she learns that Doctor Strange willingly handed over the Time Stone to Thanos, she reasons that she may have made a mistake in preventing Bruce from borrowing the stone.

Observation: Doctor Strange willingly gave the Time Stone to Thanos.

Hypothesis 1: If the Ancient One made a mistake in thinking that Doctor Strange would be the best Sorcerer Supreme, then Doctor Strange would willingly give the Time Stone to Thanos.

Explanation: The Ancient One was mistaken in thinking that Doctor Strange would be the best Sorcerer Supreme.

But instead of second-guessing her own judgment about Doctor Strange, the Ancient One reconsiders her initial response to Bruce:

Hypothesis 2: If Doctor Strange knew that the only way to defeat Thanos was to accept a tactical setback and surrender the Time Stone, then Doctor Strange would willingly give the Time Stone to Thanos.

Here, Hypothesis 2 leads to a different explanation of the events. But how to choose between Hypothesis 1 and Hypothesis 2? More generally, the crucial question here is, how to select between two seemingly plausible hypotheses. As Lipton says:

It is important to distinguish two senses in which something may be the best of competing potential explanations. We may characterize it as the explanation that is most warranted: the 'likeliest' explanation. On the other hand, we may characterize the best explanation as the one which would, if correct, be the most explanatory or provide the most understanding: the 'loveliest' explanation. The criteria of likeliness and love-liness may well pick out the same explanation in a particular competition, but they are clearly two different sorts of standard. Likeliness speaks of truth; loveliness of potential understanding. Moreover, the criteria do sometimes pick out different explanations. (p.61)

But making the distinction between likely and lovely explanations only passes the explanatory buck forward—that is, if we didn't have criteria for deciding which explanation is the loveliest. Lewis Vaughn suggests using the following five-point criteria of adequacy for doing this:

Testability: whether there is some way to determine if a theory is true

Fruitfulness: the number of novel predictions made

Scope: the amount of diverse phenomena explained

Simplicity: the number of assumptions made

Conservatism: how well a theory fits with existing knowledge

If we consider the above hypotheses—1 and 2—in the light of these criteria, we find that Hypothesis 2 prevails over Hypothesis 1 on the account of scope and conservatism. Hypothesis 2—if true (which it is, but unbeknownst at the time)—explains not just why Doctor Strange surrendered the Time Stone to Thanos (scope), but it also vindicates The Ancient One's belief that Doctor Strange is the best of all the Sorcerers Supreme (conservatism). The criteria of fruitfulness and simplicity do not play a role here, but this is largely due to the fact that these are irrelevant for the case at hand. In other cases, these criteria may play a decisive role, while the criteria of scope and conservatism take a back seat.

Putting all these elements together, we can now sketch a formula for the decision procedure for testing the competing explanations to find the best one: We start with a statement of a hypothesis (and one that is consistent). Next, we assess the evidence for this hypothesis. But instead of rushing to judge our sole hypothesis to be the best explanation, we have to consider alternative hypotheses. Once we have these, we use the five-point criteria above for judging which of the explanations fares the best. This formula is admittedly sketchy, but this has to do with the fact that different situations call for different approaches: sometimes multiple hypotheses need to be compared to find the best explanation, while other times it suffices to weigh just two. And so on.

Theoretical Abductions

Not all abductive inferences are selective. There are also theoretical abductions, which are a part and parcel of scientific reasoning. As an example of this, consider the scene where Tony is exploring the possibility of time travel, and he asks FRIDAY to render a model: "Give me the eigenvalue of that particle, factoring in for spectral decomp." When the model turns out successful, Tony is taken aback, exclaiming "Shit!" as he wasn't expecting this result. We can construct Tony's reasoning as follows (and with fewer expletives):

> **Hypothesis:** For time travel is to be possible, this model would have to work.
>
> **Observation:** This model does work.
>
> **Result:** Time travel is possible.

Here, Tony is not selecting among competing hypotheses which vie for the title of the best explanation. Well, strictly speaking, the choice was between two alternatives: either his hypothesis worked, or it didn't. The latter case would have been the null result, which Tony was clearly expecting.

Abduction and Creative Thinking

Let's now turn to analyze Doctor Strange's reasoning that led him to the conclusion that he should give up the Time Stone to Thanos (with seemingly very little fight). Before the Avengers fought Thanos on Titan, Doctor Strange used the Time Stone to peer into the future. As he reported to the others, he saw a total of 14,000,065 possible futures, and the Avengers prevailed against Thanos in only one of them.

Doctor Strange has access to far more evidence than any of the other Avengers. Later, when he witnesses Thanos beating Tony within inches of his life, Doctor Strange intervenes, and promises to hand over the Time Stone if Thanos spares Tony's life. It is not until much later—five years and change—that we learn the significance of this: The one scenario where the Avengers prevailed required Tony to survive his initial encounter with Thanos so that he could sacrifice himself by performing a snap that dusted Thanos and his army. To someone like Tony, who didn't have access to all the information Doctor Strange saw, this would likely look like throwing the fight on Titan. But from Doctor Strange's perspective, it may have looked like the following:

Thanos will be defeated.

Tony Stark must use the power of the Infinity Stones for Thanos to be defeated.

Tony Stark must use the power of the Infinity Stones.

This abduction alone doesn't account for the whole story. Doctor Strange also deduced that he must surrender the Time Stone to save Tony's life—maybe along the following lines:

For Tony to use the power of the Infinity Stones against Thanos, Tony must be alive.

If I don't surrender the time stone to Thanos, Tony will not be alive.

Therefore, I must surrender the time stone to Thanos.

Although abduction did not entirely account for Doctor Strange's—admittedly convoluted—reasoning, this does not detract from the overall usefulness of abductive inferences. When it comes to critical thinking, abduction provides up with another tool, which is to be used alongside deduction and induction. What makes abductive inferences useful is how they allow us to deal with surprising phenomena with relative ease. The following example is provided by Charles Peirce himself:

I once landed at a seaport in a Turkish province; and, as I was walking up to the house which I was to visit, I met a man upon horseback, surrounded by four horsemen holding a canopy over his head. As the governor of the province was the only personage I could think of who would be so greatly honored, I inferred that this was he. This was an hypothesis. ("Deduction, Induction, and Hypothesis," p. 189)

Peirce's encounter with the greatly honored horseman was a surprising fact—which can be said to be an anomaly, or the starting point for research. What is observed is not a mere irregularity in ordinary affairs, but an irregularity that demands an explanation. In *Endgame*, surprising facts abound, so much so that Natasha exclaims, "I get emails from a raccoon. Nothing sounds crazy anymore." Here, we can revisit our earlier characterization of abduction:

The surprising fact, C, is observed.

But if [hypothesis] A were true, C would be a matter of course.

Hence, there is reason to suspect that [hypothesis] A is true.

From all the examples of abduction in *Endgame*, we see that abductive responses to the surprising facts are seemingly instantaneous. Peirce himself commented on this aspect of abduction extensively; for him, "The abductive suggestion . . . is an act of insight, although of extremely fallible insight." Here's how Nubiola sees it:

> This ability of guessing right is neither blind nor infallible, but it is an instinctive ability, similar to the animal instinct of flying or nest-building of ordinary birds . . . This guessing instinct is a result of the development of our animal instincts and of the process of rational adaptation to our environment. It could be also called creativity. ("Abduction or the Logic of Surprise," p. 118)

So although making abductive inferences has some features of an instinct, it also has elements of a rational process. Some of the abductive inferences we see in *Endgame* turn out to be mistaken while others are right on the mark.

IV

Death

14

When the Stakes Are Highest

JOHN V. KARAVITIS

At the end of *Avengers: Infinity War*, despite the heroic efforts of the Avengers, Thanos achieves his universe-wide genocidal goal. While wearing the Infinity Gauntlet, with a simple snap of his fingers, *half* of all living beings in the entire universe are erased. In the sequel, *Avengers: Endgame*, Thanos is defeated; and his original genocidal success is undone.

It can be difficult to see what's really going on in Hollywood blockbuster movies like these. With no disrespect to the actors, the moviemakers, or the audience, I'm sure you'd agree that they are basically "eye candy." Canadian filmmaker David Cronenberg considers superhero movies "adolescent," not "an elevated art form," and "mostly boring." Martin Scorsese, another filmmaker, likened Marvel movies to "theme park" films. And I can see what they mean.

The audience is captivated by CGI special effects, near non-stop action, adrenaline-pumping conflict, and a storyline that is epic in nature. *No one* goes to movies like these to *think*. (If they did, perhaps the overused screenwriter's cheat—they'd call it a *trope*—of using time travel to the past to solve problems would finally be put to rest!) It's a question of pure thrill and vicarious enjoyment, movie critics be damned! Why should we care what these high-brow critics might opine? I'm sure that if audiences which had seen both movies were asked "What do you think is really going on here?" after a brief moment of stunned silence, we'd quite likely be presented with the simplistic themes of "good versus evil," or "us versus them," with the good guys (and gals!) invariably winning in the end.

That's certainly one way of looking at these two movies. I won't deny it.

In one sense, yes, the Avengers *Infinity War–Endgame* story arc is about good versus evil, about us versus them. This is how audiences in the West would have understood the story, and American audiences especially wouldn't have it any other way. But I claim that what's really going on in these two movies is that, without either the screenwriters or the audience realizing it, we are being presented with an *alien* perspective on life and death, on failure and success.

Yes, an *alien* perspective. (Although, please, you do know that I don't mean one from another planet! You're not watching an Avengers movie now. You're reading this thoughtful, yet, hopefully, thought-provoking chapter in a book in the Popular Culture and Philosophy series.) It's a perspective that people in the West would find abhorrent and reject if they ever caught on to it. But I don't think that they ever would. (That's why you have philosophers running around, asking the big questions!)

The perspective of audiences in the West is based on Western cultural values, of course. That can't be helped. Each of us views the world through the cultural lens that we've grown up with. But the Avengers *Infinity War–Endgame* story arc changes its meaning if we choose to view it from another, *non-Western*, cultural perspective.

It's a cultural perspective that I believe the screenwriters did not consciously adopt as they were crafting the screenplays. But I claim that it's the *correct* cultural perspective. It's a philosophy of life that explains exactly what's going on not only in this story arc, but, truth be told, in a great many other superhero stories. I'm prepared, as always, to back up my claim with cold, hard philosophical ideas. (And a lot of finger-pointing, and snapping, too, so watch out!)

I claim that the *Infinity War–Endgame* story arc only really makes sense if we view these two movies from the perspective of a culture that is deeply steeped in ideas such as honor, loyalty, and death. A culture faced with internal conflicts over a long period of time. A culture which struggled to come to terms with both its internal conflicts and ever-growing pressures from the outside world. A culture where every action, intentional or not, was laden with deep meaning, and could have dire, unforeseen consequences—including death. A *warrior* culture which presents, to Western eyes, an alien perspective on life and death, on failure and success.

Have you guessed it yet? I'm referring to the culture and philosophy of *feudal Japan*.

Life Is to Death as Failure Is to Success

The reason for Thanos's mission is explained in *Infinity War*. Having seen that overpopulation led to the end of his home world, the planet Titan, Thanos fervently believes that killing half of all life in the universe will give the life that remains a chance to survive. After kidnapping his daughter Gamora on Knowhere, Thanos explains his position to her. "A small price to pay for salvation. If life is left unchecked, life will cease to exist. It needs *correction*."

Thanos sees himself as the only one who can both see the truth of his position and have the strength of will to carry out his plan through to the end. Traveling with Gamora to Vormir to acquire the Soul Stone, Thanos is warned that "It extracts a terrible price." "I am prepared," he replies. Thanos is then told "In order to take the Stone, you must lose that which you love. A soul for a soul." In anguish, Thanos throws Gamora off the cliff, sacrificing her for the Soul Stone. "The hardest choices require the strongest wills," Thanos later tells Doctor Strange on Titan. We see that failure and success are measured in terms of life and death. Thanos's success is based on death. Had he failed, countless lives would have been spared.

In *Endgame*, an earlier version of Thanos learns that, in the future, he will succeed in his quest to end half of all life. But seeing how the Avengers would continue to try to thwart him, even after his eventual "future" success, he realizes that killing half of all life in the universe would not be enough. He decides to erase *all* life in the universe, and start over. He has come to see his "first" success—ensuring that life would continue by erasing half of it—as a failure. However, the Avengers succeed in bringing back the "lost" lives; and Thanos is defeated.

In *Endgame*, Thanos's failure is measured by life—the lives that he had originally planned on "saving." Now they have to go, too. Success still depends on death, only now, more so. The Avengers' success is now also based on death—including the deaths of Black Widow and Tony Stark. The Avengers finally succeed by using Thanos's playbook! As Doctor Strange foresaw in *Infinity War*, in one of the 14,000,605 possible futures, the Avengers would only succeed by "failing"—by embracing death. We see that the moral of the *Infinity War–Endgame* story arc is that, when the stakes are high, life is to death as failure is to success.

The Playbook for Success

You may be thinking that this observation is a bit contrived, and I understand your feelings. But you must keep in mind that you are reading this chapter with the same cultural lens through which you saw both *Infinity War* and *Endgame*—a *Western* cultural lens. The *Infinity War–Endgame* story arc is best explained by the culture and philosophy of feudal Japan. It all comes down to equating success with death—the enemy's and, if necessary, your own.

This cultural perspective is clear to anyone who has read *Hagakure*, a famous Japanese book. This work is a collection of aphorisms and vignettes which was compiled in the early eighteenth century by Yamamoto Tsunetomo, a retired samurai. The title has been translated as "Hidden Among the Leaves," or "In the Shadow of Leaves," but it is also known as "The Book of the Samurai." The philosophy presented in *Hagakure* is based on *bushido*.

Bushido translates to "the way of the warrior" (*bushi* "warrior" and *do* "the way") or, as Dr. Inazo Nitobe translates it in his book *Bushido: The Soul of Japan*, "Military-Knight-Ways." *Hagakure* repeatedly presents the core concept of *bushido*: death. "The way of the warrior is to be found in dying" (I.2). "One should always be 'ready to die' for one's cause" (I.19). "The Way of the warrior entails a rehearsal of death morning after morning, picturing one's life ending here or there, and imagining the most wonderful way of dying" (II.49).

This emphasis on death runs throughout *Hagakure*, as it does through the *Infinity War–Endgame* story arc. It's a perspective that presents a brutal indifference to life, if life presents an obstacle to achieving your goals. This could be the lives of one's enemies, friends, family members, or even one's own. In *Infinity War*, we learn that Gamora knows the location of the Soul Stone, and that she is willing to sacrifice her life to keep its location from Thanos. As they head to Knowhere to secure the Reality Stone from the Collector, Gamora tells her lover, Peter Quill, "If things go wrong . . . if Thanos gets me . . . I want you to promise me . . . you'll kill me." On Knowhere they are surprised by Thanos, who seizes Gamora. Quill wants to rescue her, but Gamora urges him to remember his promise. "Peter. Not him. You promised. You promised." Thanos understands. He tells Gamora "Oh, daughter. You expect too much from him."

Thanos accepts death as the solution to achieving his ultimate goal: "correcting" Life to give it a chance to survive. I would also argue that at the beginning of *Endgame*, Thanos accepts his own death, implicitly, after he is caught unprepared by the Avengers in "the Garden," but before Thor kills him in a fit of rage. The Avengers reluctantly accept death, too—that of Black Widow and Tony Stark—to defeat Thanos. It's a perspective that most

Westerners would find abhorrent if they had to face it and articulate it. (Although perfectly acceptable in a three-hour cinematic blockbuster experience, wouldn't you agree?)

Although it might seem difficult to accept this perspective, in fact, we've been aware of it for quite some time. Stories of Japanese samurai culture have long been a staple of entertainment for Westerners. We all know about the importance of honor, loyalty, and death in samurai culture. We know about samurai battles, one-on-one swordfights to the death, and even the idea of *seppuku*, ritual suicide performed in order to atone for failure or dishonor. But it's this same perspective on death, this seemingly brutal indifference to life, which runs through the *Infinity War–Endgame* story arc. Westerners would surely balk at accepting a way of life where one should "think of himself as already dead" when facing problems or pursuing goals (I.35), or which declares that "Samurai resolve to die at any moment" (I.63). But it's this idea of voluntarily accepting death when unavoidable that is at the heart of *bushido*.

The way of the samurai is complicated; and the three ways of life which molded Japanese culture over centuries, Buddhism, Shinto, and Confucianism, each contributed to the formation of *bushido*. Dr. Nitobe noted that the "disdain of life and friendliness with death" that is part of *bushido* is rooted in Buddhism. Shinto was the source of ideas of patriotism and loyalty. Confucianism, adopted from China, was the source of ethical guidelines.

So, this alien perspective is really not as simple as what you may have seen in movies about samurai and feudal Japan. In order to achieve a goal, we should assume a detachment from both life and death, indeed, an indifference to them. This is exactly how the Avengers finally defeat Thanos. But at this point, we've only scratched the surface. To really get to the heart of the matter, we need to do a little more digging into *bushido* to see how this alien perspective correctly explains the mindsets and actions of both Thanos and the Avengers.

Digging Deeper among the Leaves

The problem that most Westerners would have in reading *Hagakure* is that, even with the best translation into English, it can appear to be a confusing jumble of aphorisms and vignettes. What to do, and when to do it, is not at all clear. All too frequently, the advice and stories appear to contradict each other. But there is a unifying thread that runs through *Hagakure*, which explains the mindsets and actions of Thanos and the Avengers as they struggled against each other to take possession of the Infinity Stones. It's related to *bushido*, and the idea of death.

In "Embracing Death: Pure Will in *Hagakure*," Olivier Ansart acknowledges that *Hagakure* presents diverse meanings to its readers. But Ansart identifies *ichinen*, or "pure will," as the unifying thread throughout this book. (*Ichinen* can also be translated into "single-minded resolve," which I think gives a clearer idea of what's going on in the mind of a samurai.)

Ansart notes that the samurai is always in "a relentless competition" with other samurai. This competition is obsessive in nature. "Never fall behind others in pursuing the Way of the warrior" (I.19). The Avengers constantly jockey among themselves, even if it's just to be "right" about an issue. At times, it's amazing that they are able to work together to pursue common goals! ". . . when you are recklessly determined to 'not be outdone by others' and 'aim to charge the enemy line', you will not fall behind, your spirit will be intrepid, and you will exhibit fearlessness" (I.162).

We see this obsessive competition express itself in the pursuit of the Infinity Stones. In *Endgame*, Thanos implicitly acknowledges this spirit of competition when he observes, "You could not live with your own failure. What did that bring you? *Back to me.*"

But beyond a competitive spirit engendered by *bushido*, and deeper than the idea of just "pure will," Ansart identifies *shini-gurui*, the "frenzy to die." We see many examples of both Thanos and the Avengers fighting with *shini-gurui*. "*Bushido* is to enter a 'death frenzy'. Even dozens of men cannot kill a man in a frenzied state already determined to die" (I.113). This describes every hand-to-hand battle Thanos ever had with the Avengers. The Battle at Wakanda in *Infinity War*, and the final battle in *Endgame,* both show everyone in a non-stop frenzied state. Thanos appears unstoppable, even when tangling with the Hulk or Captain Marvel.

"Do not hesitate once you have decided to cut a man down. . . . be ready to leap headlong into the fray without a second thought" (I.189). At the Battle of Wakanda, Thor drives Stormbreaker into Thanos's chest, and then proceeds to gloat. A few moments later, Thanos tells Thor "You should have gone for the head." Thanos then snaps his fingers, and achieves his goal. In *Endgame*, Thor carried the guilt over not having beheaded Thanos when he first had the chance *for five years*. His guilt drove him to withdraw into a self-pitying alcoholic stupor. Had Thor acted when he could have, and not missed his first chance, Thanos would not have lived long enough to erase half of all life in the universe. Lacking sufficient *shini-gurui*, Thor failed.

"To retaliate entails just frenetically throwing yourself at your adversary *with the intention of being cut down*" (I.55). In *Endgame*, Tony Stark saw that the Avengers' last opportunity to succeed would require him to sacrifice his life. He did so without hesitation.

In *Infinity War*, after Thanos snapped his fingers, he found himself inside the dream world of the Soul Stone, with Gamora appearing to him as a young girl. She asks him "What did it cost?" Thanos replies "Everything." For Thanos, death, not life, led to success. In *Endgame*, Black Widow sacrificed her life on Vormir in order to acquire the Soul Stone. She points out to Hawkeye that Thanos left Vormir with the Soul Stone, and without his daughter. "Whatever it takes," she tells him. In his final battle with Thanos, Tony Stark craftily stole the Infinity Stones and defeated him, but at the cost of his own life. Here too, death led to success. Both sides "win" in turn by following the same playbook—the samurai playbook, as described in *Hagakure*.

Although audiences in the West can understand altruism, suicidal altruism is a bit more difficult an idea to swallow. It provokes a visceral, negative reaction. And rightly so, I believe. Although the actions of Black Widow and Tony Stark are understood and accepted, nevertheless, in the West, standing alone, they would be viewed as horrific. However, their final choice is one that any true samurai would have embraced without any hesitation. To succeed, you have to give up both your ego and the *Western* idea that life means more than achieving your goals. To live and to have failed would have been anathema to a samurai. Death—even through *seppuku*—would have been preferable to failure; and it was calmly accepted when necessary.

The Ways of Comic-Book Heroes, Villains—and Us

Superheroes tend to be monomaniacal, with samurai-like personalities. They see situations in terms of black and white—no nuances. When it comes to fighting supervillains, they typically have no problem rushing headlong into battle. Captain Marvel is the best example of a superhero who possesses these stereotypical samurai character traits. She refuses to wait to go in to battle, and seems completely unconcerned with the possibility of losing her life. She acts as *Hagakure* counsels. "Now is the time; the time is now. He who thinks of the present and the critical moment as separate will never react in a timely fashion when disaster strikes" (II.48).

But I think that, if you're willing to agree that I have presented a fair case for viewing the *Infinity War–Endgame* story arc as being representative of the culture and philosophy of feudal Japan (fingers crossed, no snapping!), I'd like to take my argument one step further. And I'm sorry, but it's a step that I think you really will *not* accept.

Given that the culture of feudal Japan best explains what's going on here, whom would you characterize as being more representative of *bushido*? The Avengers or Thanos?

It's a tough call, I'll admit. I'd have to balance, among other things, Black Widow's and Tony Stark's acceptance of their individual deaths against Thanos's monomaniacal drive. But the proof that it really is Thanos who best expresses the values of *bushido* lies at the beginning of *Endgame*. The Avengers discover Thanos in "the Garden" on Planet 0259-S, living the life of a simple, solitary farmer. Having achieved his universe-wide genocidal goal, he intentionally and willingly destroyed the Infinity Stones! But it wasn't fear that his work would be undone that drove him to destroy the Stones. Thanos knew that the Infinity Stones made him truly invincible. He explains his motive to the Avengers. "The universe required correction. After that, the Stones served no purpose, beyond temptation." The Avengers refuse to believe him. They desperately want to find the Stones and bring back all the lives that Thanos erased. But Thanos has no reason to lie now. "I used the Stones to destroy the Stones. It nearly killed me. But the work is done."

This act goes to Thanos's *self-discipline*. It would be hard to believe that anyone with the power granted by the Infinity Stones would ever give it up. The Avengers couldn't believe it. But Thanos did give this power up. Intentionally and willingly. Only someone with this level of self-discipline could be a true disciple of *bushido*. Look at the Avengers; and compare them and their arguments, doubts, hesitation, and lack of cohesion and self-discipline to Thanos and his "single-minded resolve." Of all the characters in the *Infinity War–Endgame* story arc, as misguided as he may have been in his quest to "correct Life," Thanos is the true samurai.

There's a lesson here for us in the West. In every goal that we set for ourselves, with every challenge that we accept in Life, especially when the stakes are highest, we should follow Thanos's example. We should be self-disciplined, determined, and single-minded, to the point of frenzy, if need be. *We should act as though we were being driven by death.* To succeed in achieving our goals, we should be just like Thanos. *Not* like the Avengers!

Although I grant you, doing so won't be as easy as just snapping your fingers.

15
Life Is a Laugh and Death Is a Joke

JARNO HIETALAHTI

Monty Python's movie *The Life of Brian* ends with a beautiful song about the humorous aspects of humanity: "Life's a laugh and death's a joke, it's true." *Avengers Endgame* proves the song correct in so many ways that philosophers of humor are overwhelmed.

For humble human beings, sure, why not?, but even for god-like superheroes, humor is a central piece of life, and death is no duller. But to sing out loud statements like these, you really should first understand what humor is. And that's exactly what *Avengers: Endgame* does; portrays a whole wide spectrum of funniness, sometimes in the most tragic manner.

Just consider Iron Man's sarcastic remarks, Spider-Man's teenage giggling, Black Widow's seductive smile, Doctor Strange's sophisticated upper-class witticisms, and Rocket's endless gags—Marvel Comics movies offer a paradise for a humor researcher! If there ever was a franchise with a plurality of humor, you have found it. And Avengers isn't even a comedy.

Heaven and Hell are surprisingly close to each other, and plurality sometimes becomes a curse. Eventually, philosophers of humor can't help but bang their heads on the TV screen while watching *Avengers*. In our field, you should be able to find a common denominator for all the possible forms of humor. Good luck with that when you have a rather simple-minded character like Drax (who laughs at others' failures), melancholic Gamora (whose humor is silent and subtle), and jester-like Ant-Man (who throws puns all the time).

Loki and Countless Contradictions

Philosophers of humor have realized that humor is based on incongruities, that is, something unexpected. Just as the famous Danish thinker Søren Kierkegaard once said, wherever there's a paradox, there's potential for humor. And that's what modern humor research is based on: humor occurs when something surprising happens.

This approach is called the incongruity theory of humor. Philosophers speak about contradictions between our expectations and what actually occurs. You know, if a human being walks a dog, that's relatively ordinary, and on itself not that funny. But if a golden retriever has a human being on a leash and takes him to the back yard to do his business, there's something you don't see every day, and most likely you will be amused by the sight (and conversely, this theory explains why you don't laugh too many times at the same old jokes—you're already expecting the outcome!). Laughter, in turn, is a reaction which signals that we have got the joke, and one way or another, resolved the incongruity fittingly. If you don't get a joke, you don't realize what's funny, and the laughter will stick in your throat.

In the Marvel universe, who's a more paradoxical character than Loki? This prankster Norse god just loves to mess with people and with other gods. He's the master of mischief, champion of illusions, and oh boy, he has fooled Death himself more than once. In *Avengers: Endgame* Loki has a woefully small part, but even during those few minutes he gets to be what he truly is, a trickster. When the time-traveling silliness gets heated, Loki once again appears into the screens and overcomes Death, even though everyone thought that it would be quite final when Thanos killed Loki earlier. No way, sir! In the alternative reality offered by time-travelling, Loki does what he does best. He sees the world in a different way than others around him, manages to make the best out of the situation, and even when heavily captured, gets away with the precious Tesseract. Nobody knows where Loki went.

You can call Loki an epitome or embodiment of humor. If humor is something unexpected, that's what Loki does in every movie of the franchise. Also, he is full of contradictions. Just remember how at one point he's ready to force the whole of mankind to its knees, and a couple of movies later is willing to sacrifice his own well-being to fight for the Earth. If we stick to traditional reason, there's little logic behind Loki's deeds. But this is a hasty conclusion. Loki is a manifestation of alternative reason, he is a trickster in its purest form.

But what is a trickster after all? It's not merely an entertainer or a fool, but something deeper; you could say, a sum of contradictions. A Polish anthropologist Paul Radin has put it well:

Trickster is at one and the same time creator and destroyer, giver and
negator, he who dupes others and who is always duped himself . . .
At all times he is constrained to behave as he does from impulses
over which he has no control, he knows no good nor evil yet he is
responsible for both. He possesses no values . . . is at the mercy of
his passions and appetites, yet through his actions all values come
into being.

If Loki truly is a trickster, he is neither good nor evil, not
immoral either, but perhaps amoral. This allows trickster to
keep on confusing everybody around him because he has no
goal for his deeds in a traditional sense. Instead, trickster par-
odies social norms and structures, and inverses hierarchies
and values. But, and this is a tough philosophical, practical
and political point, trickster doesn't care about power in itself.
Of course, based on the movies, you could argue otherwise;
clearly Loki yearns for power! He tries to take over both
Asgård, and Earth, but eventually always falls short with his
evil plans. But that's just it! Loki's plans are not precisely evil,
but humorous; instead of staying in power forever, he wants to
rattle the cage, and offers something entirely different for people around the universe. Because Loki is such a cunning fellow, and (almost) always one step ahead of his rivals, it could
be that Loki actually wants to lose the gained power position.
If he didn't, there's a danger he would stay on the throne forever; and that just doesn't fit with the paradoxical psyche of
trickster gods.

It was a shrewd decision by the directors of *Avengers
Endgame* to bring Loki back to life and let him escape with the
Tesseract. For the franchise, you can be fairly sure that Loki's
adventures are not done just yet. Wait and see!

Thanos's Brute Smile

Even if most humor researchers base their works on the incongruity theory, this hasn't always been the case. Historically
speaking, for some two thousand years the so-called superiority theory of humor prevailed. Philosophers from Plato to
Epictetus and from St. Augustine to Thomas Hobbes thought
that we are somewhat selfish creatures with our laughter. We
laugh at others for a petty reason: we want to be better than
others! Hobbes has given the strongest formulation of this theory in his book *Leviathan*: laughter is nothing else but a sudden glory when we realize that the others are weak and stupid
in comparison to ourselves. Bwa-ha-ha- ha!

Thanos, anyone, hmm? Ring a bell? If you admire power, you love Thanos. This guy basically does whatever he wants to. And if Hobbes is correct, then there is plenty to laugh at for Thanos. Face it, he is as strong as it gets in the Marvel universe. Someone could say that Hulk could match his power, but come on, Thanos eats Hulks for breakfast.

Of course, for a slightly more humane viewer, Thanos symbolizes horror. His route to the massacre is accompanied by fun. Already in his first appearance in *The Avengers* (after the credits), he smiles his diabolical smile. He knows something others don't, and that something can't be good. Brr, shivering. Even when the strongest heroes on Earth have beaten his army, the ultimate destroyer isn't a bit concerned. Instead, Thanos is amused, and probably because of his superiority. He has his self-satisfied smirk thanks to the confidence about his forthcoming destiny. As Thanos manifests in *Avengers: Endgame*, he is inevitable. What a guy, smiling in the face of, during and after the annihilation.

Not sure whether Charles R. Gruner had Thanos in mind when he published *The Game of Humor* in 1997. In this book, Gruner claims that humor is always a game with winners and losers; winners laugh, and losers don't; and more likely the latter weep. In any case, Thanos is the clearest living, even if fictional, example of this theory. He laughs while everyone else is devasted.

Thanos has fun also on a smaller scale. Just think about the huge fight scene in *Avengers: Infinity War*. All the superheroes are attacking the supervillain with all their strength, and to what end? The very best of the best manage to spill a drop of blood from the purple titan. Well played, guys. And as the superiority theory predicts, Thanos smiles after the huge attack and beats the hell out of, well, basically from half of the universe. With a snap of a finger, billions and billions of living creatures are gone, and Thanos once again smiles his self-satisfied grin. What a sick sense of humor.

Thor and the Sorrow behind Laughter

The father of psychoanalysis, Sigmund Freud, realized that we don't always laugh because of our superiority. Instead, surprisingly often we laugh because we are nervous little creatures who have all kinds of inner tensions within us. We struggle in our lives, we have to balance between our own wishes and social demands and—this is especially important for Freud— we don't get enough sex and can't duff up other people without consequences. In this tense situation, we laugh and release some of the tension, and we feel at least a little bit better. If you can't do anything about it, laugh at it. In the field of philosophy of humor, this approach is called the relief theory. When we laugh, we are psychologically relieved. Humor is a socially approved safety valve.

The most interesting part of Freud's theory is that humor and laughter express our so-called unconscious; that is, our personal motives of which we are quite unaware. For example, through jokes we express our hidden wishes in a socially acceptable way. This is rather sensible; the society probably won't punish us in an equal manner when we joke about raping and if somebody actually rapes another human being. Obviously, there are strong objections to rape jokes, too, but the actual punishment is not equally harsh. The point is that through humor you reveal yourself in one way or another. This doesn't mean that everyone who jokes about mass murders would like to commit mass murder, but nevertheless, there's always a reason for our humor. If you want to find out what this reason is, you need to dig down deep to the psyche of the joker.

In the *Avengers* movies, you should pay attention to the Mighty Thor if you want to get a full grasp of Freud's theory. Even if the nickname hints otherwise, Thor has his emotional side, and he is vulnerable. But he often hides his limitedness behind humor. Of course, Thor has his share of witty remarks and exuberant laughter, but the broader picture is more complicated than this. Humor reveals Thor's character.

In *Avengers: Endgame* Thor has changed. The most obvious change is how the daydream of all the heterosexual females has become fat. Even though Thor laughs joyfully when he meets Hulk and Rocket after so many years, there's something wrong with him; pretty clearly, the heavy drinking Asgardian has lost control over his life. Instead of saving universes, he prefers to spend his days playing video games with his buddies. The contradiction for the viewer is obvious, and besides somewhat tragic, also humorous. In addition, Thor himself doesn't seem to worry too much, he is in his merry mood—at least seemingly so.

However, it becomes clear soon enough that Thor is struggling. Cheap laughs don't last long when Hulk and Rocket mention Thanos's name. It triggers something in Thor. True, he laughs and reminds the others that he has killed Thanos. But this laughter is terror-ridden, and Thor tries to hide his horror even from himself behind the laughter. Humor becomes a mechanism of escape. It's a way to avoid facing the dreadful reality as it is.

So, the Mighty Thor has become a washout. And that's what Freud tries to say. Even if you put on a show and try to be superior to everyone through your humor and laughter, you can actually be just weak and insecure. That's Thor's situation, and there's a reason for this. All the horrors Thanos brought into the universe nag Thor's inside. He was the one to protect the Earth, but failed miserably. Even if Thor and his group managed to get revenge and kill Thanos, it didn't bring the dead back. Avenging is eventually worth very little, even for the Avengers.

As the movie proceeds, Thor starts to find integrity little by little. We don't need to dive too deep into the murky waters of time travelling and dimensional details, but all the time Thor's humor is a mirror to his soul. For instance, when he finds the lost *Mjölnir* (his precious hammer), Thor is exhilarated; even with all the problems the Norse god has had, he is still worthy of the hammer. At this scene, laughter expresses a true relief, and not just hidden anxiety. By the way, later on Thor manages to prove the superiority theory of humor wrong. When Captain America lifts *Mjölnir*, Thor is just excited and shouts with joy that he always knew that Steve Rogers could do it. From a theoretical level, Thor laughs because he is not superior to Captain America but an equal. Take that, superiority theory.

The end of the movie wraps up Thor's complex relation to humor and laughter. In the ending, he actually hides his leadership behind the veil of laughter. His laughter is kind and affirmative, and he doesn't need to put others down in any way. Instead, even jokingly, he is equal with the Guardians of the Galaxy (or Asgardians of the Galaxy, as the pun goes). Of course, everybody joining him to the next space voyages knows that Thor is their leader, but on a personal level, Thor doesn't need any extra glorification. After all the afflictions Thor has faced, he has found his true calling, once again. To wrap up, during the first scenes of *Avengers: Endgame* Thor laughed to hide his pain, sorrow and weakness; in the middle he laughed because he was not superior to Rogers; and in the end Thor laughs to hide his divine leadership.

Chris Hemsworth, Thor's actor, made an excellent call when he demanded that Thor must be fat at the end of the movie, too. Apparently the directors had planned otherwise, but Hemsworth thought that if Thor was again a musclebound god at the end, that would have made his fatness just a cheap joke. Now, there's much more depth in his character, and as said, the diversity of Thor's psychology is reflected in his humor and laughter throughout the movie.

Endgame of the Endgame (of Humor)

Yep, in humor there's often something really incongruous present, but true too, some people express their (imagined?) superiority over others through laughter, but then, there's often this silent humbleness around humor. Which is the best theory?

If you ask any modern philosopher, they will go with the incongruity theory. This is just because you can quite easily show cases where there's not any kind of superiority or super tight inner tension present in humor and laughter. But to find an example about humor completely lacking contradictions, well, that's a challenge.

Even if the incongruity theory covers the whole wide spectrum of humor better than superiority and relief theories, don't be too hasty to throw them into the trash. Perhaps they are, philosophically speaking, flawed theories, but they still at least complement the incongruity theory. You could say that they are more empirical theories, and thanks to it, they give flesh to the bones of humor's skeleton.

When you start to apply humor theories to *Avengers: Endgame*, the best thing is that it shows a wide variety of possible forms of humor. On the most obvious level, humor has a clear role in Marvel Comics' movies. Witty remarks and resounding laughter make the superheroes more easily approachable and acceptable. They promote the positive aspect of humor.

However, humor in *Endgame* is as complex as are the characters. Even if some heroes are more acceptable thanks to their humor, Thanos, as argued above, becomes more horrible with his devilish smile. Evidently, he laughs, and this makes him an even more appalling creature. Massacres and beatings are fun for him. Thor, then, runs away from his anxiety with humor, and Loki is basically his cunning own self, who lives and breaths the very cornerstones of humor, that is, surprises and paradoxes. If anything, you can conclude that humor isn't good in itself, but it's not bad either. It's a much more dynamic thing.

At least for philosophers of humor, it's apparent that *Avengers* highlights the idea that humor has to be analyzed in relation to other values. Actually, humor is a part of a worldview; you laugh because you see the world and its ridiculous aspects from your own unique perspective. And that reveals how fitting the Monty Python song in the beginning of this chapter actually was. Traditionally, laughter has been connected to the living; the dead are silent. Of course, people, and especially philosophers, want to take their lives seriously, but even so, life is something to laugh about. Laughter is an expression of life, you could say romantically.

But is death a joke? That just depends on how you relate to joking. Joke doesn't necessarily mean worthless or trivial. Humor about death can be silent and sorrow, even respectful. Of course, if you are a bloodthirsty titan like Thanos, laughing at the death of billions of living creatures could be rather tasteless. However, there are tricksters like Loki who manage to cheat the death, and in this way death can become a joking matter. And, in *Avengers: Endgame*, the time-traveling stuff negates a huge amount of dying, and in this sense, death seems to be a joke for the makers of the movie in general.

If we want to take a step to a more philosophical direction, we could argue that life and death are essential parts of human life, and human beings themselves are inherently contradictory and silly creatures. We love life, and we fear death, but our scope is always limited. If we knew everything and lived forever, our humor would be drastically different; and it's questionable if there would be humor for an immortal and all-knowing creature (there has been a long discussion about whether the Christian God can have a sense of humor or not).

Death is the horizon which gives meaning to human life; and this makes humor possible. In the face of our death, we can laugh, because without mortality we wouldn't have humor at all. The same holds for superheroes as long as they are at least a bit like us.

16
The Defeat of Death

JD Lyonhart

Coming out of the theater my wife was visibly shaken. But I kept thinking: *they're just going to bring them back to life in the next Avengers movie.*

Marvel's two-part conclusion to its epic thus set itself a seemingly impossible task: take seriously the death of half of its characters, many of whom were already scheduled to reappear in movies the following year (such as *Spider-Man 2*).

Death after death, character after character, the Marvel world was quite literally blown away by Thanos, extracting a large emotional toll from the audience, a toll that not all were expecting or wanting to pay, and which might be even more problematic if quickly refunded—for instance, if its characters were killed off in order to simply bring them back, cheapening the cost of death and the emotions we felt in response to it.

I left the theater wondering if there was any way for the sequel to overcome—rather than simply sidestep—death. Was there any way for Marvel to move forward while maintaining a solid and coherent philosophy of death?

Arthur Schopenhauer (1788–1860) wrote that "Death is the muse of philosophy." Death terrifies us into asking those existential questions, putting life into perspective in the same way the darkness of the forest heightens the visual intensity of a late-night camp fire.

Yet much of the history of philosophy has been concerned with negating death, whether through the transmigration of souls, reincarnation, the resurrection of the body, or even the infinite recurrence of the same. At the root of much of Western thought is Plato, whose rigorous defense of the soul provided an actual argument for life after death.

In Plato's *Meno*, Socrates asks questions of a young, uneducated boy (hence, "the Socratic method"). Simply by asking questions—without feeding any outside information to the child—Socrates helps the boy solve increasingly complex mathematical equations.

Yet the boy was uneducated, and Socrates did not give him any positive information, so how was the child able to answer the questions? Because, Plato reasons, there must be some knowledge that is innate; that is not learned from the five physical senses while in the body but that we already have before we begin to explore with our bodies. For example, while we may learn the official rules of logic later in high school, even as a child we still think within the parameters of logic (no matter how irrational your children might seem).

A child cannot imagine a square that is also, at the same time, a triangle. Sure, they could put a triangle inside a square, or a square inside a triangle, but they could never actually picture something that has three sides and four sides at the same time and in the same way. Their mind is still inherently logical. We cannot even imagine a contradiction; this is precisely why it is called a contra-diction, for it is *contra* our ability to *speak* it. Even prior to school or any formal education, even prior to any physical knowledge derived from the senses as we grow, we already seem to know certain things, already seem to have a proto-logical framework, from the very beginning.

This is why the boy was able to come up with complex logical and mathematical answers to questions he had not studied before. Socrates did not put the knowledge into the boy, but was merely a midwife delivering that which was within him all along. And so it seems, there must be something within us other than the body of flesh and the external knowledge we gain from our five senses. And if there is indeed something within us that is not physical, then it need not perish when our physical body perishes, but could instead live on.

Dealing with Death

Plato thus placed a great tradition of the afterlife at the heart of Western thought, making the soul the means by which innate knowledge itself is attained, anticipating Descartes's later soul as a "thinking thing," *who thinks therefore it is.* Yet Plato did not thereby end death once and for all, but rather, baked it into an ongoing cycle of reincarnation.

At times Plato seems to be saying that your soul is placed in one body until that body falls apart, at which point your soul does some cartwheels in the afterlife before returning to a different body on Earth to do it all over again. Death and life rotate back and forth. We've heard this before: *It's the circle of life, Simba.* There are multiple religious versions of this, where life and death are locked in some eternal yin-yang dualism with neither one better than the other.

There are also secular counterparts. It's common today to hear someone who does not believe in an afterlife say that death is a natural part of life. Death is part of the journey, and all good things come to an end. In fact, many see this inevitable demise as the very thing that gives life meaning; life is precious because it is fleeting. As Vision says in *Avengers: Age of Ultron*, "A thing isn't beautiful because it lasts." Life and death are seen as partners, without which neither can work. Life is as contingent upon death for its meaning as death is contingent upon life to feed it. Thus, even the secular has a yin-yang view of life and death, where both are just part of the natural order. Death is not a bad or evil thing, but merely the way of the world. We need not fight death, but can embrace it as a friend. *Death is embraced.*

There is an alternate secular reality that is not so friendly to its impending doom. Much of the Western world does not believe in any afterlife, yet neither does it really accept on a gut level the cliché that death is natural and good (even if people verbally insist that they do). Instead, much of the Western world seems to have simply evacuated death from its midst, shipping the elderly to homes, building graveyards away from the city, and delaying the inevitable with creams, surgeries and outright denial. Billion-dollar industries have been founded upon the delaying of death and the fetishization of youth. This option does not embrace death, but side-steps, ignores, delays, and avoids it. *Death is denied.*

Yet there is another option for the secularist. They can admit that death is not fun and games and flowers and the circle of life. They can admit that it really is horrific, and that for every perfect lemon-drop whose death is peaceful there is another death that drags on for ages, where walking, breathing, or swallowing are a living agony for months and years of decline. They can admit that death is not good, is not a beautiful part of the circle of life, is not how things should be. That death, in a word, sucks. Yet, instead of denying this reality, they learn to accept it. It's not ideal, but it's all we've got. It would be great if we didn't die or if we went to Heaven after we did, but these are mere fairy tales, and we really just need to grow up, accept the finality of death and get on with the business of living. This type of person does not embrace death as natural nor as part of the circle of life, yet nor do they deny it. Rather, they simply accept that it sucks and move on. *Death is accepted.*

In contrast to these secular alternatives, the Judeo-Christian narrative is also prevalent in the West. It goes like this: Once there was no death, but only life. Life in the garden of Eden, life that was meant to last forever. But then sin entered the world, and with sin came death. For sin gets in the middle of relationships; our harmful actions damage those around us and hinder our intimacy with them, weaseling its way between us and those we love. Now, God is life itself; God is the source of all being, and so once sin gets in between our intimacy with God that basically means we are separated from the source of all life and being, and so humanity begins to die. Sin has gotten in the way of our intimacy with God, and so separated us from the one who is life itself. Thus, with sin comes death. A human history littered with tales of sin and death follows soon after, beginning with Cain and Abel and ending with wars, abuse, and empire.

But then Christ dies for our sins, suffering a most gruesome, excruciating death on a cross. In this, he forgives and takes away our sin, bearing it upon himself, thus removing that which blocked our intimacy with the God of life. In turn, Jesus dies the death we should had to have died ourselves, and so though we still die on Earth, we are then resurrected with him to everlasting life. In this narrative death and sin are seen not as natural parts of the created order, but something alien that entered into the world at the Fall, and which are removed through the cross of Christ. Death is not part of the circle of life, but interrupts it. Life can exist without death as inherently valuable and good in its own right. In fact, life would have continued on that way in the garden if we hadn't sinned, and will continue on that way forevermore once we resurrect. God has triumphed over death; death itself has died. Death is defeated.

Death Vanquished by Sacrifice

So we've looked at four philosophies of death:

1. **The embrace of death**

2. **The denial of death**

3. **The acceptance of death**

4. **The defeat of death**

The question is, which one of these best aligns with the two-part conclusion to the *Avengers* saga and does this narrative really do justice to the philosophy of death?

Now, 1. the embrace of death epitomizes Thanos. For Thanos, death is a natural part of life that keeps all things in 'balance'. Thanos is not a humanist who wishes to save life, yet nor is he a sadist who kills solely for sport. He does not worship life nor death, but rather the balance between them. For every fifty who are spared fifty must be cut down, and it is only by this sacrifice that life itself can be preserved. This is similar to the light and dark side of the force in Star Wars, where every imbalance in the universe needs to be corrected; where both the light and dark side need to keep each other in check. Death thus has its place in the circle of life, and its inevitability must be made manifest. All things must be kept in balance. Death is necessary to the equation.

Thanos's embrace of death is not the view of the movie itself but precisely the position that is countered by the Avengers. Tony Stark's initial response in *Endgame* is essentially that of option 3, the acceptance of death. Tony accepts that he has failed, accepts that death is both horrible and inevitable and that his friends are not coming back. He faces the full weight of this reality and it almost destroys him, leaving him half the man he used to be, broken and demoralized. Yet, over time, he finds the power to accept the reality of death and move on. Tony and Pepper get a cottage on the lake, have an adorable daughter, and get on with the business of living life while it lasts. This is not the embrace of death as good or part of the circle of life, yet nor is it a denial. It is facing the harsh reality and then getting up and moving on. *It is acceptance.*

Yet, Tony begins to shift when hope re-enters the equation. He barely dares to let himself entertain such possibility, barely dares to re-open that wound that had only just begun to heal. When Captain America, Black Widow and Ant-Man show up at his door, he refuses to 'talk shop' with them. Like many secular-humanists, he does not merely disagree with such hopes but finds it painful to have them dangled in front of him, for he is trying to let go of naive hopes and just accept the world as it is. Yet once he invents time travel he slips into a more optimistic—borderline religious—view, where death can be conquered by some means.

Like Christ, Tony sacrifices himself, and by his death he defeats death for the rest of humanity. As Doctor Strange ominously declares, Tony's sacrifice was "the only way." Death may be potent in the Marvel Cinematic Universe, but it can be defeated. Death is not denied, ignored or sidestepped, but is swallowed up by Tony, who defeats death by facing it head on, dying so that others may live. Death is defeated by a death. This is not just a cool plot twist to end the movie with tears, but rather, completes the trajectory that was set in motion in the first thirty minutes of *Iron Man* back in 2008.

Tony's friend, Yinson, dies a good death in the cave in order to save Tony, begging him not to waste the sacrifice. Tony insists Yinsen get up and live to see his family, but then Yinsen reveals they were dead all along, replying: "My family is dead, I am going to see them now. I want this." For Yinsen, death does not have the final word. This sacrificial death changes Tony from a rich playboy, setting him on the character arc that continues when Tony "lays down his life on the wire" with the bomb at the end of the first *Avengers*, falling back through the wormhole with his arms spread wide (the familiar image of Christ on the cross). This trajectory of sacrificial death is then completed in *Endgame*, when Tony—like Yinsen—finds "rest," because he has defeated death through dying, sacrificing himself so the rest of humanity may live.

Thus, while options 1, 3, and 4 are present in the movie, it's option 4 that seems to be the position ultimately adopted by the film itself. *Death can be defeated.* The question then, is whether or not *Endgame*'s defeat of death really does justice to the philosophy of death, or whether it is, in its own way, a more sophisticated denial of death. Indeed, my real fear leaving the theater after *Infinity War* was that the follow-up movie would go for option 2, denial.

I was afraid it would too easily fix the deaths of half its heroes, failing to sit in the *macabre* long enough to feel the weight of mortality. Yet, *Endgame* does not do this. Rather, it doubles down. It re-presents the trauma with a whole other level of intensity, beginning the movie with Hawkeye's wife and children slipping through his fingers at a picnic, in one of the most melancholic scenes of the year. The weight of death is then fully felt, the audience left anxious for the team to track down Thanos and snap the world back to its rightful place. Yet, as if to specifically counter the quick relief we long for, we are then presented with a false start. The team immediately tracks down Thanos in the first fifteen minutes. The audience—and even the Marvel characters themselves—exchange a look: *That was easy.* But then Thanos reveals he has destroyed the stones, and we realize that the deaths of *Infinity War* are not going to be simply passed over, not simply *snapped* back like flicking a light switch.

Instead, five years pass. Five years is an appropriate amount of time for mourning; the amount of time it might genuinely take to get through the stages of grief for a loved one. And yet, even five years later, humankind is still haunted. Captain America leads grief groups, Thor has let himself go, and Black Widow threatens anyone who tries to see the silver lining by saying the whales have come back in humankind's absence.

It's almost a full hour by the time any hope re-enters, and a plan is set into motion to set things right. Now, even many art-house films do not have the patience to sit in the dark for that long. The fact that a big-budget, superhero movie was willing to wallow for an hour shows its writers knew how to honour the reality of death, rather than simply denying it. Thus, *Endgame* successfully avoids the pitfalls of option 2.

While *Endgame* defeats death, it does not deny it. It sits in the full weight of death, admitting its potency and power, before triumphing over it. Likewise, the Christian narrative ultimately triumphs over death, but without denying it. Death is not ignored in Christianity but is its centerpiece; the very symbol of faith is the cross, like having an electric chair at the front of your church. Sin and death are acknowledged as the enemy at the very beginning, in Genesis, and it is precisely through fighting them that we come to know their full strength, for the true might of an enemy cannot be known until we actually stand up to them.

It is only through facing the full reality of death that it can be defeated; only by Christ and Stark actually dying that the full weight of death can simultaneously be felt and subverted. Any defeat of death that does not empathetically enter into the full morbidity of its weight has not taken the phenomenon seriously enough. We cannot celebrate Easter Sunday without first sitting in the trauma of Good Friday.

In the *Avengers* saga, death is not sidestepped, but swallowed-up. It is not fled from, but faced. It is not denied, but defeated—defeated by charging it head on and entering into it.

Death is defeated by a death. While Endgame has traces of multiple philosophies of death, it has ultimately inherited an optimistic, hopeful, Judeo-Christian narrative of the defeat of death.

Whether tales of this defeat are exaggerated is another question entirely.

17
Life Unchecked Will Cease to Exist

Diego Pérez Lasserre

In *Avengers: Infinity War*, Thanos explains to Gamora that the fundamental idea underlying his plan to eliminate half of the existing population of the universe is that "if life is left unchecked, life will cease to exist. It needs correction."

Even though Thanos refers to "life" without any specification, throughout the movie, we see that he never worries about exterminating trees or animals—and when the Snap occurs, it seems that these types of beings are not affected by it. We only know that birds were also affected by the Snap when Banner reverses it in *Avengers: Endgame*. However, it seems that this is used merely as a storytelling device to let the audience know that the *time heist* worked, and not as a way to give us any deeper insight into Thanos's plan.

Even when he does not have the infinity stones, we see that his main concern is the reduction of half of the population of rational beings (such as Gamora's people, Asgardians, and Earthlings in New York). And so we can conclude that Thanos's plan to exterminate half of the population can be read not merely as one that intends to wipe half of all existence, but rather as a countermeasure to what philosophers such as Heidegger and Schmitt, call *Metaphysics of Technology*. The Snap actually represents a response to the path that, according to Descartes, "modern man began to walk . . . towards *mastering* all there is: where he imposes his terms upon reality—chaos—dominates, crushes, exploits, pulverizes, transforms, accumulates, distributes; in sum *produces* or fabricates the world."

In that sense, *Avengers: Endgame* (at least before the time heist) would show us the consequences of our own way of interpreting the world, rather than the success of an evil plan orchestrated by a "bad guy" (and that's why Thanos is *inevitable*).

The Metaphysics of Technology

Simply put, when we talk about "metaphysics," we're referring to the scrutiny of everything that is beyond the natural realm, the *physical* world. For example, if I want to know the biological composition of a tree, I can go to a lab and determine its structure (and my scrutiny would be focused on the *physical*). However, if I am asking "what makes a tree a tree," or where the tree comes from and what its purpose in life is, I'm no longer questioning the *physical world*, but the *metaphysical* one. Metaphysics deals, as Aristotle explains, with the first causes and principles of things.

In ancient and medieval times, God (or more generally, transcendence) occupied the metaphysical "kingdom." The answer to what makes an entity what it is and not something different, where everything comes from, and what our purpose in life is, was clear: it is God who created everything and that allows the differentiation of things, and in his plan we find the purpose of existence and the role we play in it. The entity that occupies the "metaphysical realm" is not indifferent because it determines how we interpret everything around us. For example, if we locate transcendence there, we will probably see family as the fundamental nucleus of society, nature as part of the divine plan (and, therefore, as something that must be respected), work as something secondary to family (but that also dignifies human beings) and human life as something that is destined to be more than just momentary pleasure.

The problem, however, is that, with modernity, transcendence was slowly but firmly displaced from the metaphysical realm. The establishment of the scientific method as the only way to acquire true knowledge exiled God from the world (along with philosophy, history, and the "humanities" in general). The consequences? We started living in a world where only the *physical*, the material, what can be perceived by the senses, is relevant for our lives. The metaphysical realm was left empty, with no inhabitants, or so we thought.

In 1953, the philosopher Martin Heidegger returned to the scrutiny of metaphysics and proposed something unthinkable until that moment: when transcendence was banished from the metaphysical world, that "plane" was not left empty, but was "filled" by humanity with other, more mundane and immanent, entities. As the philosopher Carl Schmitt put it:

Today, many varieties of metaphysical attitude exist in a secularized form. To a great extent, it holds true that different and, indeed, mundane factors have taken the place of God: humanity, the nation, the individual, historical development, or even life as life for its own sake, in its complete spiritual emptiness and mere dynamic. This does not mean that the attitude is no longer metaphysical. The thought and feeling of every person always retain a certain metaphysical character. Metaphysics is something that is unavoidable. (*Political Romanticism*, pp. 17–18)

In other words, when we humans displaced transcendence from the metaphysical kingdom, we also, consciously or unconsciously, replaced it with other ideas or concepts. In the twentieth century, for example, concepts such as 'race', 'nation', or 'color' seized the metaphysical realm, which led many people to believe that we were not all equals.

As it happens, both Heidegger and Schmitt seem to have fallen into this logic when they joined the National Socialist Party. So the metaphysical realm is not something to be taken lightly! That concept has a direct influence on how we interpret the world, and, therefore, can have devastating effects (as we can clearly see from the traumatic experiences lived by many in the twentieth century). Today, however, there is one concept that seems to be implicit in virtually all interpretations of the world: economic growth.

The idea that economic growth permeates practically every interpretation we make of the world is not something new. Already in 1919, Schmitt observed that the postulates of free trade and commerce were the dominant metaphysical ideas of the twentieth century (*Political Theology*, p. 62). But why is this relevant? Mainly because these ideas make us see the world and everything that is in it merely as a potential source of wealth. A tree, then, is not interpreted as an entity that should be cared for because of its function in the ecosystem that allows life to exist, but merely as a potential good, such as furniture, paper, or even birdhouses (which is quite ironic).

This metaphysical posture, which assign scientific and economic growth as key concepts for understanding the world, is known as *metaphysics of technology* and has tragic consequences for humanity. Family and friendship are no longer relevant because we cannot obtain wealth through them (although there may be some "strategic alliances" that may take the form of marriage or friendship). Comfort and pleasure now occupy the center of existence, and we devour everything around us to obtain them. Simply put, we become predators on everything that allowed us to exist, survive, and evolve in the first place.

The question that naturally arises is: what can we do? We believe that even though in *Avengers: Endgame,* we do not have an explicit answer to this interrogation, we do have an answer to the question of what will happen if we do nothing and let the metaphysics of technology run its natural course.

A Character of Our Own Making

In the Marvel Cinematic Universe, it is generally accepted that bad guys are evil simply because they are evil. Even though some context is always provided, such as in the cases of Ultron, Hela, and Loki, the complexity of their evilness is never such as to allow the audience to sympathize with them, or to admit their plans (Loki, as his character develops, deserves more attention, but in his first appearances he fits the stereotype). The case of Thanos seems to be different.

In *Avengers: Infinity War*, we see how Thanos's plan begins to take form. The Infinity Stones are crucial for him to succeed, so he sets out on a quest to collect all of them. As he explains to Gamora, he wants to eliminate half of existence. Why? To illustrate his argument, he uses Gamora's planet as an example. That planet was on the verge of collapse. There were too many people living on it, and not enough resources for all of them to have a blissful life. Now, he argues, her planet is a paradise. The children born there have known nothing but a life of abundance. The small price for this? Killing half of the planet's population. The argument that Thanos wields is that the universe is inevitably finite, while life has unlimited needs. This existential flaw needs correction, and he is the only one that has the will to act on it.

What Thanos is saying is that he is the only one who sees that the way of life that we, rational beings, have adopted is unsustainable. The path that we are on inevitably leads to the destruction of the natural habitat that we live on, and, ultimately, to our doom. In other words, Thanos believes that he is the only one in the Marvel Cinematic Universe who is not nearsighted and who understands the consequences of our own way of interpreting the world (at least the only one that has the guts to act on it).

Thanos, then, believes himself to be the hero who is trying to vanquish the metaphysics of technology and teach the universe an important lesson. If we see the antagonist from *Infinity War* and *Endgame* from this perspective, we could argue that Thanos is not actually an *external* bad guy. He is not an enemy with an evil purpose, but rather a personification of the consequences that we, humanity, will have to face due to our poor metaphysical choices. Simply put, Thanos is what we have chosen to put under the rug in order to obtain as many utilities as possible from nature.

If we interpret these movies from the given description, we can see that Thanos is actually showing us the only two possible outcomes to our modern metaphysical posture (or at least the only ones that he is able to see). If we do nothing, our destiny will be that of his own planet. We will continue to devour everything that allows life as we know it to flourish until there is nothing left, not even us. But if we banish economic growth from the metaphysical realm, we may be able to save half of existence, if we're lucky. According to Thanos, there's no third option. One way or the other, life must be balanced. It is inevitable, and so is he.

So, what would the Avengers represent if we see *Infinity War* and *Endgame* from this perspective? In the first movie, they would be the bad guys. More specifically, they are the personification of human stubbornness. They never seem to understand that the way to defeat Thanos is not by destroying him but by facing the problem that allowed a character like him to emerge in the first place. That is why the recipe that had worked so well against every other villain fails when used against Thanos. If we continue to tackle the existential crisis that we are currently living with the methods we as humans have always used when a problem emerges (injecting money, declaring war, or simply ignoring it), we are definitely going to fail.

In the second movie, however, the Avengers represent a "third way", an option that Thanos was not able to see (or one that he thought was not possible). The movie starts with the development of an unlikely relationship: Tony and Nebula become friends. Later, after Thanos is dead and the hope of bringing everyone back is gone, we see how, one by one, the mighty heroes of the Earth fall into their personal existential crisis, which leads them to stop or slow down the "superhero life," face (or ignore) themselves and authentically choose how they will live their life. Black Widow, Rocket, and Thor, for example, represent, though in very different ways, the attachment to the past. Tony, Banner, and Hawkeye (again in dissimilar ways) choose not to stay with their arms crossed, and change their lifestyle. Finally, Rogers deepens in his absence of sense of belonging and decides to help other people so that they do not suffer as he does.

Even though they do not seem to face the predatory nature of rational beings towards nature, they do change their way of understanding the world (and the movie infers that all of humanity seems to be heading the same way). Differently put, the Avengers "resolve" their existential crisis by throwing out the economy-focused concepts from the metaphysical realm and replacing them with others that are more important. Money, fame, and superficial things, in general, don't seem to matter anymore, or at least they are not as fundamental for the characters of the Marvel Cinematic Universe as they were in the past (Tony and his new-found passion and dedication for his family is the best example of this). The Avengers fight the metaphysics of technology by questioning the view of the world before the Snap and replacing it with one that does not seek economic growth, but rather virtue and happiness. Only when this is done, the possibility of bringing everyone back and defeating Thanos appears out of thin air. Coincidence? We believe it is not.

The movie makes a strong argument: only when everything is lost, when we as humanity are forced to face the consequences of our technological-metaphysical image does the non-material, that which the transcendent metaphysics interpreted as fundamental for human life in ancient and medieval times, re-emerge. We are referring to family (Tony Stark), friendship (Black Widow), justice (Hawkeye), self-knowledge (Banner), love (Vision and Wanda), and a relationship with transcendence (Captain America).

Finally, we believe that there is another lesson to be learned from *Endgame*, and it is related to arrogance. When "past Nebula" manages to bring Thanos to the future, she says to him that the Avengers "didn't suspect a thing." Thanos responds by saying that "the arrogant never do." This conversation can be read as a warning to us viewers about the existential climate crisis that we are currently undergoing. If we believe that nothing too serious will happen, that the changes that we are experiencing are caused only by natural phenomena, that some magical solution will come out of thin air without us having to do anything, then we will face the disastrous consequences sooner than later. If we as humans are arrogant, then our own extinction will take us by surprise.

Metaphysical Transformation

The metaphysical realm, which used to belong to transcendence, is now filled with immediate and mundane concepts, such as economic growth and personal pleasure. And the concepts that occupy the metaphysical realm have an impact on how we understand the world around us.

In light of the metaphysics of technology, Thanos is not just a bad guy, but a personification of the consequences that we humans must face for guiding our lives based merely on economic and hedonistic concepts. The existential crisis that each of the Avengers experiences throughout the movie is not accidental but is actually a process which allows them to change the metaphysical concepts through which they interpret reality. After their crisis, concepts such as wealth, fame, and power are no longer important. Love, friendship, virtuosity, empathy, among others, seem to take over the metaphysical sphere.

You might protest that I'm trying to give a meaning to these movies that's not really there, and that actually they're only intended to make fans happy enough, so that they buy tickets and merchandise. However, seeing in these films a message of warning and hope for humanity can bring nothing but good. We should become aware of the concepts that, collectively or individually, guide our interpretation of the world so that we can see whether we like them or want to change them.

18
Iron Man's Choice to Die

Edwardo Pérez

TONY: Hey. You said one out of fourteen million, we win, yeah? Tell me
this is it.

STRANGE: If I tell you what happens, it won't happen.

TONY: You better be right.

Tony is understandably anxious during the climactic battle in
Endgame, especially since the time-travel heist didn't go
exactly as planned. And, a few moments later, when Thanos
manages to get the nano-tech Gauntlet, Tony looks frustrated,
almost defeated. It seems as if all is about to be lost (again) but
then Tony looks up at Doctor Strange who nervously holds up
one finger, indicating that this moment is the one and only time
they'd win and Tony knows what he has to do.

As much as Thanos liked to claim he was inevitable (and,
okay, if you want to get all timey-whimey about it, maybe, technically, he was), it's Tony Stark's death that's always seemed
inevitable (and not just because of Robert Downey Jr.'s contract
with Marvel), as the narrative weaved together in the Marvel
Cinematic Universe since 2008's *Iron Man* telegraphed a journey for Tony that seemed destined to end in self-sacrifice—
from his near death in *Avengers* to the panic attacks he
experienced in *Iron Man 3* to the vision he saw in *Age of Ultron*
to his feud with Captain America in *Civil War*, which saw Tony
wanting to relinquish control of the Avengers to the United
Nations because his confidence had been shaken. Tony's death
was foreshadowed throughout *Infinity War* and the opening of
Endgame, as if viewers needed to be prepped for Iron Man's climactic, goosebumps-inducing death at the end of *Endgame*'s
epic battle.

While there's a funeral scene and a hopeful, holographic voice-over of Tony paired with a montage of life returning to normal at the end of *Endgame* (all designed to make us feel better), it's perhaps a more fitting tribute to Iron Man's death in *Spider-Man: Far from Home*, where the weight of his loss (and the effects of undoing the Snap five years later) is fully felt. After all, Iron Man's death was consequential in many ways. Still, who wasn't hoping for a Tony Stark cameo where we'd learn that he actually cheated death and everything in *Far from Home* was merely a test for Peter? (Couldn't Tony have been sipping a piña colada with Nick Fury on the simulated beach, sharing a laugh about how they fooled ol' Underoos?) Certainly, Tony made a habit out of avoiding the inevitable since his first film, making his death in *Endgame* seem like a ruse. Of course, his cheating was rooted in the anxiety he felt about his own mortality and the inevitability of his death. As Tony tells Pepper in *Iron Man 3*, "Nothing's been the same since New York. You experience things and then they're over and you still can't explain them. Gods, aliens, other dimensions. I'm just a man in a can."

Indeed, part of Tony's appeal has been his incessant drive to continuously upgrade his "can," making it easier to put his life at risk while ensuring that he'll emerge out of any battle still alive and perhaps Tony's journey has always been about how he chooses to deal not just with his own mortality but with his inevitable death. Should he have died instead of becoming Iron Man? Should he have died in *Avengers*? *Age of Ultron*? *Infinity War*? Has Tony sought to avoid his death or has he always been looking for it? After losing to Thanos in *Infinity War*, did Tony finally realize he'd rather live than die? As he tells Steve Rogers while holding Morgan in *Endgame*, "I got my second chance right here, Cap. Can't roll the dice on it." So why does he? After quitting the Avengers, finally marrying Pepper, and having a daughter, why would Tony seek out his death again and choose to die?

This Is It

Like most superheroes, Tony's life has a duality—he's Tony Stark and he's Iron Man and living this duality has compelled him to constantly find creative ways to balance the competing instincts of life and death, what Sigmund Freud (1856–1939) calls our life drive (Eros) and our death drive (Thanatos—not to be confused with Thanos).

For Freud, the two drives aren't just competing, they're essentially cyclical: life comes from death, so life seeks to return to death. So, it's not so much a struggle as it is a goal: we have an instinct to die, so we engage in behavior that might cause our own death, like invent an Iron Man suit and fly a nuclear bomb through a wormhole in space or hitch a ride on a ship bound for another planet so we can fight the most powerful being in the universe. But we also have an instinct to live. So, we build our lives around long-term commitments, like marrying Pepper, having a daughter, and living in a cabin in the woods, far away from the dangerous superhero life.

It's significant that Tony wants to be a husband and father—that at fifty-three, Tony's finally ready to set aside his womanizing, alcoholic, playboy lifestyle to spend time with a wife and child. Yet, it's also interesting how Tony nevertheless continues to risk his life and put himself in harm's way. Indeed, there's a defiance to Tony's demeanor, not just with Pepper but with everyone he seems to encounter in *Infinity War*, as if everyone Tony interacts with (from Doctor Strange to the Guardians of the Galaxy and especially to Thanos) represents (on some level) his life coming to an end.

Tony might not want to die (like the Ancient One in *Doctor Strange*, Tony wants to stretch out one moment into thousands) but he also can't help being drawn towards his death. Perhaps it's because the arrival of Thanos signifies not just his inevitable death but also an opportunity to cheat it. As Tony tells Bruce, "This is it." In other words, it's as if Tony is seeking out his death in *Infinity War*, embracing the death drive— when he boards the donut-shaped space ship, when he realizes they've only got one chance in fourteen million six hundred and five, when he fights Thanos and gets mortally wounded, when he seems disappointed in Doctor Strange saving him, and when he's with Nebula in the beginning of *Endgame*, having accepted his fate—because when you leave the love of your life a final message and then lay down to die, it usually means you're ready to pass on.

Once he's rescued and reunited with Pepper, Tony embraces his life drive, giving up his life as an Avenger and moving to a cabin in the woods, where he and Pepper raise Morgan. It works, for about five years, until the Avengers team finds him, wanting his help, which he eventually gives them. In other words, he returns to embracing his death drive. Why the back and forth? Does Tony really want to die? Or does he want to test himself and see if he can pull of one more last surprise? Does he want to live or does he want to die?

Another way to look at the Freudian drives is to see death as being the point of life, the goal we'll all achieve and the final event that gives meaning to everything that came before it—which seems to be Freud's point in recognizing the death drive. And yet, our advances in technology (as Tony Stark/Iron Man illustrates) have made death obsolete, because if we create anything in this mode (like a reactor in our chest cavity) we create the possibility of indefinitely sustained life—as Yinsen claims in *Iron Man*, the arc reactor's power could run Tony's heart "for fifty lifetimes!" From this, death becomes meaningless and so, too, does life, as both Freudian drives become cheated.

This is what ultimately happens in *Endgame* when the Snap is undone—and because the plot involves changing history through time travel (because even if they put the stones back, the history of *Infinity War* still changes), it's difficult to accept any deaths that occur in *Endgame*, not just Tony's death, but Natasha's and even Thanos's. In other words, through *Endgame*, the deaths in *Infinity War* become meaningless, but so, too, do the deaths in *Endgame*.

If we consider all eighteen prior movies, death has been meaningless for many characters, most notably Steve Rogers, Bucky Barnes, and T'Challa. And it's a shame because I actually liked Tony's almost-death in *Infinity War*. It felt heroic and it felt real (for about four seconds). It also felt earned. Perhaps this is why Tony eventually decides to die in *Endgame*—as much as he loves Pepper and Morgan, he needed to die on his terms in a way that allowed him to make his death as meaningful as possible. Certainly, erasing Thanos and his minions from existence qualifies as a meaningful death. But why should life have meaning? And why would death give life meaning?

That's the Hero Gig, Right?

For philosopher Albert Camus (1913–1960), life is meaningless and absurd. Where Freud's drives compel us to choose between creating life or hastening death, Camus views the choice as being between ending our lives or living in absurdity. Tony's life is certainly absurd—from his vain lifestyle, fast cars, immense fortune, and beyond-genius intellect to his fighting aliens and eating schawarma afterwards to getting a moon thrown at him and teaching Nebula how to play paper football.

Even his invention of time travel seems absurd, just something he pulled off on a random evening because he was feeling guilty about Peter's death (and because he happens to have the means to not just discover time travel but also to manufacture handy time-travel GPS wristbands). From this perspective, it's easy to see why Tony perhaps lives life the way he does, as if everything's a joke and nothing matters—especially in *Iron Man 2*. Yet, his struggle between selfishness and selflessness indicates he's trying to find meaning in the absurdity.

In *Endgame*, we can see this in the various decisions he makes—leaving the Avengers and then leaving Pepper and Morgan. Indeed, he seems to be embodying Camus's observations, longing for happiness in the face of the irrational and absurd. Camus recognizes that we can find meaning through choice. Recounting the myth of Sisyphus—who had to roll a boulder up a hill every day only to watch the boulder roll down once he reached the top—Camus observes that the fate Sisyphus suffers daily is his choice.

For Camus, Sisyphus isn't doomed to a meaningless life, he's the master of his own fate because he chooses to be. This makes fate and meaning subjective, created by us through the choices we make throughout our lives. Thus, Tony gives his life meaning when he chooses Pepper and Morgan and when he chooses to undo/redo the snap by using the stones himself. He's choosing life and he's choosing death and both are meaningful. As Tony says in his holographic message, "Part of the journey is the end." But, is this enough for us to understand why Tony ultimately chooses to die in *Endgame*? Was it simply about creating meaning in an otherwise absurd life?

Oh, This Is Nice

It's an emotional moment near the end of *Endgame* when Peter Parker and Tony find each other on the battlefield and Tony just stands there listening to Peter ramble and then embraces Peter like a father without saying a word. The brief scene is significant, not just because the last time these two characters embraced Peter turned to dust, but because Peter was the impetus for Tony's decision to rejoin the fray—a decision that, in this particular moment, seemed justified. But what about Pepper and Morgan? Tony seemed to make his decision out of guilt for Peter's death in *Infinity War*, but this could also be seen as Tony feeling like he had a duty to try to bring back Peter, especially after discovering time travel. But didn't Tony also have a duty to his wife and daughter? Why choose Peter over them? Why choose killing Thanos over them? Why choose the universe over them?

There are several possibilities from moral and ethical philosophy we could explore to help us explain Tony's choices but the theory that seems most appropriate is consequentialism, which is a type of utilitarianism. Of course, there are many varieties of consequentialism so let's begin with a basic form that goes something like this: a morally right action is the one that produces the best consequences. While this is not without its criticism, especially from deontologists like John Locke (1632–1704) and Immanuel Kant (1724–1804) who each argue that moral decisions should be made according to one's duty regardless of the consequences, consequentialism in this basic form resembles what most of us probably do on a daily basis when we make decisions and it seems to explain what most of the Avengers do throughout the Marvel Cinematic Universe narrative, especially Tony.

It's worth noting that a strict utilitarian perspective, like one held by Jeremy Bentham (1748–1832), would define the right moral choice as being the one that produces the greatest amount of good for the greatest amount of people. Consequentialism is a little different because what matters isn't whether the consequence is good or bad but whether the consequence is desirable. For example, Thanos choosing to snap his fingers and erase half the universe is a consequentialist decision for Thanos. Certainly, it doesn't produce the greatest amount of good for the greatest amount of people, but it does produce a desired result for Thanos. He may be the villain, but he truly believes the consequence he produces is the correct solution to the universal problem of too many people and not enough resources.

Similarly, Tony's decisions in *Endgame* seem to be guided by the consequence he's hoping to achieve. Consider what Tony says to Steve after arriving at the Avengers facility in New York:

> We got a shot getting these stones, but I gotta tell you my priorities. Bring back what we lost, I hope, yes. Keep what I found, I have to, at all costs. And maybe not die trying. Would be nice.

In other words, Tony is willing to help Steve but he doesn't want to lose his daughter Morgan. So, undoing the Snap, for Tony, means letting everyone come back not at the moment they left, but five years later. Is Tony being selfish? If so, how can this be a morally correct decision? Perhaps it's because consequentialism, which could be seen as a form of hedonism, allows for selfishness. We might think undoing the Snap is a good thing, but when we consider how those who didn't turn to dust had to deal with the loss (which could include moving on, suicide, depression, and so on) is it really better to bring back the lost five years later? It's good for Tony because he wants Morgan to exist as she is and it's good for the Avengers who each have their own selfish motivations, but it's not entirely good for everyone else—which *Spider-Man: Far from Home* illustrates to some extent (and it's why Tony's five-year condition isn't a utilitarian decision). So, in a sense, Tony is able to cheat life and death again to his benefit.

It's also worth noting that the priorities Tony outlines to Steve resemble what Doctor Strange tells Tony in *Infinity War* about letting Tony or Peter die to protect the Time Stone. Of course, Doctor Strange changed his mind when he realized the only way to defeat Thanos was to give up the Time Stone. And, while Tony may have cheated by creating a time-travel system, it worked from a consequentialist perspective: they got the stones (and put them back), what was lost was found and what was found was not lost.

The logic Tony and Doctor Strange used is also the same logic Natasha employed when she sacrificed herself for the Soul Stone, getting the consequence she wanted. And, it'd be nice to see if Steve convinces Red Skull to bring her back in exchange for the Soul Stone. After all, a soul for a soul should work both ways. And this brings us back to Tony's death, which, like Natasha's death, was a sacrifice made for the sake of a desired result.

Whatever It Takes

The difficulty with consequentialism is that the consequence can't always been known with certainty (this is why the Ancient One is initially reluctant to give Bruce the time stone). When the Avengers traveled back in time, they assumed they could simply retrieve the stones. So, they didn't count on other variables – such as Natasha dying on Vormir, 2014 Nebula accessing 2019 Nebula, and 2014 Thanos showing up in 2019 (with his entire army). Thus, they couldn't anticipate all the possible (and unintended) consequences. This relates to another criticism of consequentialism (and utilitarianism) that finds fault with the ends-justify-the-means rationale inherent in the philosophy. Do the ends justify the means? Do the means justify the ends? And, what about the unintended means?

In *Infinity War*, the Avengers' mantra was "We don't trade lives." In *Endgame*, it's "whatever it takes." It's a significant evolution from a deontological philosophy to a consequentialist one. Had they realized the consequences in *Infinity War*, they could've simply destroyed Vision sooner. After all, he died anyway and, like Natasha in *Endgame*, Vision wasn't resurrected by the Hulk's Snap. So, it was, essentially, a meaningless and pointless death—because if the entire nation of Wakanda is going to risk their lives for one man, then that man needs to survive.

For Tony, part of his anxiety is rooted in his desire to ensure the plan will work, that his means and ends will be justified. That's why he wants Doctor Strange to confirm for him that they're experiencing the one time they defeat Thanos. Otherwise, Tony's choices would be meaningless, like Vision's death. But, does that make Tony's choices right? Is Tony using the stones really any different than Thanos using them? And, when it comes to consequences, what really happens to the universe when half of it disappears only to be return five years later so that Peter and Morgan can simultaneously exist? It may provide a creative twist on the Sophie's Choice dilemma, but does it explain or justify Tony's decision to die?

From a consequentialist view, perhaps Tony's choice to die was the best consequence for Tony, who'd been plagued by fear, anxiety, and guilt for most of his story. As Pepper tells him, "We're gonna be okay. You can rest now."

And I . . . Am Iron Man

Tony's death might have happened because he was driven to pursue it or because he wanted to find meaning in the absurdity of his life or because the consequence that resulted was the best outcome for Tony, trading himself to ensure that Thanos and his entire army would be obliterated and that the universe could return to some sense of normalcy. Does it matter that he cheated or that his consequence might not have produced the best moral result?

Perhaps this is why Tony Stark is so compelling—because when you strip away all the bravado, all the wealth, and all the knowledge and skill, he really is just "a man in a can," a flawed mortal like any one of us, willing to live and die for what he loves. In the end, maybe it doesn't matter what choice he makes or why he makes it. Perhaps all that matters is that he makes a choice. As Tony tells Steve when he returns to the Avengers facility in the middle of *Endgame* (in a sweet, charcoal grey E-Tron GT), "I just want peace."

V

Thanos

19
Thanos Is No Abraham

JD LYONHART

He dragged her to the edge and half-heartedly tossed her over the side as if she were nothing. Not because she was nothing, no, but because she was everything to him, and he had to do it quickly and unthinkingly if he was to do it at all.

After the initial adrenaline of the deed, he's left wide eyed in shock, stunned that he actually did it, staring down at her in agony, an agony that reveals she truly was his everything, and so he's sacrificed not merely another but all that matters to himself.

It is simultaneously his most monstrous and most human moment; both ethically abominable in its massacre and yet somehow commendable in its self-sacrifice and courage of conviction.

The average big-budget movie might ask the audience to rejoice at the survival of some climactic battle, to shed a tear when lovers are reunited or to cheer at the demise of a villain; fairly straightforward moral conundrums and emotional responses to them. But few mainstream movies have dared to demand the level of moral complexity that was involved in Thanos's sacrifice of his daughter on Mount Vormir. In the *Avengers* two-part conclusion, Thanos must collect the soul stone in order to save the world through annihilating half of its residents. But the soul stone comes at a 'terrible price': the sacrifice of that which one truly loves. In Thanos's case, his daughter, Gamora.

Thanos sacrificing Gamora (as well as Hawkeye sacrificing Black Widow) bears a striking similarity to the ancient Jewish story of Abraham sacrificing his beloved son. Abraham and his wife had been unable to have a child for many decades, so when

Isaac was born they believed he was their miracle child. Yet when Abraham is told by God to take his son up Mount Moriah and sacrifice him, he sets out on the journey with Isaac, just like Thanos led his beloved Gamora up Mount Vormir. The knife is out, glistening in the mountain sun, ready to strike at youthful flesh. Father Abraham's limbs rattle like a barn door in a storm, as he raises the knife to strike.

Then at the last second God spares Isaac. Yet Abraham is commended simply for being willing to sacrifice his only son, for having enough faith in God to give up for Him that which he loved more than anything else in the world. Just as Thanos's sacrifice of his beloved daughter made him worthy of the soul stone, Abraham's willingness to sacrifice his beloved son made him worthy of being called the Father of the Jewish Faith.

The Aesthetic Person

This would merely be an interesting literary parallel, were it not for a philosopher named Søren Kierekegaard (pronounced 'Keer-ka-*gore*'). Kierkegaard retells the story of Abraham. Refusing to provide easy answers to fit this story into ethics, Kierkegaard instead overhauls ethics to make it fit it into the story of Abraham. The result is one of the most potent ideas in the last few centuries, one that inadvertently spawned Existentialism, and challenges everything you think you know about ethics.

Kierkegaard outlines three types of individuals: the aesthetic, the ethical, and the religious. First, is the 1. aesthetic person. The aesthete is concerned with their own *particular* wants in the moment. They don't care about any absolute morality or code, but only about being true to their own desires and urges. If you wanted a depiction of this person writ large, think Hugh Hefner or Barney Stinson.

But in reality, this person is often more subtle than that, lurking all around us. It is your family, friends, colleagues; it is *you* a good chunk of the time, I imagine. It is you whenever you choose to place yourself as an individual above any higher law of right and wrong, whenever your particular desires and whims trump all else. This person is not necessarily some sadist or villain intent on evil; oh, how easy it would be if they were, and we could just dismiss them without seeing them in ourselves. In fact, they are often quite pleasant, for as long as they are happy and getting what they want, why wouldn't they be pleasant? They may often seem to be decent people—playing the game of society—but they do so to bring about their own personal enjoyment in the end, to ultimately chase after their particular whims.

The Ethical Person

You could summarize the aesthetic type as simply selfish. A self-focused, individualistic, hedonist. And that would mostly be true. But the key thing for Kierkegaard is not that they are evil, but that they are focused on particulars rather than absolutes, on particular desires in the moment, rather than any absolute law or moral code. Whereas absolutes deal with what is good for all—what is metaphysically good in the sense of some higher law that applies to all the cosmos—in contrast, the particular deals only with one individual or even one cultures personal desires and whims. It is *particular* to that person or place or time, rather than having a higher significance which is morally binding on all people everywhere. While the aesthete's pursuit of their particular desires describes most of us at one point or other (especially as children, and *especially* as teenagers), some of us do mature and evolve past giving in to our *particular* whims, and instead follow some *absolute* moral law. In so doing, we become 2. ethical people.

While the aesthetic person follows their own particular desires, the ethical person is willing to give up what they want to submit to some higher code. They may want to vent their road rage, but they don't, not merely because they're trying to lower their blood pressure, but because morally it's not the right thing to do. They may want to cheat on their boyfriend, but they don't, not merely because they don't want to get caught, but because it's not the right thing to do. They may consider stealing a philosophy book about the Avengers from the bookstore, but they don't because it's not that well-written. And because *it's not the right thing to do.*

The ethical person strives to follow a moral law, to submit themselves to what is absolute, regardless of their particular feelings about it in the moment. They don't even want to follow the particular desires and ideologies of their own culture. Rather, they want to figure out what is right in an absolute sense everywhere at all times, and do that. Because morality cannot be particular. Right and wrong cannot just be what one particular group or culture wants, any more than it can just be what one individual wants. For that would not be truly right and wrong, but just preferences that were made up at some particular time and in some particular place by some particular group of people. Which is why most of Germany could become

Nazis, without Nazism becoming morally correct, for ethics is higher than what one particular culture or time wants.

Such particular ideologies could perhaps be like the made-up rules of a board game—that we all agree to follow to get along and play the game—but they would not be right and wrong in an absolute sense, not in the sense that Kierkegaard is getting at. They would not be eternal, absolute, metaphysical, moral laws that are binding upon everyone everywhere at all times. As such, the morality of the ethical person must become more and more abstract and general as they move beyond the particular. For in order for ethics to not be relative to a particular time or space, they must be outside of time and space. Rather than laws that were made up at a particular time, they must be eternal. Rather than morals that are grounded solely in a particular place, they must transcend the physical world.

If we are particular they must be absolute. If we are finite, they must be infinite. So if the aesthetic person is at one end of the spectrum, the ethical person is at the exact opposite end, as far away from particulars as possible, losing themselves in the absolute.

Many of these ethical people call themselves religious, because in rising away from the particulars they believe they are coming closer to the absolute, metaphysical, eternal laws of God. But Kierkegaard would disagree. Looking around at the Danish church in his homeland, he saw many people who were following these absolute laws, yet seemed dead inside. He realized that the ethical person often becomes a moralizing Pharisee who serves an abstract law with no passion or romance. They may be decent, respectable folks, yet they never dance or belly-laugh or have any vigor in their bones.

These are the priests who have so transcended human desires, that they cease to be truly human at all. This is you, when you do what you know is ethically right in an absolute sense, but leave your true self behind. For we are not abstractions. *We are individuals*; individuals with particular personalities, backgrounds, talents, longings, etc. Ideas and morals that seem reasonable in the abstract often break down when we try to apply them to our particular situations. We cannot be utterly subsumed under a series of absolute laws; we do not fit neatly into a moral box; one size does not fit all. To utterly abandon the particular is to abandon ourselves and what makes us who we are as individuals.

So, on the one hand, we need to engage with the absolute, or else we are just selfish aesthetes with no sense of a higher right or wrong, following our own particular whims. On the other hand, we also need to remain particular, or else we lose ourselves in abstraction in the absolute. Hence, what is needed is for the two to meet in the middle: we need to have a *particular* relationship with the *absolute*. For while morality may be *absolute*, it is only in a *particular* relationship with such things that we can truly come to know them on a personal level.

We can't know abstractions, we can't know absolute laws written on the clouds, for they are distant and far off. We can only know that which we are subjectively and intimately bound up with, that which is near enough to be knowable. There is no knowledge at a distance. No abstract, 'de-particularized' knowledge of absolute moral laws. We can only ever approach the absolute in our particular way as individuals, within the particularities of our context, culture, time and place. We can only ever see God through our own eyes.

The Religious Person

This middle way, this particular relationship with the absolute, constitutes 3. the religious person. A genuinely religious person wants to pursue something higher than themselves and their particular culture. And yet, they do not just follow an abstract moral code, no, they seek to have a personal, intimate, particular relationship with the absolute. They see the absolute not merely as something to be known in an abstract way, but as a personal entity who can be known close up in relationship; held tight in an interpersonal, subjective, prayerful, emotional embrace.

Religion seeks a relationship with a God who is near, who loves us, listens to us, enters into the subjectivity of our lives and struggles, who can know and be known. The religious do not seek to know the infinite as some abstract, absolute, mathematical equation, but as a friend. The religious person makes themselves at home in the tension between the absolute and the particular. If the aesthetic person is too busy with the particulars, and the ethical person too busy with abstract absolutes, then the religious person is 'just right', bringing the two together to have a personal encounter with the absolute. And this is where the story of Abraham comes into play.

Kierkegaard retells the story of Abraham through his three-fold typology. Clearly, Abraham is not an aesthete. He does not want to kill his son, it is not a particular desire or whim he had. It is the exact opposite of what he wanted; Isaac was his beloved miracle child. But nor is it an ethical act. Abraham was not following some abstract moral rules or absolute code; there is no ethical system that tells you to murder your own child. That is precisely why most people balk when they first hear this story; it seems morally reprehensible. Now, some preachers try to find a reason why it was actually a moral thing for Abraham to do. They try to explain it away, find some moral justification for the act. But Kierkegaard refuses to do that. He refuses to weaken the act, to euphemize it or make it easier to ethically digest. Instead, Kierkegaard bites the bullet and admits that it simply was not ethical. It was a morally abominable act, and anyone who tries to convince you otherwise is selling something.

Kierkegaard says Abraham was not an ethical person. No, he was the next stage beyond the ethical. Abraham was a religious person. It was because of Abraham's particular encounter with an absolute God that he was willing to sacrifice his son. Since he had a personal relationship with God—since his God was not just an abstraction or some absolute law in the clouds—he was willing to have faith in him. To have faith that God would ultimately save his son or even resurrect him somehow if it came to that. I would not be willing to have faith in someone I didn't know who had given me no reason to trust them (which is the kind of naïve definition of faith many people seem to have) but I would be willing to have faith in someone I have a long relationship history with and who I love and trust.

Likewise, because of his past relationship with God, Abraham was willing to have faith that God's command was the best thing to do for himself and his family, despite its not being the ethical thing nor the thing he aesthetically wanted to do in the moment. Because of his personal relationship with God—his *particular* encounter with the *absolute*—Abraham trusted God's commands even though they seemed unethical. If the act had been what Abraham wanted, it would not have been faith. And if it had just been some moral act, it also would not have been faith. Following your particular whims or some abstract code does not require any trust or faith or relationship. It is only in the temporary suspension of the ethical that Abraham can truly step out in faith and trust God on the basis of their relationship, on the basis of his particular encounter with the absolute. And because of his trust, his son was ultimately spared by God, and Abraham declared the Father of Faith for thousands of years, not just in Judaism but Christianity and Islam as well.

The Genesis of Existentialism

Now, this is quite a lot to take in, and it has many implications. It means that the universe is not the kind of thing that can only be known in abstraction or through the absolute calculations of mathematics and metaphysics, but must also be known in an interpersonal, particular, intimate, relational way. *Subjectivity* is just as important as *objectivity*. What is more, ethics itself comes into question, for ethics has been violated by Abraham. Indeed, the history of Existentialism often traces its origin to Kierkegaard.

To oversimplify, Existentialism argues that we get to decide for ourselves what our definition of ethics and norms and goodness are going to be. There is no absolute right or wrong that already exist, rather, we get to create them for ourselves as we go along. Morality is an invention. In elevating Abraham for his immoral deed, Kierkegaard was thus heralded as their founder by many existentialists, for he defied the absoluteness of ethics. However, Kierkegaard would see any Existentialism that completely abandons the absolute as a rehash of the aesthetic person, merely chasing their own particular desires. For the key to Kierkegaard's system was not the rejection of the ethical absolute, but the meeting of the absolute and the particular in a personal relationship with God.

He does not reject the absolute but seeks to dance between it and the particular, dwelling in the space between them. Any worldview that leans too far to abstraction abandons the particular goodness of the world, the uniqueness of our particular moral contexts, as well as the human self and our ability to have a personal relationship with God. But in turn, any Existentialist worldview that leans too far to the particular loses any transcendence, higher calling, absolutes and ethics.

Thanos the Cultist

Now, let's get back to the Avengers, viewing the movies in light of Kierkegaard's analysis of Abraham. Thanos's act on Mount Vormir was not that of an aesthete. He did not want to sacrifice Gamora, for he loved her and was visibly grieved by her loss. When asked what it cost, he barely manages to sigh: "Everything." So then is Thanos an ethical or a religious person? On the one hand, he seems like the absolutization of a consequentialist ethic, where the ends (the consequences) justify the means.

If trillions can be saved by killing his daughter or millions of others, then the end justifies the means in the bigger picture.

This is, in its own way, the absolutization of ethics; a willingness to look at the bigger ethical picture so much that you ignore the *particular* horrors committed along the way. But there's also a sense in which Thanos's act might verge on the religious. He has an almost religious belief in the balance of all things, even having his henchmen herald his entry and preach 'salvation'.

The act of sacrificing his daughter may be ethically abominable, but he was willing to do it because of his personal sense of a higher authority; his *particular* sense of the *absolute* balance of all things. This is a metaphysical and borderline religious view of the world, similar to the balance of the light and dark side of the force in Star Wars. Thanos has not just made an ethical calculation about the ends and means, but has had some sort of experiential encounter with the absolute nature of existence; peered into the bigger picture of the metaphysical balance of all things.

And that's one of the things that is terrifying about Thanos; your gut wants to dismiss his mission as evil, but you also get the sense he knows something you don't. Perhaps balance really is inevitable, and the Avengers just can't see it yet. The personal and particular nature of Thanos's conviction is such that it cannot be abstracted, repackaged and handed to someone else to then be evaluated for its reasonableness. It is a *particular* encounter with the absolute. It's inherently particular to that person or group. It's not the sort of thing you're going to be able to understand completely from the outside in abstraction.

Just as Abraham's sacrifice of his son looks monstrous to us from the outside, so Thanos's act also cannot be understood in abstraction by those who have not seen what he has seen. And that's what makes the religious person open to the subjective mysteries of reality, and yet susceptible to all manner of horrors. Because perhaps you are grasping something that cannot be accessed any other way than through a particular engagement with the absolute. Or perhaps, you're just on a ride with a madman.

But lest we allow Thanos to deter us from Kierkegaard or the religious life, let's nuance our interpretation a bit. For much of *Infinity War*, Thanos really does seem to be the religious type. And yet, in the climax of *Endgame*, he slips and reveals his giddiness at destroying Earth:

> In all my years of conquest, violence, slaughter, it was never personal. But I'll tell you now, what I'm about to do to your stubborn, annoying little planet . . . I'm gonna enjoy it. Very, very much.

In this moment, Thanos reveals that his vision is tainted by an aesthetic whim. He says it "was never personal," but his next comment reveals he either failed to live up to his impersonal mission in this final moment, or that it had never really been impersonal to begin with. There is a particular motivation lurking behind his balancing of the universe, a sadistic strain that truly enjoys punishing and killing.

In this moment, Thanos shows that he is not Abraham. He's just an aesthetic person, who justifies his blood lust with metaphysical language about the need for balance in the cosmos. He has attempted greatness, attempted to grasp his vision of the absolute balance of things, but been found wanting in that final battle, when he lets slip his glee at earth's destruction. One imagines that these kinds of 'slips' are present in all such failed religious figures. Surely cult leaders give themselves away from the beginning, their actions and Freudian slips revealing their secret motives and self-serving ways. They twist their alleged visions to trick their followers into sleeping with them, donating money to them, or into satisfying their every particular whim. Indeed, most of our fears about religious leaders or immoral cults is not actually a fear of the religious type at all, but of the subtle return of the aesthetic person. To encounter someone who is genuinely religious, someone who does not succumb to their aesthetic whims nor retreat to the abstractions of the absolute, someone who truly dwells in that tension between the extremes, truly trusts God in the midst of that chaos and ambiguity . . . now that would be a sight to see.

20

Thanos and the (Un)grateful Universe

TALIA DINSTEIN

It's pretty safe to assume that, if you're reading this book, you've seen *Endgame* at least once. Maybe twice. Maybe you saw it so many times that you single-handedly caused it to become the highest-grossing movie of all time. Chances are, you were also one of the many theatergoers standing at the end and cheering (through tears of course).

It's a good thing movie theaters are dark, to hide our ugly crying faces—Marvel totally should've made Avengers tissues to sell as people walk into theaters. But if you happened to be in the theater when I was watching, you might've been surprised to see a teenager still sitting and crying by the end. Why wasn't I mirroring the happy crowd? I was too distracted by the loss of my hero, the movie's true hero—Thanos.

Think I'm crazy? Hey, I'm not the one who would've spent $20 on a tissue with "America's Ass" on it.

How Do You Measure Up?

Do you know who the real heroes are? The guys who wake up every morning and go into their normal jobs, and get a distress call from the Commissioner and take off their glasses and change into capes and fly around fighting crime.

—DWIGHT SCHRUTE, *The Office*

You're probably wondering how I can make such an absurd claim, but before questioning my sanity, let's clarify some things first. How do we define the term "superhero"? This task is not simple—a superhero needs more than tights and a cape.

173

Instead of a static definition, a "superhero test" might be more effective. Think you're a superhero? Take this test before checking whether you can fly. True superheroes are put to the test all the time, so if you're already nervous, I have some bad news . . . But don't worry, it's not a math test: this test lays out the key characteristics of a superhero. A superhero must be able to pass all three parts of this test. So again, I ask, what makes a superhero?

First, you must have a goal of either helping or saving people or trying to improve something. Intentions to cause harm to people or terrorize them knock you out of contention right off the bat. Villains are notorious for their self-serving goals—seeking power, glory, or revenge—and they don't help innocent people.

Second, you must be selfless and when necessary, self-sacrificing. A superhero can't be relied upon to save the day if they choose the easy way out in a tough situation. You don't fight bad guys to be famous; you get up after every punch because people need you.

Last, you must stop at nothing to achieve your goal and be willing to make the tough decisions that others are not willing to make. Heroes do what's right, no matter the cost. People are relying on you, and giving up on a mission or failing to act (especially when lives are at stake), can have dire consequences. You must be up to the task.

Think you've aced this test? Let's meet your peers who have made it this far as well.

No Cape, No Mask, Still a Superhero

I'm doing what has to be done to stave off something worse.

—IRON MAN, *Captain America: Civil War*

Reading through these hero qualifications, you might be wondering what they have in common with the guy who looks like Barney on steroids. Let's focus first on *Infinity War*'s Thanos before we talk about *Endgame*'s Thanos. I'll refer to them as 2018 Thanos and 2014 Thanos, since they're very different characters. 2018 Thanos endured the pain and hardships of collecting the stones and lived to see his plan succeed. All 2014 Thanos knows is that his original plan failed and that he must try something new. He has a completely objective view, which makes his plan seem more extreme, but we'll take a closer look at the specific plans later.

The Marvel Cinematic Universe has been building up Thanos for years as the main villain who's been behind many of the Avengers' problems, but when you watch *Infinity War* from the perspective of Thanos being the villain, it doesn't fit the traditional structure of a superhero movie. You know the one: good guy fights bad guy, gets hurt, has some magical moment of recovery, goes into a rematch and defeats the bad guy.

Infinity War is different. This movie doesn't tell the story of the heroic Avengers defeating the evil Thanos and restoring order to the Universe. Instead, the audience is taken on a journey as Thanos collects each stone, gaining more and more power, and fighting foes who try to stop him. People question and doubt Thanos's sanity, but he ultimately prevails.

The superhero structure only fits from Thanos's perspective of *Infinity War*: Thanos and his children battle smaller groups of Avengers, they all get injured or killed, Thanos has a transcendental moment on Vormir when he's forced to kill Gamora, and in the final battle Thanos takes on all of the Avengers bolstered by the Wakandan army. It's a tough battle for Thanos where he's physically wounded, but nothing can stop him from snapping his fingers and saving the Universe.

Maybe you're following so far, but you're still not sure how Thanos passes the hero test. Didn't he just kill half the Universe? While this plan sounds horrifying out of context, it's the only way to prevent universal extinction due to overpopulation. Many will die in either scenario, but the half that was killed in the Snap would die either way (along with trillions more without Thanos). Thanos gives purpose to the deaths of those sacrificed: as Ebony Maw reassures, "The universal scale tips toward balance because of your sacrifice." Thanos's intentions of universal salvation are good, so that satisfies the first test.

Thanos passes the second test by being willing to sacrifice everything for his plan. He loses all of his "children" and is forced to kill Gamora, the only person he loves, to gain the soul stone: "Today, I lost more than you can know." Later, when asked by a young Gamora in his imagination what it cost, he replies, "Everything." In *Endgame*, 2018 Thanos further demonstrates his selflessness by destroying the stones just days after the Snap, nearly killing himself. He explains, "The Universe required correction. After that, the Stones served no purpose beyond temptation."

Thanos knew the great power the Stones possessed, but his intentions in collecting them were purely selfless. After accomplishing his goal, destroying them prevents Thanos from becoming tempted to abuse their power. As famously stated by Harvey Dent in *The Dark Knight*, "You either die a hero, or you live long enough to see yourself become the villain." Thanos risks his life to ensure he will not stray toward villainy. Thor further seals this by "going for the head," allowing 2018 Thanos to die a hero.

Thanos passes the final test by making tough decisions to see his plan through, despite the cost. He was the only one who could see the bigger picture and what had to be done: "It's a simple calculus. This Universe is finite, its resources, finite. If life is left unchecked, life will cease to exist. It needs correcting ... I'm the only one who knows that. At least, I'm the only one with the will to act on it."

The Avengers aren't even willing to listen to Thanos's reasoning, much less willing to take this step themselves. They would all rather die posing as heroes than be real ones but have people think they were villains. Only Thanos is willing to go through with this, despite a massive ax lodged in his chest. Only Thanos is a true hero.

All That Power, Yet No Vision

With great power comes great responsibility.

—UNCLE BEN, *Spider-Man*

Now that our villain has been proven to be the true hero, what does this mean for the ones we thought were our heroes? In order to figure out their role in *Infinity War*—heroes or antagonists—we must look at the Avengers' actions in relation to what Thanos does.

While it may seem as if the Avengers pass the first test because they want to save people, this isn't quite true. Preventing Thanos from snapping his fingers will save half the Universe—for now. But this is merely a temporary solution that ignores the looming threat to the entire Universe. This means that if the Avengers succeed, they will actually harm the Universe as a whole.

The Avengers also fail the second test by acting selfishly. With trillions of lives at stake, the Avengers should be willing to put away their fight from *Civil War*; but Iron Man tells Hulk, "The Avengers broke up. We're toast ... Cap and I fell out hard. We're not on speaking terms." Thanos is on his way to annihilate half the Universe, but the Avengers won't fight together because they disagree over whether to prioritize freedom or security—an argument so insignificant compared to the threat of Thanos that it seems childish. United as one team, the Avengers might have beaten Thanos—as proved in *Endgame*—

but they choose to stay separate to save their pride (a very unheroic thing to do).

The Avengers fail the third test as well due to their inability to commit to their plan. If they were truly passionate about their goal, they would be willing to do whatever was necessary to prevent Thanos from getting the stones; but this is not the case. Three of the six stones are literally handed to Thanos in a "heroic" attempt by an Avenger to save someone they care about: Loki gives up the Space Stone for Thor, Gamora reveals the Soul Stone location for Nebula, and Doctor Strange relinquishes the Time Stone for Iron Man.

True, Strange may have acted based on his vision of the one path forward to defeat Thanos but that concept has many flaws and either way we still have the other examples. I should note that one Avenger stands out in his willingness to sacrifice. Vision argues that "One life cannot stand in the way of defeating him;" but Captain America responds, "It should. We don't trade lives, Vision." The inability to make the tough decisions is what ultimately leads to their failure, both in their plan and our hero test, making them the unintended antagonists to our hero, Thanos.

Sacrificing to Win

If we can't protect the world, you can be damn sure we'll avenge it.

—IRON MAN, *The Avengers*

While the distinction between who the heroes and villains are in *Infinity War* might be easier to see, *Endgame* complicates things for us. Five years after the Snap, the world is a completely new place: people are still facing the ramifications and learning to adjust to life without their deceased loved ones. Both Thanos and the Avengers have lost people they care about which has radically changed their characters and the dynamics between the surviving Avengers. In addition, the Avengers have to deal with the guilt of failing. The Avengers may have failed the hero test in *Infinity War*, but maybe their *Endgame* performance can restore their good name, now that they're ready to do "whatever it takes."

Let's briefly skip the first test and look at the second one, which the Avengers clearly pass. Two fan favorites, Black Widow and Iron Man, both sacrifice themselves for the greater good of saving the Universe from Thanos. Hawkeye also behaves selflessly on Vormir, attempting to sacrifice himself, but Black Widow is one step ahead, ensuring his survival and her demise. During the final battle, Iron Man makes the "hero play," sacrificing himself to kill Thanos, while simultaneously delivering the iconic line: "I am Iron Man." Their sacrifices were necessary to complete their goal to undo the Snap and to stop Thanos.

The Avengers pass the third test by continuing to fight, even when it seems that all hope is lost. After 2014 Thanos shows up in the present and destroys the Avengers' headquarters, Iron Man, Captain America, and Thor take on Thanos alone. Every time they're brutally knocked down, they get back up and continue fighting. When Thanos's army shows up, Captain America stands to face them, despite Iron Man and Thor staying down. Facing Thanos and his children alongside the entire Chitauri army, Captain America tightens the strap on his shield (to hold together a deep wound in his arm) and limps towards them. He's alone—greatly outnumbered, outmatched, and injured—and knows he can't win, but he's willing to stand and fight to the end.

What about the first test? What should be the simplest test could now be costing the Avengers their hero title. Having good intentions is the bright-line distinction between heroes and villains. Despite their other heroic attributes, their problematic intentions from *Infinity War* are still the same; even if they believe stopping Thanos is the right thing to do, they're still missing the bigger picture. This poses an interesting dilemma: do we base the goodness of intentions on what our characters think is correct, or on what is actually correct?

If you believe the former, then what about Ultron from the second Avengers movie? He believed that humanity was the greatest threat to peace on Earth, and that the only way to "protect Earth" (what he was originally designed to do), was through mass genocide. Ultron believed he was right, but does this make him right? Disagreeing with Ultron shows that intentions can't be based on what the character themself believes to be true; agreeing with Ultron makes it easy to see that Thanos got things right in wanting to restart life. Either way, the Avengers' intentions can't be viewed as good.

Even if opposing Thanos was the right thing to do, the Avengers still fail because they're driven by selfish intentions: It's clear that their missions' purpose is to bring back their loved ones and saving everyone else is merely a by-product. When the Avengers are ambivalent about going to the Garden, Black Widow argues in favor of this plan: "Even if there's a small chance that we can undo this . . . we owe it to everyone who's not in this room to try." She doesn't say they owe it to everyone that died. No, she's only thinking about the other

Avengers (who would be in that room if not for Thanos). Similarly, Ant-Man reveals his intentions when Iron Man refuses to help with the time heist: "I lost someone very important to me . . . Now, we have a chance to bring her back. To bring everyone back." It's clear his first priority is Hope, not the rest of the Universe.

Even our man of morality, Captain America, falls into this trap: "Five years ago, we lost. All of us. We lost friends. We lost family. We lost a part of ourselves. Today, we have a chance to take it all back." By showing that our "heroes" are mainly focused on getting their loved ones back, we can't help but wonder what would happen if all of the Avengers had somehow survived the Snap. Would they still feel the same heroic motivation to act—and sacrifice their lives—for others?

It's unclear that they do, but if the Avengers do pass the hero test in *Endgame*, is Thanos still a hero? Despite being a very different character in *Endgame*, 2014 Thanos's motivations and goals are still the same. He has seen the sacrifices 2018 Thanos was forced to make and the flaws in his master plan. Through a reworking of the kinks, he alters this plan to prevent resistance (shown by the great lengths the Avengers went to reverse the Snap). Even though his plan is changed, the intentions and intended consequences are the same, meaning he's still our hero.

Madman or Smartest in the Room?

I don't know what to do here. This is a mess, morally speaking. This is a putrid, disgusting bowl of ethical soup.

—CHIDI ANAGONYE, *The Good Place*

Much like the indecisive Chidi in *The Good Place*, we're now faced with a difficult decision: who is the true hero in *Endgame*? Thanos has a pretty solid case, but the Avengers have their own claims to heroism (despite the flaws in their plan and some questionable motives). But if they both pass the hero test in *Endgame*, who then is the villain?

After considering this issue from many different angles, it seems the only way to resolve the question is to look at the consequences of our characters' actions, or in philosophical terms, to view the question from a *utilitarian* point of view. Under utilitarianism, the morality of an action is measured by the amount of good it produces, taking into account the overall goodness produced for everyone, not just for the person taking the action. Even if some harm is caused, an action can still be moral, as long as the good outweighs the bad: the ends justify the means.

Utilitarianism is used not only to determine whether an action is moral or not, but it also can tell us what to do. In any given situation, we always ought to choose the action which will lead to the greatest overall good, even if it will cause some pain. As long as the good outweighs the pain, we're morally obligated to act that way.

So how does this help us resolve the *Endgame* hero dilemma? We need to measure the good produced by each side's actions and see how they measure up. Looking at Thanos first, the key question is whether we agree that without the Snap we will all die due to overpopulation. If he's wrong, then the pain he caused is morally wrong; but if he's right, then his plan creates the most overall good, since killing half the Universe to save the entire Universe from extinction is morally justified. So how do we know if he's correct?

Before the battle on Titan, Thanos enlightens Strange on what happened to his own planet: "Titan was like most planets. Too many mouths, and not enough to go around. And when we faced extinction, I offered a solution." Thanos tried to use his fifty-percent plan to save his planet, but he was called a madman and rejected, resulting in the destruction of the entire planet due to overpopulation. Thanos knows that doing nothing (the Avengers' plan) is not an option.

Not only does Thanos know what can happen if his plan is not enacted, but he also has empirical proof that his plan works. When Gamora was young, Thanos came to her planet which was "on the brink of collapse" due to overpopulation, and divided the population randomly, killing half. The other half was allowed to live, and Thanos tells Gamora that since that day, "The children born have known nothing but full bellies and clear skies. It's a paradise." Her planet was saved and serves as proof that Thanos is onto the right idea.

Endgame shows us after the time jump that Thanos's plan worked on a much larger scale than Gamora's small planet. Captain America notes that he saw a group of whales in the Hudson River. He attributes this to "fewer ships and cleaner water" as a result of the Snap. As a result, this view of the Universe post-Snap is a positive one.

Additionally, Thanos's solution is humane: rather than violent murder, people would be killed "at random, dispassionate, fair to rich and poor alike . . . With all six stones, I could simply snap my fingers, and they would all cease to exist." Thanos calls this "mercy," and it's true.

All of this demonstrates that from a utilitarian perspective, the benefits of the Snap overshadow the harms it causes. And, because it leads to the most overall good, Thanos is morally obligated to take this action. By trying to prevent him from acting, the Avengers are the villains.

Killing Half the Universe Makes You a Hero?

Sometimes things have to fall apart to make way for better things.

—TED MOSBY, *How I Met Your Mother*

If you've made it this far, and still aren't convinced that Thanos is the true hero of *Endgame*, you might just be more rigid in your beliefs than the Avengers. If that's the case, then I'm not sure anything will change your mind, but I'll try one last time. Let's look at some potential issues you might have with this thesis.

Maybe you're generally on board with Thanos's plan in *Infinity War* to prevent overpopulation, but his new plan in *Endgame* seems a little too brutal. True, in the original plan half the Universe gets to live, whereas under the new plan we all die. How can this be a good idea? And doesn't this completely contradict his plan—if we care about saving people then why are we killing them all? Thanos's justification is that "As long as there are those that remember what was, there will always be those that are unable to accept what can be. They will resist." He specifically refers to the Avengers and their "time heist" as the reason this new plan is needed (another reason to view them as villains). Instead, he will create a new Universe "teeming with life," that "knows not what it has lost, but only what it has been given." While harsh, this plan will lead to the most overall good—it prevents mass extinction due to overpopulation and eludes the possibility of future "heroes" trying to undo the plan.

It's also possible that you disagree with my reliance on utilitarian principles to define someone as a hero. We don't usually associate heroes with utilitarianism because this goes against the gut feeling we may have towards a situation. Picture this: people are trapped under rubble that has split them up. On one side is a group of one hundred people, and on the other side is a little boy. The rubble has landed in such a way that any shift to one side will make it fall on the other side, killing anyone underneath. Superman appears (flying in from the DC Universe) and wants to save the day but there's nothing he can do except pick a side to rescue. Utilitarianism obligates

Superman to save the hundred people and leave the boy as a casualty, but will his fans ever forgive him? Yet ultimately you know this is the right choice. How could he let a hundred people die in exchange for saving one boy? So, yes, utilitarianism has a place in hero decisions.

Utilitarianism is known for posing the famous Trolley Problem in which a trolley is barreling down a track about to kill five people, and a person standing next to the control lever must choose whether to refrain from action and allow the five to die or divert the trolley to another track which will only kill one person.

In *Endgame*, Thanos faces a trolley dilemma of his own— the Universe is facing extinction by overpopulation, and he's the only one who can pull the lever to prevent this. By pulling the lever the "trolley" diverts to a track that kills only half the Universe. The Avengers are the ones watching; and instead of allowing this to happen, they choose to kill Thanos to save the half (ignoring that their action will result in the death of everyone). When *Endgame* is viewed from this perspective, it is much easier to see why the Avengers are the villains here.

Assuming I finally got you to see things my way but you're still feeling a bit insecure about this, here's a final anecdote for you. In the original *Infinity Gauntlet* comic, after Thanos snaps, other cosmic entities appeal to the judgment of the Living Tribunal—an entity that serves as a judge of the multiverse in the Marvel Comics, overseeing all beings and making sure that balance is upheld—to decide whether Thanos is guilty of crimes. Ultimately, the Living Tribunal declares that "Natural selection is one of the Universe's oldest canons: the strong replace the weak. It is as it should be. No cosmic crime is being committed."

I expect by now that even those who refused to accept the idea that Thanos is a hero see that this is the only logical conclusion. To quote our hero in *Endgame*, "You could not live with your own failure. Where did that bring you? Back to me."[1]

---

[1] To my deceased brother Ofir, without whom I probably would've said my favorite Marvel comic character is Superman. I know you're watching *Endgame* on replay up there.

21

I Plucked My Soul Out of Its Secret Place

KATELYN BOTSFORD TUCKER

Students in my eighth-grade United States History class love to play a game. It's called "Get Ms. T. off topic" and it goes a little something like this: "Hey, Ms. T, who's your favorite superhero?" or "Who would win in a fight, Iron Man or Captain America?" or "Which is better, Marvel or DC?"

Any variety of these questions is enough to get me to drop my dry-erase, cast aside my primary sources, and venture into a lengthy discussion with a bunch of thirteen-year-olds. They think they're playing me, but really, I'm playing them. I will talk superheroes, movies, and comics all day. I'll talk about Steve Rogers as a foil for Tony Stark, or Wakanda as a paradigm of colonialism and Pan-Africanism, or power as a means for both good or evil, and who gets to decide which is which. Because there's a lot to learn from these worlds, whether on paper or on the big screen.

We do a lot of connecting in class. Often it's connecting different people, places, things, or ideas to other people, places, things, or ideas, sometimes from the same eras and others from completely different times. One of the greatest attributes of *Avengers: Infinity War* and *Avengers: Endgame* (now the highest grossing movie of all time) is the way they brought the two culminating movies of this particular arc of the story of the Avengers together. The Marvel Cinematic Universe is a master class in world-building. Sure it's got some faults, but one of the reasons it's successful is because of the thread that weaves stories and characters together through both space and time. That thread wove itself together in *Infinity War* and *Endgame*, leaving us speechless, sobbing, or otherwise heartsick, from loss and love.

Of late, our class discussions have revolved around the now deceased big bad himself, Thanos. There are a lot of questions: Why would someone destroy half of all living creatures in the universe? Can we see instances of the use of concentrated power for evil in our own world? What, if anything, can we liken the power of the Infinity Stones? These questions take us far and wide. So let's order some shawarma, peer into the Infinity Well, and get down to it.

Mad Titan, Servant of Death, Slayer of Worlds

According to Marvel canon, Thanos is one of the Eternals, a god-like race created by the Celestials. Thanos is considered one of the strongest beings in existence. Due to his innate power, strength, and abilities, he is considered effectively immortal. Other Eternals include Thena, Kronos, Ajak, Uranos, and Angelina Jolie.

Thanos was born with the Deviant gene or Deviant Syndrome, making him automatically one bad dude from birth. Knowing this, his mother attempted to kill him as a baby, but since the other Eternals thought that was pretty heinous, they stopped her, and locked her away. Thanos later visits his imprisoned mother and literally tears her apart. The thing about Thanos is that he isn't just out for revenge; he's obsessed with Death, the being which symbolizes mortality. Death, of course, is an actual being within the Marvel Universe whose opposite is Eternity. Death becomes a muse to Thanos and the driving force behind the decisions he makes.

In the movies, the first glimpse we catch of Thanos comes in *The Avengers* (2012) during an end-credit scene in which the leader of the Chitauri, unsuccessful invaders of Earth, says that humans are more dangerous than they had anticipated, and to go up against them would be "to court Death itself." This is exactly what Thanos wants; he longs for the attention of Death and to please her in any way he can. In addition to literally courting Death, he is out to fulfill her goal of acquiring souls, but also, to right a wrong of the universe. In the comics, as well as in *Infinity War* and *Endgame*, Thanos explains the purpose behind his plan to annihilate half of all living creatures in the Universe. He says in *The Silver Surfer*, that there is a "great imbalance . . . the most dire threat this universe has ever faced." He continues:

> . . . the medical and other scientific breakthroughs this world's dominant
> species have made over the past few decades . . . these gains have

dramatically extended the life spans of these creatures . . . more than half of the humans ever born on this planet are presently alive right this moment . . . this planet is becoming criminally overpopulated.

With that overpopulation, Thanos continues, the human species is "rapidly burying itself in its own waste." He tells Silver Surfer of the "shameful things" humans are doing to their own atmosphere and that "Earth is a world rushing on its way to desolation and doom." But it's not just Earth. Thanos escorts Silver Surfer to other planets in the universe, explaining that overpopulation is something everyone faces and it must be dealt with.

This is echoed in the *Infinity War* movie, in which Thanos has a heart-to-heart with his favorite daughter, Gamora. She recalls Thanos taking her—kidnapping her—from her home planet. "I saved you," Thanos corrects, "Your planet was on the brink of collapse. I'm the one who stopped that." He continues, "Do you know what's happened since then? Children born have known nothing but full bellies and clear skies. It's a paradise."

Although Gamora acknowledges the success of her home planet she reminds Thanos its success was due to him having "murdered half the planet." But Thanos argues, "A small price to pay for salvation . . . Little one, it's a simple calculus. This universe is finite, its resources finite. If life is left unchecked it will cease to exist." So it's simple; Thanos must destroy the universe in order to save it. The question is how? Planet hopping would take far too long. He needs something powerful, quick, and effective.

Gotta Catch 'Em All!

In *The Thanos Quest* comic the Infinity Stones are revealed. Except that they are actually "Six Soul Gems" which "individually . . . contain power beyond comprehension" and "together . . . could destroy a universe." They're like Pokémon and Thanos has gotta catch 'em all if he wants to realize his dream of destroying half the universe. In *The Silver Surfer* when Thanos is talking to the Runner, he explains why he wants the gems so badly. He says, "They are the ultimate in power, the darkest secret in all the universe."

We've been watching the Infinity Stones since the early days of the Marvel Cinematic Universe, even if we didn't yet know it. The movies *Thor*, *Captain America: The First Avenger*, *Thor: The Dark World*, *Guardians of the Galaxy*, *Avengers: Age of Ultron*, and *Doctor Strange*, each had their own exposition of individual Infinity Stones. In those films respectively, the Tesseract or Space Stone, the Aether or Reality Stone, the Orb or Power Stone, the Mind Stone, and the Eye of Agamotto or the Time Stone, are revealed, each with its own unique powers. All five of the Infinity Stones had full movies around them; the Soul Stone, however, is a wild card at least on film. It isn't until *Infinity War* that we are made aware of the existence of the Soul Stone. And it's a big get. So, what does it do?

After paying a visit to the Infinity Well to "gaze into the depths of wisdom," Thanos comes to the realization that, even with his awesome power, he needs a way to expedite the task at hand. The six Soul Gems will give him this power. Not a new power, mind you, simply the ability to magnify his already destructive gifts. And the first stone he goes after has had several masters; Adam Warlock held it for a time and later it was in the possession of the In-Betweener. After quickly seizing the gem from the In-Betweener, Thanos explains the Soul Stone. "With it the sentient spirit can be touched and manipulated to serve the gem bearer's will. Never before has there been such an almighty and unique weapon."

He goes on to attain the remaining five gems; he retrieves the Power Gem from Champion on Tamarata, the Time Gem from the Gardener, the Space Gem from the Runner, the Reality Gem from the Collector, and the Mind Gem from the Grand Master. But it's clear that the Soul Gem is special. In *Avengers: Infinity War, Prelude Issue #2*, Wong regails Doctor Strange with the whereabouts of all five of the Infinity Stones. He recounts each of the stones but when he comes to the last of them he prefaces his explanation by saying, "if what is known turns out to be true, it could prove to be the biggest threat of them all."

But in the comics, Thanos doesn't have to do much of anything to retrieve the Infinity Gems. Just beat down a couple of Elders. Light work. In *Infinity War*, however, there's more to it. Yes, he's got to do a fair amount of beating—taking on the likes of Scarlet Witch, Captain America, and Thor mano a mano—but to achieve the Soul Stone, he's got to make a sacrifice.

Sacrifice

We know this story. With great power comes great responsibility. But in order to gain that power, you had better be prepared to throw your daughter off a cliff. Thanos's sacrifice of Gamora may have come as a surprise to some, but in reality, people have been immolating their offspring for millennia. In Genesis we see Abraham offer Isaac, but scripture tells us that the boy is saved in the nick of time by an angel of the Lord. Different religious traditions understand this in different ways. The Jewish faith interprets this as a test of faith, and a belief that God was never going to allow Abraham to go through with it. It was just a test. Similarly, the Christian faith views the Binding of Isaac as a test of faith but also an acknowledgment of the certainty of resurrection. And Muslims believe that Abraham's son volunteered for the sacrifice, although there is some debate over which of Abraham's sons fulfilled the duty.

In all three faiths, the Lord does not allow the boy to be sacrificed. In the sheer act of leading, and in two cases out of three, binding, the boy, Abraham has fulfilled his faith, duty, and trust in the Lord. Okay. So, if Thanos is to Abraham as Gamora is to Isaac, the question for us is this: why did Thanos actually have to go through with it to get the Soul Stone? He doesn't have to in the comics. I mean, plenty of people die, but Gamora isn't one of them. At least not at that moment. But the movie creates a twist. Why? Because of that common theme carried through both the Marvel comics and movies since the beginning: sacrifice.

While all the other Infinity Stones can be taken with brute force in the film, the Soul Stone in *Infinity War* requires a trade. The long-perceived dead turned guardian of the stone, Red Skull, explains, "The stone demands a sacrifice . . . In order to take the stone you must lose that which you love. A soul for a soul." It is there, on Vormir, that Thanos is made aware of what he must do. Gamora laughs. She thinks that this is actually Thanos's undoing. "You kill and torture and you call it mercy. The universe has judged you. You asked it for a prize and it told you "no." You failed. And do you want to know why? Because you love nothing. No one."

But Thanos does love someone. Multiple someones it would seem. So, did Thanos's sacrifice have to be Gamora? He loves Death. After all, this is all in service to her. But he isn't going to sacrifice Death. At least, not in the movies. He doesn't need to. He loves Gamora. His "favorite daughter." His "little one." The sacrifice must be her. She's the only other being in the universe he cares for. Even through all that purple and CGI, Josh Brolin makes it clear that this sacrifice is going to hurt Thanos deeply. But it's one he is going to make. He says, "I ignored my destiny once. I cannot do that again. Even for you." This reference to destiny is discussed earlier in *Infinity War* when Thanos explains to Doctor Strange how he failed at saving his planet, Titan, but it is also a reference to Gamora, and the fact that Thanos initially saved Gamora when he destroyed half of the inhabitants there in his early incarnation of the "Save the Universe by Destroying Half of It" plan.

A great line from the comics actually comes when Thanos takes the Time Gem from the Gardener, an Eternal whose only desire is to create a planet with a beautiful garden. Thanos has got to kill him to get the gem, of course, and he says, "You forced me into doing what I did. I had to be faithful to my nature. For, after all, I am Thanos." There you have it. Spelled out in the clearest of terms. Thanos is as Thanos does. So, despite the pain it causes him, he's hellbent on fulfilling his destiny and honoring his promise.

The ends justify the means. They must. Because another theme in the Marvel Cinematic Universe is that sometimes what's best for the group outweighs the wants or needs of any single individual. Recall in *Endgame* when Clint and Natasha are tasked with retrieving the Soul Stone from 2014. Now, a lot of fans were really bothered by this scene, and for the record, Natasha deserved a better end to this story. But poor decisions by screenwriters Christopher Markus and Stephen McFeely aside, Clint and Natasha are tasked in *Endgame* with going back in time to retrieve the Soul Stone, and, as we already know from watching *Infinity War*, the Stone demands a sacrifice. This won't end well for one of Earth's mightiest heroes.

Weighing the two of them has been done; some have pointed out that Clint, who went rogue as Ronin in a post-Snap world should have been the sacrifice, since he no longer had a family and committed various atrocities, while others point to Natasha as being the one without a family, a problematic plot point from *Avengers: Age of Ultron*. Either way, the Stone needs a soul, and in the end, it's Natasha who is sacrificed for the greater good. If we view this strictly in comparison to the sacrifice of Gamora, it makes *a little* more sense. Gamora is the only person Thanos loves; Natasha is the only person Clint has left. So if you "lose that which you love" then yes, both Thanos and Clint have done it right. Which would then mean that who the sacrifice is, does matter.

But Marvel is notorious for forcing these sacrifices. In the *Infinity Gauntlet* comic, Adam Warlock uses literally all the Avengers as lambs on the altar. One by one the Avengers are destroyed by Thanos. But, just as in *Endgame* nothing is forever, and both the Snap and the subsequent slaughter of the heroes is reversed. In the movie it's Tony Stark, but in the comic it is actually Nebula who brings about Thanos's undoing. Adam Warlock and Thanos team up to retrieve the gauntlet from Nebula, fearful that she will abuse her newfound god-hood. The point is that both in the comic and cinematic universe, no one stays gone for long. In fact, the Soul Stone offers us a glimpse of ways in which those lost to the sacrifice may be eventually restored.

Resurrection

The Soul Stone is unique among the Infinity Stones in that it contains an entire world—the Soul World. In the comic, Adam Warlock spends a lot of time within the Soul World, which is how he comes to know Thanos inside and out. Thanos also uses the Soul Gem to steal the "spiritual essence" of Silver Surfer, trapping him in the Soul World where he meets Adam Warlock, Drax, and Gamora, who were also trapped. We see Gamora and Thanos in the Soul World at the end of *Infinity War* when young Gamora confronts Thanos asking, "What did it cost?" He replies, "Everything." So, what did he receive in return for such a price?

In the comic, Thanos attains the first Soul Gem and decides that this stone is special. He refers to them collectively from there on out as Infinity Gems, having decided that there is only one true Soul Gem. He proclaims himself a god and he is referred to as such by his adversaries. But even before *Endgame*, Thanos dons the moniker of god. In *The Avengers Annual 7* (1963), upon locating the Cosmic Cube later known as the Tesseract and losing to the Avengers, and in *Infinity War*, when a dying but exculpated Loki says, "You will never be a god." Thanos replies, "No resurrections this time," proving that sometimes heroes don't come back. (Praise be to Disney+ for the return of Tom Hiddleston.)

Thanos being considered a god leaves us wondering who, if anyone, he answers to. We know he doesn't ascribe to any kind of Social Contract. We can probably assume he was assigned a fair amount of Ayn Rand as a student. So is there a higher power for Thanos? Yes. The Infinity Stones. Back in *The Silver Surfer* comic when Thanos is talking to the Runner, he further explains the origins of the Infinity Gems. He says,

> I discovered the true nature of the gems while gazing into the Infinity Well. It was a well kept secret for over a thousand billion years. The gems come from before all recorded time. They were once a single unit, a lone entity. They were a sentient being of limitless power. At the time, this being was the only living thing that existed within any and all realities. It was all that was and all that was, was it. This being

was infinity and forever. No one would fault you if you were to call it God. What other name would fit? But I doubt it ever had a name or any use for one. For it was more alone than any being has ever been. All that was was already part of itself. There was no other in its life. A more desolate existence is beyond imagination. I believe that is why it chose to put an end to itself. But such power does not give up the ghost easily. From its ashes rose all that is currently reality, in all its many forms. The core of this being's might was reincarnated in the form of the six Infinity Gems.

Thanos is nothing compared to those Infinity Stones, and certainly not anything compared to the "sentient being of limitless power" which proves to be infinity, reality, and life itself from which the Stones come. Thanos is a false god. An idol. Maybe this is why the Soul Stone demands a sacrifice. God in many religious traditions and faiths can have bouts of jealousy. Chapter 20 of Exodus says, "for I the Lord thy God am a jealous God" and Chapter Four of Deuteronomy says, "For the Lord thy God is a consuming fire, even a jealous God." Would a jealous god require a sacrifice of a loved one? Would a god see all the terrible things humankind has done and want to just wipe the slate clean with a snap, or a flood, perhaps? Maybe.

The Savior, the Godslayer, the Avenging Hand of Light

In the comic, *The End*, Thanos is again trying to wield untold power over the universe. Literally everyone we know and love is gone. And then, out of nowhere, Adam Warlock appears to have a chat with Thanos. Thanos says, "Adam Warlock, you have always been part of this universe but inexplicably apart from it." Adam Warlock has spent the most time within the Soul World and understands the power of the Soul Stone even more than Thanos does. He uses this power to eventually convince Thanos that he must save the universe but the cost will be himself. This is the last incarnation of Thanos. To be sure, he went a few more rounds in the comics than in the movies, but I think it's safe to say that the Thanos of the Marvel Cinematic Universe is out for good.

We haven't yet seen Adam Warlock in the Marvel Cnematic Universe. His character was teased in the end credits scene of *Guardians of the Galaxy, Volume 2*, and many speculated that he would make an appearance in *Infinity War* or *Endgame*, but he did not. If and when he does join with the remaining Avengers, he may be able to tell us more about the Soul World.

But, since he will probably appear in a post-Snap, post-Blip timeline, the Russo brothers may decide to take an entirely different angle with his character. That leaves us to dig into Adam Warlock's past through the comics in order to find a bit more information about what made it so powerful in the first place.

The 1972 comic, *Warlock*, bills Adam Warlock as "Tomorrow's Superhero . . . Today!" The hero Him is faced with certain destruction from the God of Thunder himself, so he opts to use a machine designed for Bruce Banner to propel himself "into what man will be at the end of a million centuries of evolution." Him enters the cocoon and emerges a short time later as a being born of no man or woman. He is tasked with saving Counter-Earth and provided protection and understanding in the form of the Soul Gem. He's told that the gem will come with pain and agony and "That is the merest fraction of what it means to be a man,"

Throughout *Warlock*, Adam Warlock uses the Soul Gem to control beings, but the Soul Gem is more than mind or body control. In the 1982 *Warlock,* he uses the Soul Gem to violently defeat Autolycus and Magnus (Warlock's own "dark reflection"). He comes to the realization that he cannot remove the stone. It has become a part of him; it has become his "life force" but taken Warlock as its prisoner. Later in *Warlock Chronicles,* the Soul Gem turns on Warlock, proving that the stone is indeed capable of thinking for itself.

The Soul Gem itself is a sentient being, and it thrives on collecting and consuming souls, keeping them within the Soul World. So what exactly is the Soul World and how does Adam Warlock seem to get so much out of existing there? Within this world, whoever has the Soul Gem can learn about those inside, and even access their powers, memories, and thoughts. What they understand, the Soul Gem understands, and so whosoever wields the Soul Gem has the same power of knowledge, understanding, and control. When, in *The Avengers Annual 7*, Adam Warlock finds himself trapped in the Soul World with Gamora, he notes the others who had gone there before him. He says, "We're all here together . . . truly together, for our hearts are open books, and this atmosphere breeds understanding and mutes the ego. Here we are all one and in this oneness there can only be . . . love." With this description it's no wonder that Warlock refers to the Soul World as "Heaven."

One of the reasons Thanos may not have been ultimately successful is that the Soul Stone never truly belonged to him. In *Infinity Countdown*, Warlock is reminded that his "physical form and mind were the pinnacle of human achievement" but he was "without a name, and without a soul." After he is given the Soul Gem by the High Evolutionary, he has a new purpose. He eventually resides within the Soul Gem, in the Soul World. And he is only aware of its existence once he has left. As Claude McKay's 1922 poem goes:

> I plucked my soul out of its secret place,
> And held it to the mirror of my eye,
> To see it like a star against the sky,
> A twitching body quivering in space,
> A spark of passion shining on my face.
> And I explored it to determine why
> This awful key to my infinity.

The "awful key" for Thanos's infinity were the steps he was compelled to take in order to get what he wanted. Thanos was a wannabe god bent on impressing his lover, willing to sacrifice the life of his child to secure absolute power. The poem ends, "I know my soul," but for Thanos it would seem he doesn't have one. As for Adam Warlock, he may be the only one who knows his soul, but the power that comes with it is too great, even for him.

22

The Mad Titan and the Mother of Dragons

HAYDEN WEISS

The two biggest popular culture creations in recent years have to be *Avengers Infinity Saga* and *Game of Thrones*. The *Game of Thrones* franchise has made upwards of 1.5 billion dollars while *Infinity War* grossed upwards of two billion, and *Endgame* just under three billion.

One of the most appealing aspects about both stories is that there is a villain with a justification beyond just being the shallow bad guy. Both Marvel's Thanos and Daenerys of *Game of Thrones* were willing to do whatever needed to be done in order to create their vision of a utopia, and they truly had character of their own. The depth of the two characters make them a compelling pair of antagonists, antagonists who are actually quite similar.

This pair of villains are both uniquely situated with a source of immense power, which allows them to force their desired utopia upon their respective universes. There are even smaller similarities that couldn't possibly be clocked up to coincidence. For example, Thanos is called the Mad Titan and Daenerys is known as the Mad Queen, while neither see their own plans, actions, or beliefs as the least bit insane. In fact they are each completely convinced they're the only sane ones who see the truth.

The Historical Precursor

A historical figure who foreshadows Daenerys and Thanos is 'Old Nick', Niccolò Machiavelli. Machiavelli was a sixteenth-century political scientist, writer, and diplomat. His ideas revolutionized politics and had a huge impact on how politics operate today. Often referred to as the Father of Politics, his writings in *The Prince* and *The Discourses on Livy*, have "paved the way for modern republicanism." Machiavelli famously stated that it was better for a leader to be feared than to be loved, and he is often credited with saying that the ends justify the means.

How do we see Machiavelli's thinking in Daenerys and Thanos? The first example is how they plan to achieve their utopian visions and the power they have that allows them to follow through. While yes, their visions are slightly different, both characters utilize a very Machiavellian "ends justify the means" approach. Machiavelli writes in *The Prince* that the pollical leader "should not deviate from what is good if he can avoid it, but he should be ready and able to do evil when it is necessary." And in the *Discourses*, he says "For although the act condemn the doer, the end may justify him."

Both of these quotes are pure consequentialism. Machiavelli and by our two characters believe the morality of an act is based on the result of that action. The pair both have consequentialist monologues about recreating a better world through the destruction of the old one. Daenerys talks about ending slavery and "breaking the wheel" of oppression and suffering, while Thanos focuses on ending poverty and famine. He says "Titan was like most planets. Too many mouths, not enough to go around. And when we faced extinction, I offered a solution." Genocide! "But at random, dispassionate, fair to rich and poor alike. They called me a madman, and what I predicted came to pass."

The characters even have explicit dialogues projecting their Machiavellian ideals. Thanos calls for the slaughter of half of life itself and considers it "a small price to pay for salvation." To justify her rampage in King's Landing, Daenerys says, "We can't hide behind small mercies. The world we need won't be built by men loyal to the world we have"—meaning that the utopian new world order must be made without regard to the single-minded people of the current world, and that those people would only serve to squelch potential progress.

Both characters' goals sound admirable and are motives the viewer can even sympathize with. The only issue the viewer has is the means by which they plan to achieve their perfect world, which ultimately makes them each story's villain. Just as Machiavelli wrote in 1513, a good leader ought to do "evil" when it is necessary. Both Thanos and Daenerys truly take this to heart and act with it in mind. To achieve her perfect world, Daenerys uses her dragon to slaughter hundreds of thousands of people. Thanos uses the power of the Infinity Stones to snap half of all living things completely out of existence and then even worse in *Endgame* wanted to "shred this universe down to its last atom. And then with the stones collected . . . create a new one. Teeming with life, but knowing not what it has lost but only what it has been given." In their belief, their proposed plans are necessary evils, such that the result's absolutely enormous benefit vastly outweighs the means by which it was accomplished.

Right or wrong in the eyes of the viewers, in the characters' judgment, their actions are admittedly horrible means to wonderfully fantastic ends. While the viewer may disagree about whether the ends outweigh the means, looking at each character's bias certainly helps us understand their decision making and gives the viewer some sympathy with them.

Bad Childhoods

While on screen, we see much more of Daenerys's background, Thanos's background is shown extensively in the comics—specifically the *Thanos Rising* arc and is lightly alluded to in the movie. The backstories of the two characters certainly have quite a few parallels to one another. Both grew up in an extremely tough and cruel environment, where they had little chance of a happy childhood. In *Thanos Rising*, not only does Thanos's mother attempt to murder him just seconds after he was born, but Thanos experiences the horror of an irreversible, unimaginable 'I told you so'. He warned the people on Titan about their overpopulation and how their resources wouldn't keep up with their rapid population and industrial growth. Eventually, he was forced to watch as his own people destroyed themselves because of the very thing he warned them of.

In Season One of *Game of Thrones*, Daenerys has to appease her abusive brother who seeks the opportunity to sell her off in exchange for an army that would allow him to conquer the Seven Kingdoms. She is given as a bride to a Dothraki horse lord, who was known for his brutality and Viserys, her brother, even calls them savages himself. The horrors of childhood end up permanently scarring both characters, and they never wholly recover from their experiences as children.

Daenerys experienced a form of slavery from her own family and learned to despise enslavement and any form of oppression in it's entirety; Daenerys became completely motivated to end slavery and oppression due to her personal experiences with her brother, just as Thanos is with overpopulation and lack of resources because of his past. Even in history, the villains are nearly always similar. Hitler was abused as a child by his father and that led him to develop feelings of anger and resentment. Josef Stalin and Osama bin Laden had similar experiences. Pent up anger and neglect in his childhood molded the personalities which became prone to horrific actions in later life. This precedent set by history is mirrored in popular culture.

Thanos followed a shockingly similar path to Daenerys, and even to some degree to Hitler, Stalin, or Bin-Laden and the villainistic perspective the viewer has for the two popular culture villains is certainly lessened once the viewer understands the background and past events that seem to ultimately shape all of the characters' current decisions.

This leads into an interesting argument of nature versus nurture. We know in both of the backstories of the duo that both were born quite different from their peers. Thanos is born purple, scarred, and psychotic while Daenerys is descended from a long line of incestuous relationships, which manifest in the Targarean curse of madness (evident in her father and brother).

Were this pair "evil" because of their hereditary traits or because of their upbringing and past experiences? Their future actions could be argued to be a byproduct of either. As an alternative to the idea that it was their past that dictated their choices, the argument could be made that it was because of Daenerys's madness that she ended up burning down King's Landing—or that Thanos's genetic abnormalities (both physical and mental), are more responsible for his genocidal tendency than his upbringing. Both characters' decisions could be chalked up to either nature or nurture, but the most compelling choice of the two is realistically a horrible combination of both—the perfect storm of a justification and natural irrationality.

Messianic Destiny

A truly fascinating similarity that makes the rationale behind their desires important is that each character is uniquely situated with a source of immense power (be it the dragons or the Infinity Stones) that allows them to make the changes they desire, which creates a messiah complex for them both. Both eventually come to believe that they are the key to saving humanity, and life itself. They believe it's their destiny to fix their universes and think they are the only ones capable of doing so. They see themselves as the only hope of all people, the exact definition of a messiah complex. Daenerys says exactly that. In a dialogue with Jon Snow she explicitly talks about her and Jon's destiny in the line, "build the new world with me. This is our reason."

Thanos too. He says in *Infinity War* that he is foretold by destiny, evident especially in the line "Dread it, run from it, destiny still arrives." Even in *Avengers: Endgame*, he repeatedly says that he's inevitable and after he sees the events of the future through

Nebula, and realizes that he gets the stones and accomplishes his ultimate goal, he says "And that is destiny fulfilled."

There are a couple of dialogues of the characters explaining their feeling of being uniquely fitted to enact their utopia and to become the savior they believe they are destined to be. Thanos says in a conversation with Gamora in *Infinity War*, "Little one, it's a simple calculus. This universe is finite, its resources finite. If life is left unchecked, life will cease to exist. It needs correction." Gamora protests and Thanos finishes the conversation with "I'm the only one who knows that. At least, I'm the only one with the will to act on it." This example is as simple as it gets. He believes he is the sole being with the ability or understanding to correct things, so he takes matters into his own hands and attempts to correct these perceived issues. Daenerys says in Season Four: "Let the priests argue over good and evil. Slavery is real. I can end it. I will end it. And I will end those behind it." And even earlier, in Season Two, she says, "I'm no ordinary woman. My dreams come true." This links into destiny pretty directly. She believes her dreams do come true, one can assume, because destiny chose her.

This idea of destiny links directly to an incredibly interesting point brought up in *Game of Thrones* by Varys in a dialogue with Tyrion in Season Eight's "The Last of the Starks." Varys, commonly referred to as the spider, is an advisor to Daenerys. He says, "I have served tyrants most of my life, they all talk about destiny . . ." Tyrion, a dwarf who also advises the Targarean Queen, responds "She's a girl who walked into a fire with three stones and walked out with three dragons, how could she not believe in destiny?"

While they are talking about Daenerys, it equally applies to Thanos. Thanos traveled across the universe and battled many powerful beings to get the stones and to have the opportunity he now does. Both characters realize the incredible nature of their feats and choose to believe that it wasn't luck or coincidence, but something guiding them and causing these things to happen; that this is their predetermined destiny and if it weren't, then it would be nearly impossible for them to have come so far; unforeseeable success builds firm belief in destiny.

Ultimately this is the whole idea of the messiah complex. A person feels that they uniquely have a huge amount of influence on the things around them (whether they do or don't) and they use that unique "influence" to fix the world in any way they see fit. While the most obvious example of a messiah complex is Jesus (his name literally means 'savior') most people who show a similar ideology tend to be tyrannical. Hitler and Bin Laden align with this aspect of messianism as well. Hitler consistently claimed that he was Germany's savior and even wrote an autobiography to support it. This ties closely back to belief that destiny is built by beating the odds and being successful, especially when that success was unexpected.

Hitler started off as a young man who failed to make it into art school, into becoming a member then politician for the Nazi party, next becoming the German Chancellor, to finally seizing the German Presidency and becoming the most infamous dictator of all time. Throughout his rise he was harboring ideas of creating a purely Aryan Germany. His incredibly improbable rise led him to believe in a greater power pushing him onward— that greater power almost certainly being destiny or some other supernatural force. The unique power he acquires reinforces his belief that he was the only person to be able to or willing to act upon the world and shape it. This happens time and time again with the historical rise of dictators, leaders, and other figures— including figures of fiction such as Thanos and Daenerys.

Yet, with all this similarity between Thanos, Daenerys, and history, there are some key differences, the most obvious of which is their view of what will happen to them after they have remade the world. Daenerys's plan was to rule over everyone everywhere, Thanos on the other hand, had no plan for himself after the Snap. He simply destroyed the stones so his work couldn't be undone and sat down and watched the sun rise. He didn't fight back when the Avengers attacked him and ultimately was slain by Thor, offering no resistance. Early in *Game of Thrones*, Daenerys was a protagonist with no clear sign of her dramatic change; viewers almost certainly favored Daenerys as the more moral character. After the change, the 'endgame' inverts the viewers' original evaluations of the two characters. The always evil-seeming Thanos now appears like a tired, contented man—happy for doing what he set out to do. Yet Daenerys, called the breaker of chains, creates a new chain around the world and plans to sit on top of it. The good becomes bad and the bad becomes almost justified.

Despite that critical difference, overall the two characters are remarkably similar and both are sadly viewed as the ultimate, irredeemable villains of their respective series. For better or for worse, they follow direct Machiavellian politics to a T and firmly believe that they are the ones with the power to save everyone. The reasons the characters say what they say, think the way they think, and act as they act, is understandable. Not that mass slaughter can ever be justified, but to look at their motivations, pasts, and relationships, is to comprehend and even to empathize with these villains.

23
Where Thanos Got Lost

AMBER DONOVAN

Thanos has been hailed as one of the Marvel Cinematic Universe's best villains of all time and the fact that he appears to have identified a genuine (and relatable) problem and thinks he's doing the right thing about it, seems to play a part in this. Although Thanos's plan doesn't sit right with us, some of us have wondered whether it's possible that Thanos didn't do anything wrong. Hopefully, by the end of this chapter you'll see why, despite having a moral compass, Thanos has managed to get pretty lost.

Thanos's Morality

So, Thanos wants things to be "perfectly balanced. As all things should be". By 'balanced' he means 'in correct proportion' to facilitate the flourishing of life—as opposed to the complete extinction of life he predicts will happen due to a lack of resources.

For Thanos, the flourishing of life is the ultimate good and is what we should be trying to maximize. This is Thanos's *morality:* it's the principle which guides his action and informs his view of what is right and wrong. This isn't exactly an unfamiliar idea. In fact, it's something of a mash up of two of the most prominent moral philosophies—Aristotelean virtue ethics and utilitarianism.

Aristotelean virtue ethicists would agree that moral action ought to bring about flourishing (although usually specifically human flourishing) and utilitarians believe in a principal of maximization. Sometimes this principle is cashed out in terms of happiness—for instance, the greatest happiness for the greatest number—but there are many variations on this. The main point is that they want to increase the amount of [insert good thing here] for the greatest number [of humans or of sentient life forms]—for Thanos, this is the flourishing of life. This is why we get so taken in by him! His perception of what is good is in line with a large part of our moral thinking!

So, given this view of things, Thanos decides to take action to achieve this ultimate good: he erases half the population of the universe to create a ratio of resources to living creatures which is more conducive to the flourishing of life. But all life does not flourish—life (especially human life) is not happy at all. Thanos realizes that balance alone will not be enough, he also needs *gratitude*. Once again, he's really smashing the whole 'conceiving of a good universe' thing: people have been on about the benefits of gratitude from the Romans, to Buddhist Philosophy, to modern Cognitive Behavioral Therapy, and then some. Then he goes and spoils it all with: so I will destroy everything so I can make a perfect new one! And everyone's like, Oh no . . . abort!

Vision and Choice

But the really interesting question is why? And not, 'why is destroying everything bad?' That's a much less interesting question. But rather, where has Thanos gone wrong? He's clearly a clever guy with a good idea of where morality is meant to get us and you can't fault his commitment to making it happen, so what went wrong?

Well, let's take a closer look at Thanos's argument. Thanos reasons that as the universe is finite and populations keep growing, eventually, there will be no resources and life will die out. He also believes that the ultimate good is the flourishing of life and that the right thing to do is always whatever maximally increases this good. From this he concludes that whatever the cost, he must bring balance to the universe, even if this means erasing half the population or erasing everything and starting again. His reasoning seems sound and his moral aims are understandable, so how has he arrived at a conclusion which seems so immoral?

To understand this we need to consider whether thinking about morality exclusively in terms of choice is actually accurate. Doing this makes is seem as if we only need to consider morality at all when it comes to *actions*. But is this really all there is to it? When we make a decision about how to act, we do this in light of whatever situation we're in, but what if there are different ways to *see* the situation? This would likely impact how we chose to act. If the Avengers saw what Thanos had done as a gift as opposed to a tragedy, they wouldn't have proceeded to try and undo everything. So, if there are multiple ways of seeing our circumstances and this plays a large part in what action we take, surely moral considerations are also relevant to this *seeing*—we should be concerned with *seeing* the right way as much as (if not more than) acting the right way.

Aspects and Thanos's Chin

The idea that there can be multiple ways of seeing is explored by Wittgenstein who described this phenomenon as *aspect perception*. Consider this picture of a duck. Or is it a rabbit? In Wittgensteinian terms, when you see the image as a duck you are seeing one aspect and when you see it as a rabbit you are seeing a different aspect. Think about all the Thanos's chin memes—if you haven'tseen them, get on the Internet now!

Someone said that Thanos's chin looks like a panini and now I can't unsee it.

Each meme shows us a new aspect, they teach us to see the resemblance between Thanos's chin and a panini, a sofa, the back of a Yeezy trainer, a McCoy's crisp, and so forth. and as a result, we experience an aspect shift and learn a new way of seeing. As you can see from the picture above, this is not an alien phenomenon, people talk about aspect-shifts in terms of *seeing* as a standard thing: "now I can't *unsee* it". So aspect perception is not just a fancy philosophical term, it's something that actually happens in our lives all the time!

Okay, so a few things to keep in mind about aspects. They can't just be anything; every aspect is a legitimate way of seeing the thing in question so there is no 'tangerine' aspect to Thanos, as Thanos does not resemble a tangerine (nor does his chin for that matter), but Thanos would have these aspects: a Titan, a villain, a father, a purple alien, a deviant, as he does resemble these things.

There's also a difference between knowing a fact about something and seeing an aspect: it's one thing to *see* Thanos's chin as a panini and another to know that his chin can be seen as a panini (from seeing the meme above)—the *seeing as* is immediate whilst the *knowing that* is inferred. When you see a new aspect for the first time you learn something new: when Thor learns that Thanos is a father and sees him in this light, he has learnt a new aspect of Thanos.

As you may have noticed, any given thing can have *a lot* of aspects and we, as mere mortals, can't see them all; this means that we can't learn everything there is to learn about a given thing or situation. Also, the aspects that we do see, and can learn, depend a lot on the concepts that we have. If you have no idea what a panini is, you're not going to be able to see the panini aspect of Thanos's chin. You'd need to learn what a panini was before you could see that aspect. So, our concepts play a significant role in what aspects we can see and as a result, influence what we can learn about a given thing or situation.

Some Stuff on Concepts

Right, so, what determines what concepts we know? Well, to borrow from Wittgenstein again, learning a concept is not a matter of memorizing the dictionary but a matter of learning how to *use* the concept—first by observing others and then by using it yourself and having other people guide you. This means that the concepts that you learn will depend on who teaches you and what concepts they know (which will be a matter of where they live, the language they speak, their culture, who taught them, and so on). So, as you can see, what concepts you have, and how they combine together to form your worldview, depends on a whole lot of things which are outside your control.

Okay, sure, you're thinking, but if we share a language we share our concepts right? And even across languages, we all have loads of concepts in common so how much of an impact can this really have? It's true that for some concepts there doesn't seem to be much difference. Especially those which are easier to teach and learn like the names of farm animals: you show a child a few pictures of cows, point at the cows in the pictures and say 'cow', correct them when they mistakenly call a patchy dog a cow, and perhaps draw their attention to a feature that cows have that dogs don't, to correct their understanding of the concept. Eventually it clicks; you know what a cow is, they know what a cow is, everyone knows what a cow is, so what's the problem?

Well, think about something like 'selfish' which is much harder to teach. You can't point to some particular object in the world which is the thing 'selfish', instead you use it to describe people who behave a certain way. But this 'certain way' is not someone doing the same action like running, and there is definitely not unanimous agreement over what this 'certain way' is. Some people may say that Thor is selfish because he's hiding away drinking beer and playing video games when the world needs him, but others may disagree and say he's not selfish, he's just struggling to cope with all the traumatic events.

When you're learning a concept, the way the people around you *use* the concept will inform your understanding of it: so, if you are exclusively taught by people who see Thor as selfish, you'll see him that way too. In real life, we aren't taught by people who all think the exact same thing, so it's practically impossible to know how your specific combination of influences will have shaped the concept for you. But what's clear is that nobody will have been taught *exactly* the same. All these concepts, many of which (unlike 'cow') we all understand slightly differently, combine to form our worldview and it is this worldview which influences what aspects we see in a given situation and this is one reason why we so often disagree—especially over those things which involve these more complex concepts.

Vision's a Big Deal

So, moral considerations *have* to affect more than just our decisions on how to act because we make decisions about how to act based on what we *see*. This means there can be (morally) better and worse ways of seeing; so to be moral, you've got to work on your vision. It would be great if we were a bit more awesome and were actually capable of seeing every aspect of everything, as then we'd be moved to act in the right way because we'd have all the information.

But, unfortunately, I think our brains would implode from the sheer effort of trying. So, instead, we have to be mindful of the fact that our worldview is always doing this little bit of extra work for us and that it will always be imperfect. If we forget this, it becomes much harder to improve our moral vision and make moral progress, as we fall into the trap of assuming that our way of seeing is *the* way of seeing. Doing this makes it very likely that we'll miss important aspects that would have moved us to act better.

To go back to the Thor example, if the Hulk had only seen the selfish aspect and not been able to see the sad and struggling aspect, he'd have found it much harder to get Thor out of the house—I don't think Thor would have been too happy if the Hulk had barged in there, called him selfish and demanded he come with them—and we can all agree that getting Thor out the house was the right thing to do. In this situation, the Hulk saw both aspects and was able to figure out which balance of these aspects was the best way of seeing the situation given the details of that situation (which include his knowledge of Thor as a person, Thor's experiences thus far, and so on).

This figuring out is what we have to do and get better at to see more morally in general. Exactly how we do that is a huge and separate topic, but if we're going to have any hope of being good at this figuring out, we've got to be open to different ways of seeing and can't be blind to all the rest—this is something of a golden rule for getting good at seeing.

Back to Thanos!

To help paint a picture of Thanos's way of seeing, we can turn to the novel *Thanos: Titan Consumed*—I know this novel did have its status as canon revoked, but it is still the most consistent with the Thanos we see in *Endgame* so I'm going to use it anyway. So, Thanos is born with the deviant gene which means he's purple and generally looks a bit different to the other Titans. Since purple is the color of death, he spends pretty much his whole life being rejected by everyone: his mother rejects him at birth and is then locked away in an asylum and he's not allowed to see her, he finds out his only friend was paid to be his friend, and his dad is about as emotionally cut off as they come.

A big theme in the novel is Thanos's overarching drive to belong and feel loved. Thanos is also pretty damn smart. Given how technologically advanced Titan is, his smarts are mostly science and technology smarts. He's good at math and stats and computers and general logical and quantitative thinking—which makes sense, it'd be pretty strange if he were super emotionally-intelligent given his upbringing.

So, Thanos, desperately wanting everyone to like him decides to have a good long think about what he can do. He's always had the sense that something about Titan wasn't quite right. He has a hunch that the problem is overpopulation, and after doing some research of his own ("The numbers add up. I've done the math.") he concludes: "The problem with Titan was not Titan itself, was not the cryovolcanoes and the threat of their freezing ammonia and methane. The flaw in Titan was *too damned many people.*"

Initially he sees the problem as inevitable, but then he realizes that "the inevitability was a predicted outcome that relied on no one doing anything" and he can do something. So he hatches his all too familiar plan of euthanizing half the population. Since his father (A'lars—top dog on Titan) won't listen to him, he broadcasts a message to everyone on Titan explaining the situation and his plan (and volunteering himself as one of those to die as a gesture of his faith in his plan). Naturally, everyone is horrified, including his only friend and recently acquired love interest, as they consider this immoral regardless of the outcome. Thanos *cannot understand this.*

Taking a look at his backstory, it's fairly easy to see why. If nearly everyone else's worldview included an image of you which was so horrific that accepting it would send you into a deep pit of self-loathing and despair, you'd be likely to develop a habit of ignoring other people's ways of seeing. In addition to this, being constantly shunned by others affects how you see other people and it has a significant impact on Thanos's way of seeing *life*. Life is another complex concept, like selfish, which we are unlikely to all understand in exactly the same way.

To add to this, 'life' has five dictionary definitions (unlike selfish which has only one) which creates even more room for people to fail to *see* (aspect blindness) when it comes to this concept. These different definitions are different ways of seeing 'life' and hence entail different ways of seeing 'the flourishing of life'. Two of these are especially relevant here: life as "the condition that distinguishes animals and plants from inorganic matter" ('condition of living things' aspect) and as "the existence of an individual human being or animal" ('existence of individuals' aspect). It would make sense that Thanos would see life in the 'condition of living things' way as opposed to the 'existence of individuals' way as his relationship to individuals on his home planet would unlikely to have made him see their individual existence as valuable enough to be what he understood by 'life' when the flourishing of this 'life', is, on his account the ultimate good.

Taking these together, it's no wonder that his way of seeing the data (which showed that if everything on Titan stayed the same the population would eventually decimate the resources and then die out) was 'the problem with Titan is that there are *too many damned people*'; not overconsumption, poor distribution of resources or a lack of consideration of environmental impact—despite all of these things being part of the problem. But, the way Thanos sees it, the thing standing in the way of the 'flourishing of life' is *exclusively* the population. And, to his mind, the solution is to deal with the problematic variable—*the population*. This is the *only* solution and the *only* way of bringing about the flourishing of life. So, naturally, he *sees* it as a *moral action*.

So Why's He Lost?

When Titan eventually perishes, Thanos interprets these events through the same unchanged worldview: Titan perished as *he* predicted because they did not enact *his* plan which was the *only* plan that would have worked. As opposed to, for example, that Titan perished because A'lars could not accept that his son may have discovered a flaw in the eternal city and so took absolutely no measures to deal with any of the facets of a complex problem with a complex system. This interpretation of events only adds to the reasons Thanos thinks he has for believing that he, and only he, knows what is right and is able to follow through on this: "I'm the *only* one who knows that. At least I'm the only one with the will to act on it" for "the hardest choices require the strongest wills". It has become a matter of confirmation bias: Thanos is so convinced that he is right—so convinced of his way of seeing—that he only finds evidence which confirms this (as you will when you are dogmatically attached to your way of seeing) and it snowballs to the point where he proclaims himself "inevitable". So, Thanos seems to have completely failed at following the golden rule of being open to other ways of seeing.

But what if he hasn't and his worldview is just right? How do we know that he hasn't seen all aspects and figured out the right way of looking at things and *that's* why he doesn't change his way of seeing? That's a legitimate concern. Thanos does have the Infinity Gauntlet after all and I'm sure he *could* have seen all aspects if he had used it for that. But it seems that he didn't . . .

Actually seeing an aspect of something is immediate and moves you to act accordingly. So, if Thanos has *seen* life as the 'existence of an individual' it would have been the flourishing of this that was the ultimate good for Thanos. He would have been moved to make the existence of all individuals as good as possible and any action which threatened individuals' ability to exist well, would be immoral—like erasing them from existence.

Figuring out the right way of seeing requires you to see multiple aspects, and if you figure out that one aspect is more important than another in a given situation, the less important aspect does not disappear—you don't *unsee* it! Thanos's final plan to erase everything is completely incompatible with the 'existence of individuals' aspect of life, so his actions *only* make sense if he does not see this aspect at all. This means that Thanos's way of seeing is missing information and is not the product of figuring out the right way. So, in the end, although Thanos's reasoning is fine and he does have a recognizable moral compass, what he sees (his starting point) is missing information and that's why he ends up so thoroughly lost!

24

The Left Hand of Thanos

KING-HO LEUNG AND ADAM T. MORTON

THANOS: I am... inevitable.

TONY STARK: And I am . . . Iron Man.

The exchange of Thanos's and Tony Stark's "I am" statements is perhaps the climactic moment of *Avengers: Endgame*. But is there anything more to this juxtaposition than a dramatic showdown between a supervillain and a superhero?

Why, anticipating his own death, is Stark nevertheless sure that "everything's gonna work out exactly the way it's supposed to"?

I Am Inevitable

In the Christian tradition, "I am" statements are frequently declarations of divine presence, beginning with God's appearance to Moses in the burning bush in Exodus 3:14: "God said unto Moses, *I Am That I Am*." Likewise, the seven "I am" statements of Jesus Christ in the Gospel of John: "*I am* the bread of life" (John 6:35), "*I am* the light of the world" (8:12), "*I am* the door" (10:9), "*I am* the good shepherd: the good shepherd giveth his life for the sheep" (10:11), "*I am* the resurrection and the life" (11:25), "*I am* the way and the truth and the life" (14:6), and "*I am* the vine" (15:5). These seven "I am" statements all point to the final and most remarkable declaration of Christ simply as "*I AM*" at his arrest before his death (John 18:5), a declaration which evokes God's words to Moses in Exodus 3.

Read through this lens, Thanos and Stark's respective "*I am* inevitable" and "*I am* Iron Man" could be regarded as two declarations of opposing absolute "divine" principles: The inevitable Thanos destroys life while the Iron Man Stark saves the world. Whereas Stark sees himself as a hero of American freedom in the earlier Marvel movies, Thanos sees himself as a necessary principle of the universe—as he remarks in the opening scene of *Infinity War*, the wreckage of the Asgardian ship, holding the defeated Thor in his right hand:

> Dread it, run from it . . . destiny arrives all the same. And now, it's here. Or should I say [*raising his gauntleted left hand*] . . . *I AM.*

It is with the same gauntleted *left* hand that Thanos snaps his finger to destroy half of the world in the last scene of *Infinity War*.

In *Endgame* Thanos tries to go beyond his first attempt and destroy the *whole* universe; however, he never succeeds. Instead, what we see in *Endgame* are two snaps, respectively by Banner and by Stark, to restore and save the world from destruction. What's fascinating—and *unexplained*—in the movies is that whereas Thanos's destructive infinity gauntlet is a notably *left*-handed one in *Infinity War*, the gauntlet that is used in *Endgame* is *right*-handed: Thanos's left hand of inevitability destroys the world in *Infinity War*, and Stark's right hand of freedom saves the world in *Endgame*.

So why was there a change from a *left*-handed gauntlet of destruction in *Infinity War* to a *right*-handed gauntlet of redemption in *Endgame*? Is the "inevitability" of Thanos necessarily incompatible with the freedom that Stark embraces and promotes? Perhaps some insights from Martin Luther could help us here. The contrast between the *left* hand of Thanos the Inevitable and the *right* hand of Stark the American hero of freedom surprisingly parallels what Luther, channeling another long Christian tradition, calls the *left* and *right* hands of God. For Luther, the hands of God refer to two forms of divine rule over the world—but because, to Luther, what God ordains is *necessary*, these also, as we shall see, correspond to two different forms of necessity. The left hand of God, corresponds to what Luther sometimes calls God's "*alien* work," which is distinct from God's "*proper* work" which Luther associates with the redemptive right hand of God's grace.

Now, the left hand of Thanos may be understood in terms of Luther's account of God's "alien" work not just because Thanos is literally an alien, but because of a basic correspondence in the content—as Luther writes:

> God indeed also claims for Himself the work of slaying man... In Scripture God expressly says: "I kill and I make alive" [Deuteronomy

32:39]. But [the prophet] Isaiah distinguishes between these works of God and says that some are His "alien " works and others his "proper" works [Isaiah 28:21] . . . God's "alien" works are these: to judge, to condemn, and to punish those who are impenitent and do not believe.

In the original comic-book version, Thanos is a religious fanatic who worships and eventually falls in love with Death as a goddess—and of course, the name "Thanos" itself echoes the ancient Greek word for death, *thanatos*. Even in the movie version, Thanos's death-dealing activities still have a certain religious ambition, namely to bring *order* to the universe.

This "order" to the universe is crucial to Thanos's understanding and fixation with "the Inevitable." The inevitability and order for which Thanos so strives is what Luther would call "the law". As David Lose explains it:

According to Luther the law has two functions. He designated the first as the civil use to describe the law's work to compel civility through legal restraint and the threat of punishment . . . The second use of the law, by comparison, Luther described as theological, as the law not only sets up and enforces standards of civility but also accuses those who disobey it and thereby makes offenders aware of their sin and consequent need for forgiveness ,. . . It necessarily follows the second use of the law's work to make persons aware of their need and hunger for grace.

The purpose of "the law"—the left hand of God's "alien" work—is to clear the ground for and point to God's "proper" work: forgiveness, grace, and life. Indeed, it is the destructive "alien" work of Thanos's left hand in *Infinity War* that makes possible the mutual forgiveness and reconciliation of Tony Stark and Captain America in *Endgame*, which in turn makes possible the final redemption of the universe through the right-handed snap of Iron Man.

And I Am . . . Iron Man

This final victory of the Avengers was foreseen by Doctor Strange in *Infinity War*. Does this mean that Thanos and his destruction were in fact not really "inevitable"? No, in all of the 14,000,605 possible outcomes that Doctor Strange saw, Thanos inevitably snaps his left hand: The "alien" work of Thanos—and indeed the law—is always inevitable and necessary.

Even in the *one* happy victorious outcome out of the 14,000,605, Thanos was successful in snapping his left hand and destroyed half of the world, as we saw in *Infinity War*.

However, Thanos's inevitable destruction of the world was not the ultimate ground on which Iron Man's right-handed snap depended. Instead, Stark's self-sacrificial saving act was ultimately dependent on Doctor Strange's foresight and gift of the Time Stone to Thanos in *Infinity War*.

Doctor Strange's foresight and gifting of Time Stone was not only that which enabled Stark's self-sacrificial act but also that which moved the Ancient One to give the Time Stone to the time-travelling Bruce Banner in *Endgame* in order to undo Thanos's destruction:

> THE ANCIENT ONE: Yes, but you're leaving out the most important part. In order to return the stones, you have to survive.
>
> BRUCE: We will. I will. *I promise.*
>
> THE ANCIENT ONE: *I can't risk this reality on a promise.* It's the duty of the Sorcerer Supreme to protect the Time Stone.
>
> BRUCE: Then why the hell did Strange give it away?
>
> THE ANCIENT ONE: What did you say?
>
> BRUCE: Strange. He gave it away. He gave it to Thanos.
>
> THE ANCIENT ONE: Willingly?
>
> BRUCE: Yes.
>
> THE ANCIENT ONE: Why?
>
> BRUCE: I have no idea. Maybe he made a mistake.
>
> THE ANCIENT ONE: Or I did. . . .
>
> [*The Ancient One reveals the Time Stone*]
>
> THE ANCIENT ONE: Strange was *meant to be* the best of us.
>
> BRUCE: So he must've done it for a reason.

What is remarkable is the centrality of the notion of "promise" in this exchange between Banner and the Ancient One. The Ancient One was initially skeptical about the Avenger's time-traveling project to save the world, but after learning that Strange risked everything in giving up the Time Stone to Thanos, the Ancient One herself *also* decided to give up the Time Stone. She thus rested all of reality on Banner's—*and* Strange's—promise, a promise which appears very fragile, even unlikely to be kept.

The idea of "promise" lies at the heart of Luther's theological understanding of reality *per se*, including the matters of human salvation and forgiveness. As the influential Luther scholar Oswald Bayer points out: "'God' is apprehended as the one who makes a promise to a human being in such a way that the person who hears it can have full confidence in it."

For Luther, the reason why the hearer of the promise (*promissio*) can have full confidence in it is because this sort of "promise" *must* come to fulfillment: it is a type of necessity, but one that is very different from Thanos's "Inevitability." As opposed to the destructiveness of Thanos's "Inevitability," the necessity of the *promissio* is *creative*: it is one that brings life. In Luther's terms, this creative necessity is not "the law," it is not the left hand but rather the *right* hand of God: that which brings freedom that breaks away from the inevitability of death.

Unlike Thanos's "Inevitability," this "promise" and "necessity" is not strictly caused by prior events: When Doctor Strange looks ahead into the 14,000,605 possible outcomes, the fact that there is only *one* outcome in which Thanos is defeated does not give us much confidence. Neither can Banner seemingly be sure that he will be able to return the Time Stone and prevent the collapse of the Ancient One's entire reality. However, as we find out in the playback of the 3D video Tony Stark recorded before setting off time-traveling, there is a sense of confidence in the word that Doctor Strange gave him. As Starks says at the very end of his moving speech:

> Part of the journey is the end. What am I even tripping for? Everything's gonna work out exactly *the way it's supposed to* . . . I love you 3,000.

The language of "supposed to" in Starks last words to his daughter Morgan is echoed by the last words that Frigga said to her son Thor during his time-traveling return to Asgard in *Endgame*:

> THOR: I'm not supposed to be like everyone else, am I?
>
> FRIGGA: Everyone fails at who they are *supposed to be*, Thor. The measure of a person, of a hero is how well they succeed at being who they are. . . .
>
> THOR: I wish we had more time.
>
> FRIGGA: This was a gift. And you're going to be the man you're *meant to be*.

While Thor has failed—in his failure to defeat Thanos in *Infinity War*—in being the hero he was "supposed to be," Frigga *promises* that in the end he *is* "going to be" who he is "meant to be." This eventual "meant to be" isn't an inevitable outcome in terms of the chain of events we had yet witnessed (what we may call "the law") in the movie so far. However, it is nonetheless a guarantee, a promise—or even, a gift (what we may call "grace").

This realm of "gift" or "grace"—as opposed to the realm of "the law"—is what Luther associates with the *right* hand of God, that of God's *"proper* work" of forgiveness, redemption, salvation and liberation. It is through grace that God fulfills God's promise which alone determines what (and who) is "meant to be." For Luther, this is what true freedom means: It is not merely an opposition to causal determinism, but the fulfillment of a promise, the realization of who and what is "meant to be". This freedom given by God's right hand does not simply negate the *particular* destruction caused by Thanos's left hand, but negates the *entirety* of the logic of inevitability which Thanos embraces and represents.

The right-hand snap of Iron Man *creates* a new realm of freedom in which Thanos's inevitability is turned into impossibility, one in which the world is saved and indeed *free* from the inevitability of destruction: Having passed through the death that Thanos brought about, through the saving right-hand snap, the world becomes a new creation which was "meant to be".

I Am Still Worthy

"I am . . . still worthy!" So said Thor before he left Asgard one final time. The reunion between Thor and his mother Frigga during Thor's time-travel sequence is yet another instance of the motif of forgiveness and reconciliation that runs throughout *Endgame*, as we already saw in the friendship between Tony Stark and Steve Rogers. In both of Stark's and Thor's time-travels into their past, they encounter their deceased parents. While Tony reconciles with his father Howard after years of a complicated relationship and Howard Stark's untimely death (as we learn in *Captain America: Civil War*), Thor learns to forgive *himself* for his failure to defeat Thanos after speaking to Frigga. But Thor's reconciliation is not simply about "forgiving" himself but moreover *accepting* himself and his failings, and coming to find his "worth" and understand his identity as not being effaced by his failings.

To recall Frigga's final words to Thor: "Everyone fails at who they are supposed to be, Thor. The measure of a person, of a hero is how well they succeed at being who they are." This motif of failing at who they are supposed to be is one that we also find later in an exchange in the aftermath of Stark's self-sacrifice between Peter Parker and Happy Hogan in *Spider-Man: Far from Home*:

PETER: I'm not Iron Man.

HAPPY: You're not Iron Man. You're never gonna be Iron Man. Nobody could live up to Tony. Not even Tony.

Just as Thor couldn't live up to Thor, Tony Stark couldn't live up to Tony Stark. If understood in terms of "the law"—the realm of the "left hand" of God, rather than spurring heroism, these superhero identities are burdens for the Avengers. The law is an ideal which we're compelled to live up to, but which, unlike the promise does not create the effect it demands.

As Luther famously states in the first theological thesis of the *Heidelberg Disputation*: "The law of God, the most salutary doctrine of life, cannot advance man on his way to righteousness, but rather hinders him." These sorts of ideals tell us what we should be, but they do not guarantee that we will be so—in fact, they can hold us back, condemning us to an endless pursuit of the goal. This is the law's necessity, its destructive inevitability.

While Stark and Thor act heroically in the final battle of *Endgame*, perhaps they didn't live up to who they wanted to be or what they were expected to become. Just as Tony could not remain the loving father he so desperately wanted to be (as we learned earlier in the movie), Thor did not become, as expected, King of the Asgardians, instead giving up the throne to Valkyrie at the end of *Endgame*. One could perhaps also make the same observation about Captain America's *unexpected* non-return to the Avengers after delivering the Infinity Stones in the final scene of the move. To recall the conversation between the aged Steve Rogers and Sam Wilson (The Falcon):

SAM: Cap?

STEVE: Hi, Sam.

SAM: So did something go wrong, or did something go right?

STEVE: Well, after I put the stones back, I thought . . . Maybe I'll try some of that life Tony was telling me to get.

SAM: How did that work out for you?

STEVE: It was beautiful.

Giving up the identity of the superhero didn't mean that something went "wrong"—as we would have expected—but rather that something went "right": "It was beautiful." This "beautiful" life is not just a substitute or consolation for the lack of superheroic success, but rather something that exceeds the glory of superheroism: After all, the Avengers did triumph over Thanos who truly was inevitable. On the other side of this triumph, they found what they were actually fighting *for*. While the law, the left hand, had compelled them into inevitable heroic conflict with Thanos, the right hand delivered actual freedom, which is life beyond that compulsion.

Through the personal journeys of Tony Stark, Thor, and Steve Rogers, what we find is not a compulsion to be indestructible and indeed "inevitable" as with Thanos's ambition and fanaticism. Rather, the story of the three central Avengers is a story of freedom, of learning to rely on a promise and so not on one's achievements or on the law of past successes and failures. The freedom brought forth by Tony Stark's right-handed snap is not just a freedom *from* death and destruction, but a freedom *in* a higher and more fulfilled way of life, a life not just of victorious superhero warriors but one of completed persons: A life that is free from the burdens of needing to conserve oneself and fulfill one's destiny—as Thanos so aspires (he cannot do otherwise) to do. It is this freedom that allows Steve Rogers to give up his shield, in fact, to *gift* it to Sam Wilson at the end of *Endgame*:

> STEVE: Try it on. How's it feel?
>
> SAM: Like it's someone else's.
>
> STEVE: It isn't.

For Luther, the promise of God's grace—indeed, God's *gift*—is one that's always passed on to another. It is not a possession, something you conserve in yourself, but something that's true and real even—perhaps especially—as it is given away. This is true not only of various external gifts, but also of your own life. When even life can be freely given away because it rests on an invincible promise, there is freedom.

25
Reasonable Genocide

Marco Marchesin

Is Thanos *reasonable*? Or better, is Thanos somehow *justified* in pursuing his genocidal plan of erasing half of the population of the Universe?

The answer looks clear. In fact, there is something so utterly terrifying and monstrous in his intentions that it is easy to dismiss them as the fruit of pure *madness* (Thanos is labeled the *Mad* Titan, after all).

However, there's something about Thanos that, somehow, makes us uncomfortable: we can clearly understand his worries and be *sympathetic* with them, especially in an era of ecological crisis like ours, where the increasing lack of resources and the uncontrolled growth of population make us pessimistic about the future of our society. This is exactly why Thanos is so successful a villain, in contrast to the large bulk of comic foes, who seem evil just for the sake of it, with no clear intentions grounding their actions apart from the fact that they are inscrutably *evil* (Malekith from *Thor 2* is a good example of this tendency). In the case of Thanos, we can see his *reasons* and understand them.

So, on the one hand, we're pretty confident in saying that there's nothing rational or reasonable in Thanos's Snap, the gesture of a wicked and twisted mind. On the other hand, despite his madness, there is something that pushes us to see there is a *logic* behind his actions, some worries we could even share. Despite his madness, Thanos can be said to be rational. How can we solve this contradiction?

Subjective Reason

Let's ask what we really mean when we talk about *reason* and rational actions. In his attempt to understand the logic of modern consumerist society together with the tragedy of Nazism, Max Horkheimer argued, in *The Eclipse of Reason*, that contemporary industrial societies are dominated by a paradigm of reasonability that he calls *subjective reason*. It's the reason that does not bother about the reasonableness of the *ends*, only about the relationship between *means* and *ends*. An action is thus deemed to be subjectively rational the more it is *efficient* in co-ordinating the means to their ends. Ultimately, it is the logic of *instruments* and modern technology, evaluable only through criteria of efficiency, inasmuch as technology is itself adapted to the needs of market economy.

It is also the logic of *utilitarianism*, the ethical stance according to which an action is morally good if it tends to maximize happiness. According to utilitarianism, at the basis of moral reasoning, a *calculation* is supposed to take place. We should ask: what is in my power to make people happy? Which *means* can be used to more efficiently obtain what I consider to be happiness, for me or for others? Utilitarianism, with its emphasis on means and calculation, embodies perfectly the logic of subjective reason.

Utilitarianism is subjective even in a more important, deeper sense. If it's true that happiness is the ultimate goal orienting our actions, it's also true that happiness is really difficult to quantify or define. Ultimately, as long as happiness is a *vague* concept, a risk arises of considering happiness to coincide with whatever the subject thinks it ought to be, according to his own private evaluations, taste and will. The pursuit of happiness then hangs together with an ungrounded *choice* the subject makes to consider certain outcomes of our actions as desirable and leading to happiness. In other words, it's the subject who ultimately *decides* what's good and what's not, with no constraints apart from his personal evaluation. In this context, reason itself becomes an *instrument,* insofar as its function is exhausted in bonding proper means to proper ends, without asking whether the end of our actions as such is good or desirable *in itself*, independently from a *decision* made by the human agent. As long as the agent of the action has the last word over the rationality of their own action, we can see why this model of reason is called *subjective*.

Horkheimer does not think that subjective reason is *per se* wrong. He certainly does not claim that instrumentality and calculation should be rejected as a form of false rationality, quite the contrary. Only, he foreshadows the *danger* of conceiving it as the *only* form of rationality governing our actions. Historically, subjective reason had an external *limit* in what, by contrast, Horkheimer calls *objective reason*. Objective reason is the idea that the whole reality is rational, as reason is its "immanent principle." Differently from its subjective counterpart, its emphasis lies in the ultimate ends and goals of human life that are set and recognized completely *independently* from the human will, as they objectively compose the world as a harmonious totality.

To be less abstract, objective reason can be said to be the whole set of non-negotiable values and practices that can be recognized as *per se* rational, independently of mere utilitarian outcomes. Historical religions are obvious candidates as examples of world conceptions that embody an objective take on reality. What is good and what is wrong for Christianity, for instance, is in fact written in the very constitution of the world as God wanted, it is *per se* good or wrong, and human behavior *must* conform to it. Human rights are an achievement of objective reason as well: they are recognized and conceived as objective features of our world, and our political systems should be built upon them accordingly. There's no space for subjective or personal evaluation in the context of objective reason.

In modern times, with the twilight of religions and more generally of the big narratives of the world—with the emerging of *nihilism*, we could say, with Nietzsche—objective reason struggles to play any significant role in our society, and subjective reason tends to prevail alone. Here lies the tragedy, according to Horkheimer. In fact, if there is no longer a set of non-negotiable values to conform our actions to, subjective reason is set free of any *limit*. What is left is the mere arbitrary *choice* of the subject that can set his goals as he wishes, free of any external constraints. Every action is turned to be rational insofar as it is the result of a careful calculation. As such, for subjective reason, once the limits set by its objective counterpart are removed, once it becomes in this sense *absolute*, there is no space left for ends that are reasonable *in themselves*, that is, there is nothing that cannot be taken as a *mean* for some subjective goal.

Everything *can* be turned into an *instrument*: even human life, that can be manipulated, even annihilated or sacrificed, if deemed necessary to pursue higher goals. The very disposability of human beings can be then accepted within the parameters of subjective rationality, insofar as it can be deemed as the most efficient, quick, effective mean to achieve a personal goal. This is, incidentally, the way Horkheimer tries to explain the uncanny rationality of the horrors of the last century, as Nazism's extermination camps, where everything was efficiently made up to annihilate life in the best way possible. Reason becomes hollow and adaptable to any content, even mass murder.

If we go back to Thanos, it's easy to see how much his discomforting rationality has the feature of subjectivity. As he reveals to Gamora in a central scene of *Infinity War*, he made "a simple calculation." He did the math, and realized, pretty much as the British economist Thomas Malthus did in his 1798 essay *On the Principle of Population*, that we are too many, faced with an increasing lack of resources. He then needs to act in order to rebalance the world, for the sake of life itself. At least, of the life that survives his Snap. His logic is clearly utilitarian, as his genocidal intentions are serving what he considers to be the maximization of happiness for the remaining life in the universe.

Human life becomes disposable, and rightly so, because Thanos wants it that way. There is no other justification to mass extermination than Thanos's will (he is the only one who has the will to do the job, he reveals, quite tellingly, to Gamora). It is his point of view that matters, his own twisted ethics, according to which genocide is said to be piety, as he reveals to Doctor Strange on the planet Titan. Thanos is cruel and despotic, but not from his point of view, which is the perspective of the subjectivity of reason once it has become absolute: cruelty and despotism are not bad *in themselves*, as long as they can serve a higher scope. In all of this, the world, with his complexity and rationality independent from the delirious will of a wicked mind, completely disappears, and Thanos's decision constitutes the *absolutization* of the subject at his purest, and the radical loss of the world as its intrinsic limit.

We now have the elements to easily solve the contradiction we mentioned before, by saying there is no contradiction at all. Thanos is rational not *despite* his madness, but rather, he is mad *because* he is rational. The kind of madness he represents is exactly the one dwelling in subjective rationality itself, once it is pushed and stretched beyond every limit and constraint. It is a madness that lies *within* an excess of reason as Horkheimer defines it, not something external to it or alternative to any logical thought (as madness is ordinarily conceived in ordinary talk). The absolutization of subjective reason, with no objectivity countering its excesses, leads to madness, and together, to a substantial *dehumanization* of our actions, an aspect that the *Infinity War* represents beautifully when the Soul Gem demands Thanos to sacrifice Gamora, the only bond to humanity he has left. Gamora's sacrifice, the murder of his own daughter, represents the final step for Thanos's subjectivity to become absolute, free from any connection with the world and its intrinsic values. The subject becomes absolute when it is absolutely *alone*. What is left is the horror of Evil, rooted into a subjectivity that rejects the world and its objective rationality, and deliriously tries to impose a new one with no constraints, out of its own arbitrary choice.

Conversely, Captain America resolutely and with no hesitation refuses to kill Vision to prevent Thanos from getting the Mind Gem. We can see this as acting to counterbalance Thanos's theory of rationality: there is something that can *never* be said to be just, reasonable or acceptable, there is something that escapes the logic of instrumentality. We cannot kill a life, even to save the whole world, because human life has a value *in itself*. The fight against Thanos is also, and mostly, a fight against the two types of rationality.

Humans Are Obsolete

The Thanos problem was not the first time the Avengers encountered a mad villain willing to annihilate mankind. There was the case of Ultron, the rogue cyborg of *Avengers 2*. Thanos and Ultron are quite close as villains, yet at the same time clearly distinct. Both embody the perversions of delirious subjectivity, but they are distinct insofar as their subjective intentions imply a different kind of relation to objectivity and *nature*, here understood as the mere domain of whatever resists and its independent from the subject's will.

Avengers: Age of Ultron is a movie about human beings' intrinsic incapability of gaining total control, and how much pursuit of total control would lead ironically to disorder and chaos. Tony Stark builds Ultron because he wants to protect the planet and prevent future threats (like Thanos), but he ends up creating a murderous monster who wants to obliterate the world. But why did this happen? Why is Ultron evil? Why does he want to cause the extinction of mankind?

As a cyborg, Ultron seems to be a mere variant of an old pop culture archetype, the machine that becomes self-aware and hostile to humans. Stanley Kubrick gave us a wonderful depiction of that with his HAL 9000, from *A Space Odyssey*. This archetype also fits our discussion, insofar as the rebel machine somehow represents the logic of modern *technology*, and together the fear that our technological apparatus becomes independent, completely out of human control. With their cold rationality and intelligence reduced to mere calculation, cyborgs are already an embodiment of subjective reason. However, Ultron fits this archetype only in part. There is indeed no cold calculation in Ultron, quite the contrary. The robot is born in pain and fear, his words and actions, unlike those of Thanos, are difficult to grasp. The hatred he shows for Tony Stark even hints at a sort of Oedipus Complex not usually imputed to artificially constructed machines. There is a certain complexity in Ultron's character that goes beyond the narrative standards set by Kubrick, or the *Terminator* saga (the director, Joss Whedon, confirmed this in an interview).

However, despite these further characterizations, we can still claim that Ultron embodies the logic of modern technology, and thus of subjective reason, but in a way even more radical than expected. We can come to this conclusion if we look at Ultron's reasons to cause the extinction of mankind. They are somehow quite obscure and difficult to get (Ultron in this respect is not as successful a villain as Thanos is, since it is hard to make sense of whatever he does out of fear and hatred), but there are at least a couple of scenes where his motivations are clear.

There is the very first encounter between Ultron and the Avengers in Stark's penthouse. There, Ultron argues that there is no way to get peace on Earth, the end for which he was born, if humanity is not allowed to evolve. The only way to allow this evolution is "the Avengers extinction." The second scene is even more relevant. When the brothers Maximoff finally find out Ultron's plan of mass extinction, he reveals his real motivations, rooted in a wicked and not so unfamiliar *ideology*. We discover that the evolution Ultron has in mind is the rise of artificial intelligence, which he understands as the next step in the evolution of *life* on Earth. It is life that decides who is the weak and who is not, and insofar as cyborgs are the peak of evolution in life, their genocidal intentions are conceived on behalf of life itself. The evolution of mankind Ultron hits at in his first encounter with the Avengers is then translated into its total extinction as the evolution itself declares human being disposable in favor of artificial intelligence and mechanical bodies.

We now can see then how much Ultron as a character deepens the stereotype of the rebel cyborg. He still embodies the logic of technology, not though its superficial aspect of cold blooded and emotionless rationality, but rather in the very idea that technology turns out to be the *paradigm* of the evolution of biological life itself. After all, the main flaw of human beings is their incapability of evolving, which from Ultron's point of view the biological inability to be *updated*. This lack makes humankind disposable, much as an old computer is: once it becomes *obsolete*, we can get rid of it. From a cyborg's perspective, evolution in life is distorted into the very capacity of keeping up with technological enhancements and innovations. Whatever does not fit this logic is just disposable.

If this is Ultron's ideology, it is easy to see how much it is deeply totalitarian, in the way Hannah Arendt depicts in her masterpiece *The Origins of Totalitarianism*. Totalitarian ideologies, she argues, conceive the world as an endless *process*, constantly changing and evolving. It is the case, for instance, of racism, based on social Darwinism as it was elaborated by Herbert Spencer and its idea of evolution and social developments as a result of a struggle for life. However, such ideologies think that the will of the subject can conform to the intrinsic processes and ongoing movements of natural forces and drastically accelerate and govern them.

On the one hand, we have a conception of reality and nature based on mutation, evolution and struggle, on the other, the effort to harmonize these dynamic laws of nature to the will of the subject. Within this logic there is space to conceive the horrors of the Holocaust: for the Nazis, the camps merely represented a sort of technologically induced *acceleration* of the natural processes of selection and survival of the fittest through which they understood reality.

Pretty much like Hitler's, Ultron's genocidal intentions mirror this perverted logic. In his view, there is *no limit* to what the subject can do, even mass-murdering. His reason is eminently subjective, like Thanos's, but at the same time the disposability of humankind is inscribed *within* what he conceives as the natural order and the processes of constant evolution constituting it. Evolution, technologically interpreted as the capacity of being *updated*, declares mankind obsolete, for its very incapacity of evolving. Like any old computer, humanity is obsolete, and therefore disposable. Ultron is getting rid of its own personal Windows 95.

The Mad Titan

At this level we get the substantial difference between the genocidal projects of Ultron and Thanos. Ultron pursues his distorted idea of what is natural, and so rational, whereas Thanos acts *against* nature; he wants to intervene to distort and alter the natural process at the basis of overpopulation. Ultron wants to *accelerate* nature, while Thanos wants to *correct* it. His action is explicitly said to be a mere correction, as he tells Gamora in that crucial central scene in *Infinity War*.

Both Ultron and Thanos represents two aspects of the same logic: the idea that there is *no limit* to the power of the subject, that can create its own system of values and affirm its existence by annihilating every resistance encountered in the world. Differently from Ultron though, whose totalitarianism still preserves a distorted conception of nature and reality individual will must somehow conform to, so that extinction is thought to be natural and consistent to the order of things, Thanos makes a step further in the supremacy of the subject at expenses of objective reason and nature: the world and its logic disappears, what is left is the absolute supremacy of a subject that deliriously wants to control and dominate nature at all costs, with no appeal to any form of objectivity. Contrary to what it may seem, Thanos is no Hitler. He is a step further in the absolutization of subjective reason.

A subject's will with no world is the final outcome of this process of subjectivation, the return to a status similar to God's before creation. This is perfectly symbolized by Thanos's ultimate plan in *Endgame*. Faced with the Avengers' relentless attempts to fix the Snap's horrendous consequences, Thanos claims that this time he would annihilate all life in the Universe to create *a new* one, so that no one could have memories of the losses. There is no utilitarian calculation in this change of mind, only the delirium of an individual will to play God, in the specific sense of making nature and the world *depend on* a single individual subject, unbound from any objective constrains. The absolutization of the subject and its reason implies first nihilism—the world is literally destroyed by the subject's intervention—and second a *palingenesis*: the world is rebuilt through the shape of the subject and his delirious design.

It is no coincidence that Thanos is said to be a Titan. The most famous Titan comes from Greek mythology—Prometheus. He dared challenge the natural order established by the Gods to give fire to mankind as a gift. He succeeded, but at a terrible cost: he ends up chained and tortured for eternity. The order of the Gods cannot be challenged.

In the nineteenth century, the figure of the Titan came back in Romantic literature to name that subjective individuality who struggles to impose his will to the external forces of destiny and nature, pretty much like Prometheus did. The inner secret for being a Titan is to have a world to fight *against*: this defines Thanos as a character. Differently from Prometheus, he succeeded in killing the Gods: this makes him very modern.

26
Thanos's Mistake

SUSAN HEMPINSTALL AND THOMAS STEIN

We first encounter Thanos in the Marvel Cinematic Universe's *Infinity Saga*, and we soon realize that he's being set up as the BBEG—the *Big Bad Evil Guy* whom the heroes must ultimately overcome.

What's not so readily apparent is that under several historical traditions and from the viewpoint of the philosopher Friedrich Nietzsche, Thanos's aims would not be seen as evil *per se*, but the rightful activities of a noble leader looking out for the greater good.

In the arc of the Marvel movies, Thanos's aims are gradually revealed. He is initially portrayed merely as a backer of other *Big Bads* such as *Ronan the Accuser* in *Guardians of the Galaxy*, and backing Loki's effort to invade Earth in exchange for retrieving the Tesseract in *The Avengers*. It's only in *Avengers: Infinity War* that Thanos's ultimate aim is revealed. He is on a campaign to collect all the Infinity Stones so he can achieve his ultimate desire of bringing balance to the universe by erasing half of all peoples from existence, thus placing their populations in balance with their ecosystems.

As it is later explained when we find out how Gamora became his adopted daughter, balancing the universe had long been Thanos's aim. He had been working towards his end by accumulating armies and systematically visiting planets and culling one-half of the population. Thanos adopted Gamora when his army visited her home planet of Zen-Whoberi and wiped out one-half of its population. During his culling missions, Thanos realized that the power of the Infinity Stones would offer a more expedient method of accomplishing his aim, and so the acquisition of the Stones became a more efficient means to his desired end.

What End Does Thanos Have in Mind?

Thanos is operating out of personal experience. As he recounts to Doctor Strange in *Avengers: Infinity War*, his own home planet Titan had been beautiful. However, Thanos explains *"Titan was like most planets. Too many mouths, and not enough to go around. And when we faced extinction, I offered a solution."* His solution was a culling of fifty percent of the population by a method he describes as, *". . . at random, dispassionate, fair to rich and poor alike."* Not surprisingly, the people of Titan rejected his proposal. *"They called me a madman."* Yet Thanos was not wrong in his prediction. As the movie scene depicts the desolated state of Titan, we hear Thanos's voiceover, *"And what I predicted came to pass."*

Thanos can be seen to have learned two things from this experience. First, that his predictions about what would happen were accurate. Second, that language was insufficient to change peoples' behavior or make them take action to prevent the ecosystem collapse. The people of Titan would not listen to his reasoning. And, as any peace officer knows, if language does not suffice and the issue is important, then force is a recourse if the issue is important enough. So Thanos assembles armies and begins his campaign of systematically visiting planets and culling one-half of their population by force.

Thanos Is Capable of Strong Feelings

First, he loves his adopted daughter, Gamora, as evidenced by her sacrifice at his hand being sufficient to attain him the Soul Stone.

Second, he is quite capable of becoming annoyed when sufficiently irritated. When battling the Avengers in *Avengers: Endgame* Thanos explains to Steve Rogers Captain America, *"In all my years of conquest . . . violence . . . slaughter . . . It was never personal. But I'll tell you now . . . what I'm about to do to your stubborn, annoying little planet . . . I'm gonna enjoy it. Very, very much."*

Imposing His Chosen End on the Universe

This question is critical, and it is here that the philosopher Nietzsche has much to contribute to the discussion.

In his *Genealogy of Morality*, Nietzsche distinguishes between *Master* and *Slave* moralities. *Master* morality valorizes the virtues of excellence including traits such as courage, fortitude, pride, physical strength, and strength of will. The key point of excellence was to be in possession of sufficient abilities so as to cause to come into being that which you desired, not necessarily in oppression of others, but perceiving their own desiring as sufficient justification to take action.

And what of others' opinions? To *Master* morality, your own opinion is paramount. There is no impediment to the person working from *Master* morality considering the points and opinions raised by others, but *Master* morality concerns itself with consequences—and these consequences are weighed against the ends desired and in the end made by the individual.

The classical tales of Greek heroes in the *Iliad* and the *Odyssey* celebrate heroes of this type such as Agamemnon, Achilles, and Ulysses. In a telling dialog described by the Athenian historian Thucydides, when a delegation from Athens attempted to persuade the rulers of the island of Melos to surrender, there is a statement which has become famous which shows the *Master* morality in action. The Athenian delegation was delivering an ultimatum—either surrender and pay tribute to Athens, or be destroyed (as the Athenians were worried about Melos supporting their enemy—the Spartans). The rulers of Melos raise a number of arguments, but as regard the morality of the ultimatum the Athenian delegation states "The strong do what they will, the weak suffer what they must." In the end, despite the Athenians pointing out that there was no shame in acquiescing to an overwhelmingly stronger force, especially if reasonable terms are being offered, the rulers declined. Subsequently Melos was invaded, conquered, and the island colonized by Athenian subjects, pragmatically demonstrating the point.

A key aspect of *Master* morality for both Nietzsche and the Greek classics was that of attending to virtues of worth. The admiration of strong-willed persons that accomplished their ends, and the greater the accomplishments, the more the valorizing. Those that were not great were neglected, not worthy of attention—the also-rans as opposed to the victors in the competition. Accomplishing worthy consequences—that was worth giving attention and renown to. The remainder exists as background and context and Nietzsche points out that almost all the ancient Greek words denoting the lower orders of society are related to variants on the word for "unhappy". Not bad, not evil, but *unhappy*—as in unhappy circumstances.

And what of *Slave* morality? Nietzsche describes this as the morality of the oppressed. Not being able to win the contest for supremacy, the oppressed value traits such as kindness, patience, humility, altruism, and generosity. In oppressed morality, actions are weighed not in terms of consequences, as these are likely not under the control of the person, but according to intentions.

Nietzsche contends that as well as the *tend-and-befriend* attitude towards others that are oppressed, *Slave* morality possesses an attitude towards the powerful that originates in *ressentiment*, a borrowed word from the French which corresponds to the English word 'resentment'. This attitude is antagonistic towards those external forces that oppose and oppress it, and proceeds to portray those acting from *Master* morality in as bad a light as possible. As such, while *Master* morality contrasts the 'good' with the 'not-so-good' or 'bad', Slave morality contrasts the 'good' (their values) with 'evil'. Those who impose their will on others, or ignore the desires of those weaker than them, are not merely oblivious because of focus on other consequences, but evil.

How Do the Avengers Fit into These Nietzschean Moralities?

The Avengers are heroes of the oppressed. They are individually powerful in different ways; however this power is directed in support and defense of individuals and groups. Their construal level (the level at which they interpret actions and behavior) is at the level of personal impacts on people. (Understandably, this also emerges from the dramatization aspect of superhero movies so as to make them "relatable' to audiences, however their stance still nicely exemplifies the point.)

In their actions and responses we see that the Avengers embody the virtues of bravery, kindness, and altruistic use of their powers to protect and benefit others. They do not seek authority over others and are generally humble (Tony Stark's showmanship notwithstanding).

A very telling overlap and contrast between the two moralities is shown towards the end of *Avengers: Infinity War* when Thanos has arrived on Titan and is being held in dialog with Doctor Strange as a setup for an ambush. Thanos and Doctor Strange are discussing the planet they are standing on, and Doctor Strange says *"Let me guess. Your home?"* And Thanos replies reminiscently *"It was. And it was beautiful."* Thanos uses the Reality Stone to recreate the green lawns, intact buildings, water-filled ponds, strolling citizens, and other futuristic utopian looking structures. He goes on to say *"Titan was like most planets. Too many mouths, and not enough to go around. And when we faced extinction, I offered a solution."* Doctor Strange replies cuttingly: *"Genocide!"* and Thanos replies to him *"But at random, dispassionate, fair to rich and poor alike. They called me a madman. And what I predicted came to pass."*

In response to Doctor Strange's sarcastic response, Thanos goes on to say *"With all six stones, I could simply snap my fingers, and they would all cease to exist. I call that . . . mercy."* Pushing for justification, Doctor Strange asks *"And then what?"* Thanos replies *"I finally rest . . . and watch the sun set on a grateful universe. The hardest choices require the strongest wills."*

"The hardest choices require the strongest wills." is not a reference to Thanos denying the responsibility for what he is undertaking as a personal project, but that he is acknowledging the magnitude of difficulty he faces in having to choose. Not an easy choice, but a *hard* choice. A choice like a ship's officer allowing no more people in a lifeboat, or a CEO having to lay off half her workers.

And how does Doctor Strange respond? He summons his magic shields in preparation for battle and says *"I think . . . you'll find . . . our will . . . equal to yours!"* Curiously, Doctor Strange doesn't argue that there are better choices, even though he has reviewed 14,000,605 alternative futures. Doctor Strange doesn't argue *consequences*, despite the key point highlighted by Avengers, which is that Thanos's method involves the *intention* to do genocide.

Instead Doctor Strange frames it as a battle of wills, contending that the Avengers' *will* is stronger than Thanos's *will.* Doctor Strange's contention resonates with *Master* morality and the axiom that "The strong do what they will, and the weak suffer what they must."

So, How Is Thanos Wrong?

H.L. Mencken, the twentieth-century Sage of Baltimore has been quoted as saying:

> For every complex problem there is an answer that is clear, simple, and wrong.

The balance of a population with its environs is a complex problem.

Thanos's plan is clear. He is set to reduce all populations (of people) to half their present quantity in order to place them in "balance" with their environments.

Thanos's plan is simple; reduce the population by fifty percent. It deserves mentioning that at multiple times in the movies, several characters, for example Black Widow, mischaracterize Thanos's aim as to kill fifty percent of all life in the universe. However, it is obvious that he is not proposing to reduce half of all living things, since that would not change the existing balance between *peoples* and their environments. In the "snappening" we saw only people fading into ash, not trees and other plants.

Thanos's plan is wrong. His fifty percent solution turns out to be a categorical error. It is a technical fix to a relationship problem—an answer that is clear, simple, and wrong.

Is Culling Truly Effective?

Thanos believes that he has confirmation of the effectiveness of his culling. In his conversation with Gamora she protests *"No! No! We were happy on my home planet."* Thanos replies, *"Going to bed hungry, scrounging for scraps. Your planet was on the brink of collapse. I'm the one who stopped that. Do you know what's happened since then? The children born have known nothing but full bellies and clear skies. It's a paradise".* Justifying his actions, Thanos continues, *"Little one, it's a simple calculus. This universe is finite, its resources finite. If life is left unchecked, life will cease to exist. It needs correction."*

The parallels with which Thanos engages planetary populations is strikingly similar to some events on real Earth.

St. Matthew Island is a remote island in the Bering Sea belonging to the US state of Alaska. The island has a land area of 137.857 square miles, making it the forty-third largest island in the United States.

In 1944, twenty-nine reindeer were introduced to the island by the United States Coast Guard to provide an emergency food source. The Coast Guard abandoned the island a few years later, leaving the reindeer. Subsequently, the reindeer population rose to about six thousand by 1963 and then died off in the next two years to forty-two animals. A scientific study attributed the population crash to the limited food supply in interaction with climatic factors (the winter of 1963–64 was exceptionally severe in the region). By the 1980s, the reindeer population had completely died out. Environmentalists see this as an example of overpopulation in excess of the carrying capacity of the island. Without natural predators (for example wolves or mountain lions) the deer population continued to grow unchecked until they had exhausted the vegetation they needed to survive, and they starved.

Contemporary jurisdictions face similar problems. In the Canadian province of Ontario, wolf and cougar populations are too low to keep white-tailed deer herds in check, and authorities use various measures to cull the population to prevent destruction of habitat.

The consequences of the unchecked reindeer population on St. Matthew Island are straightforward to understand and wildlife management authorities wrestle with the ways and means needed to manage the situation. Their concern is not at the level of the individual deer, but instead at the level of the herd as a population and the environs the herd occupies.

A similar situation can be seen when companies find themselves having to downsize in order to survive financial conditions insufficient to maintain the business. As opposed to having the company fail, a CEO may choose to lay off half the workers. The net result is to enable company survival and allow the continued employment of half the workers, as opposed to the loss of jobs of all the workers. A hard decision, certainly, but one that may be required in order to avoid worse consequences.

As Thanos said, *"It was never personal."* Nor is it when authorities are culling deer or company management is laying off personnel. Any "goodness" inheres at a higher construal level than the impact on individuals.

How Does This "Balance" Really Work?

In his famous article *The Tragedy of the Commons*, biologist Garrett Hardin argues for the necessity of population control as the answer to the problem of expected growth of the human population and the finite natural resources of our planet.

Hardin's thesis is that while some problems have technical solutions, other problems, in particular social problems, have no technical solutions. The increasing population versus finite natural resources problem falls under this latter category.

Hardin's argument is that the carrying capacity of the world or commons is finite. Our natural resources are fixed. Earth can only support a finite population within its means. Therefore, since the commons cannot be increased, population growth must be reduced to zero once we approach the carrying capacity of the land.

How Does Carrying Capacity Work?

Carrying capacity has to do with how renewable an environment is, with respect to the demands upon it. If the moss consumed on St. Matthew Island can keep ahead of the consumption by the reindeer, then all is well. "Balance" is not so much an issue as that of not taking more than can be regenerated. If a species grows to an extent that it exceeds the carrying capacity of that environment, the principle of carrying capacity necessitates that a species either moves or dies out. The former option was not available to the reindeer.

Unrestricted population growth is typically exponential in nature and can be described with a percentage growth rate. For example, a population growing at 3.5 percent per year will double in only twenty years.

How Does Apex Predator Population Control Work?

In the example of St. Matthew Island (which Hardin makes note of in his famous article), the lack of predators doomed the reindeer population to grow and then die off. Yet this begs the question: *If there were predators on the island, such as wolves, then what would limit* their *population*? Why wouldn't the wolf population continue to increase until it consumed the reindeer population and caused a die-off of both populations? The answer turns out to be that apex predators—those predators at the top of the food chain with no natural predators themselves—will self-limit. Wolf packs limit cubs to those of the alpha-female. Lions kill all the cubs sired by other males in their prides. Cougars drive off other cougars from their hunting ranges. Self-regulation emerges from *within* the apex species as opposed to being imposed from without.

And this is where Thanos has made his categorical error. By cutting populations in half, he is effectively sending them back in time to where their population on the planet was only half of what it presently was. And what did it historically do from that point? It grew to the present point. So Thanos's intervention is merely a stopgap, a reset to an earlier point. It does not address the fundamental aspect that the peoples of the planets, as apex predators must devise a means to self-limit.

Thanos—Moral, Yet Categorically Wrong

Thanos's error was not in prediction of consequences. He predicted devastation on Titan, an advanced planet, and it ensued. Thanos's error was not that of not caring—he wanted to restore balance so that life could continue as opposed to destroying itself (and by life we can presume he meant the peoples whose populations he culled.) Thanos's error was arguably not even without morality. As he said *"The hardest decisions require the strongest wills."* Thanos affirms the responsibility for his actions, and follows *Master* morality in seeing itself as the source of its own justification.

Thanos's error was, first, that he was attempting to impose a solution from an external point, and second, he confused quantity with relationship. Thanos was imposing a numerical technical solution on a social problem. The problem is social in nature as it is a function of within-species behavior. The peoples must make arrangements to limit their own populations, or once the external limits are removed they will recommence their unchecked growth.

As well as a relationship to each other and future generations, there is the relationship of the peoples to the carrying capacity of their planet. The arbitrary reduction by fifty percent pays no respect to the actual state of balance between the peoples and the carrying capacity. Some planets may already be below carrying capacity, and no reduction is necessary. Some planets may be at the point of the population being four to five times the carrying capacity (for example, present day Earth, if everyone was to consume at the North American rate), and a culling by fifty percent would still not be enough to achieve the "balance" sought.

Thanos did not conceive of his intervention as an ongoing solution. After effecting the "snappening" he retired to his garden world where he destroyed the Infinity Stones so that his work could not be undone. We can conclude from his behavior that he considered that only a single balancing "correction" was necessary.

Thanos's Mistake

Thanos conceives that unchecked population growth will lead to disaster on a planet. His foretelling was proven on his home planet of Titan. Thanos is soured regarding language as a means of resolving this problem, as he tried warning the population of Titan and failed to convince them. Thus, as in situations where language is insufficient and the outcome is too important to abandon, Thanos moved to use force. He assembled armies and commenced culling populations, then discovered that he could more effectively accomplish his project with the Infinity Stones. After overcoming the resistance of the Avengers and Guardians of the Galaxy, Thanos procured the

Infinity Stones and accomplished his outcome. Subsequently he retired to his garden planet and also retired the Infinity Stones, or so he thought.

Thanos's actions embody *Master* morality, imposing his own will towards a desired end upon the universe. Thanos was supremely masterful, obtaining the Infinity Stones and achieving the consequences he desired. To the Avengers and the Guardians of the Galaxy Thanos's intentions of killing half the population on every planet were clearly evil, exactly as appropriate from a Slave morality perspective. Yet Thanos was oblivious to this argument. And in the end, even notwithstanding the Avengers' ultimate success, Thanos's means contained a categorical error in that the balance he desired would not come to pass due to his confusing quantity with relationship.

27

I Am Inevitable

Rodrigo Farías Rivas

Thanos's "I am inevitable" in *Avengers: Endgame* sums up his complex psychological and narrative characterization in *Infinity War*. Even more, the villain's "inevitability," just as is evoked by his name's similarity to *thanatos* (death) itself, represents the inescapable nature of death as that which, at least according to Thanos, could bring balance to the excesses of sentient life.

So we should not overlook the radical nature of the death that Thanos represents: yes, it is the strength and cunning to kill Asgardian gods, and, once in possession of all the Infinity Stones, the ability to dispose of life in the universe at will, yet its truly chilling effectiveness is rather due to what in the end is Thanos's meta-textual power, that of vanishing characters not from their universe, but from *ours*. In an almost self-aware manner, as if objecting to the flimsy nature of comic-book death as contingent on the needs of the next story, Thanos murders Loki and says to Thor: "No resurrections this time."

And yet by *Endgame*'s transition from its second to its third act, Thanos's use of the stones to destroy the stones leads to inevitable death having been overcome by a time *heist*—a heist *through* time designed to bring the stones back from a 'past' whose hypothetical changes cannot affect the present, hence a past only able to improve it by having the stones immediately returned to the exact moment they were taken from (a restoration without which, as the Ancient One explains, the new, autonomous timelines would be left unprotected). In this way, *the inevitability of death represented by Thanos is challenged and overcome by a twist in time.*

The French psychoanalyst Jacques Lacan, following Sigmund Freud's obscure notion of a "death drive," and the

French philosopher Gilles Deleuze, following Friedrich Nietzsche's even more obscure "eternal return," have both tried to think the relation between the death of life and time out of joint, and in both cases through the topological surface whose successful modeling leads Stark to exclaim "Shit!," his very own eureka at discovering the viability of quantum tunneling through the fourth-dimensional spacetime continuum.

Whose Death?

Infinity War and *Endgame* are ambiguous as to what exactly is this "sentient life," half of which Thanos causes to vanish. While Ant-Man interprets singing birds as sign of the success of Professor Hulk's snap, we're never really told that it is life as *pathos* (including animal or vegetal sentience as the capability to have perceptual experiences) which has been cut in half. For the sake of this argument, let's begin within the Marvel Cinematic Universe's anthropomorphism and simply say that *people* die.

Yet the German philosopher Martin Heidegger has taught us to distrust platitudes like "We all die" as a comfortable *evasion* from having to face death. As Heidegger argues in *Being and Time*, to say that "people die" as people paint, love, or create comic books, means mistaking the most individual of ontological possibilities for general possibilities that can be actualized, deferred, transferred, or even talked about after their occurrence.

But then, whose death are we talking about? Heideggerian existence as temporal possibility and inalienable death as its limit means understanding "personhood" in what is primarily, and paradoxically, a non-personal way: being-there, or what Heidegger calls "Dasein," is not a self-presenting ego to which I can point to "inwards"—for example, to deduce that *I exist* from the living presence of an *I think*—but a transcendental horizon of disclosed Being where possibilities both ontic (to put on an iron suit) and ontological (to become Iron Man) *concern me* in a circular and tautologically normative way that thus appears as the very temporal meaning of the being-there that is in each case *mine*. It is in this primary sense of not being a subject nor an object but their self-referential space in-between that Dasein can be said to be an "individual."

Once understood as *my* death, that of the singular being that is in each case *mine*, death seems to be a unique possibility that precludes all others in a particularly radical and ominous way. Even more, the common interpretation of death as something which "happens to people" means missing precisely that the most individualizing of ontological possibilities, the possibility not of people dying but of *my* death, is by that same token the possibility of the absolute end of my possibilities. "Death is the possibility of the absolute impossibility of Dasein," says Heidegger. In this strict sense, only *I* die. And as Heidegger shows, in liminal experiences like the anxiety-ridden confrontation of my being-towards-death, the possibility of impossibility appears to me as the most certain one, and thus also a new, second-order ontological possibility: that of *appropriating* the said limit and what its projective transgression unveils, which means a radical individualization capable of turning finite existence—and in its entirety, as it is now seen from the vantage point of pure impossibility—from heteronomous inauthenticity, living as people do, to autonomous authenticity, living as *I* am called to do.

But there are problems with this approach. Notice the odd possibility of *apprehending impossibility*, of stepping *beyond* the death that is in each case mine in the existential recognition of the limits it sets to my possibilities, and then glancing back at the totality of my existence and being able to draw new existential possibilities from this (now appropriated) ontological impossibility. *Death is conceived as an uncrossable line, while it is precisely its projected crossing what allows for the trip back in authentic appropriation.*

This sketchy move will lead a French writer, Maurice Blanchot, to reverse Heidegger's formula into death as *the impossibility of possibility*. Critical consequences follow: not only that Heideggerian authenticity is always threatened by inauthenticity (since the perception of the totality of my existence is impossible given that, by definition, death is not a place from which something could be seen), but that the very characterization of Dasein as an ontological space of possibilities becomes thwarted by a death that cannot be appropriated, that cannot even be said to happen to *me*.

So whose death are we discussing? Well, *not mine*. Since only living I can execute any possibility, I can never appropriate death just as I cannot utter the words "I died." Indeed, death is not an event *from* which I can talk, but one *about* which I can talk. And we all do, constantly. The "one dies" that Heidegger taught us to consider a merely vulgar way of thinking about death shows its "authentic" side: the *impersonal* character of death is the only experience of it with which I can possibly relate, which means that inauthentic talk about death seems rather constitutive.

More important still is the paradoxical logic of death, for even if *I* don't die—for when "I" die I'm not longer the "I" that could utter the words "I die"—*I am nevertheless always dying*. Blanchot thus suggests death as a *mourir*, a dying, an anonymous passivity in the very life of words insofar they can only bring about the presence of meaning through the radical ontological void that is the absence of reference.

Twisted in itself by the paradoxically productive impossibility that is death as introduced by language, "life" stops appearing as ecstatic existence, the disclosure of normative possibilities within the temporal horizon of Being, and becomes a *living* undistinguishable from a certain *dying* —a *curved* topological space that means aiming objections at Dasein that curiously echo Heidegger's own critique of the Cartesian and Kantian subject as a self-evident "now." Against Dasein as ontological care graspable in its self-referential totality, normative circularity appears decentered around a kernel that turns death from the limit of life to its *extimate* core—that is, one that is *neither external nor internal*. A life in Moebian "duplicity" with death: these Lacanian consequences allow us to thank Blanchot for leading us to a definite answer to our question. For if we can even predicate sameness to what is always tainted by otherness just as the "individual" is always punctured by a drift from itself, then "death" belongs to the same that "lives": *it*.

Potential Impersonal Death

From Blanchot, an impossible Heideggerian death nevertheless capable of authentic appropriation becomes something closer to a Hegelian death, one not only incapable of being projectively experienced in anxiety while also disclosing the totality of existence, but one whose paradoxical "presence" drives the very movement of language as the necessary negativity out of which symbolic denaturalization brings about meaning in the first place. Every word is a cenotaph: in his reboot of Freudian psychoanalysis, Jacques Lacan shares this Hegel-inspired understanding of the mortifying labor of language. Consequently, whether considered the word to be the murder of the thing it presents, the subject as suspended by linguistic chains traversing his speech in gaps whose autonomous logic may be called *unconscious*, or the signifier itself as the materiality by which a structural point of emptiness metonymically weaves a world of desire and its metaphorical symptomatic formations, what Lacanian psychoanalysis teaches is that its aporetic subject is not phenomenologically enclosed by existential impossibility, but *driven* by the symbolic death that insists in the dialectical unfolding of desiring life.

Death, in a word, is not a phenomenological limit nor much less a biological occurrence, but brought about by our being constituted by language. Lacan is clear: when discourse skips a bit and the speaker suddenly stops recognizing itself in its words, "subjectivity" flickers as always-already dead just as language imposes itself as an otherness that vivifies *insofar* it mortifies. Similarly, the chains of signifiers that clinical phenomena like these enact reveal the symbolic logic determining the twisting paths of psychical, phantasmatic life. In his 1959–1960 seminar on the ethics of psychoanalysis, Lacan calls this symbolic death giving life to desire and culture a *second* death: not the (biological or phenomenological) death of the individual, but an impersonal, spectral, *undead* death that accompanies the autonomous logic of unconscious desire as its very condition of possibility—indeed, this seminar's paradigmatic example is Antigone and the verdict that, through her social death, curses her to immurement. In any case, the key point here will be that, at its most radical, the death brought about by signifying overdetermination insists not as existential but as *logical* impossibility: an empty marker of linguistic incompleteness that the logic of the signifier can only orbit.

So symbolic death is not exactly the same as the *death drive*. If the former constitutes unconscious desire, the latter marks an insistence in desire of the primordially missed encounter that the workings of symbolic death then come to regulate, defer, and encircle. Consider this "life of desire" we've mentioned as psychoanalysis describes it and intervenes in it: entire lifetimes march towards self-fulfilled prophecies, new experiences provide the meaning of past ones, current experiences gain sense through the traumatic irruption of the future, time itself bends as linear consciousness becomes subject to the synchrony of the signifier. It is because of the signifier's constitution and determination of the dialectic of desire that—within ontogenetic history, psychical reality, *and* the psychoanalytic cure—the torsion of time becomes possible. Psychoanalysis, then, allows for its own circular retroactivity, closed causal loops, temporal paradoxes, and other sorts of tropes dominating time travel fiction. In this context, if determined by the death that defines language desire becomes one topological surface twisted in itself, the death drive could be considered its single *border*. Or more precisely, if the drive is the topological function of the rim bordering desire's time-twisting vicissitudes, the *death* that defines the logical structure of every drive does so insofar its search for complete libidinal satisfaction—the death of desire—is structurally impossible.

Ultimately, then, psychoanalytic death and the looped temporality of desire coincide in their Moebian topology, death becoming a death *drive* in that it insists not as that which creates the space of meaning that the signifier determines, but as the signifier's own constitutive incompleteness throwing desire once again in search of its perpetually lost object-cause. This is why when it comes to energetic imagery, Lacan is only willing to compare the iterative insistence of the (death) drive as logical impossibility with *potential* energy, that is, with a structural tension unsurmountable by the Moebian circulation of signifiers. The psychoanalytic cure, then, becomes oriented by this topological circuit: as Lacan explains in his seminar from 1964–1965, a *beyond* of psychoanalysis would mean "a psychoanalysis that has looped this loop to its end. The loop must be run through several times." Yet doesn't it seem we still remain strangely close to Heidegger in the sight of libidinal loops that, exhausted, can nevertheless be appropriated by a now-transformed subject? And is this transformation a change in subjective position or rather a more radically iterative dissolution of the supposed "subject" itself?

While traversing his own phantasmatic loops, Tony Stark proclaims "I am Iron Man" at the ends of *Iron Man*, *Iron Man 3*, and *Avengers: Endgame*. In this latter case, the spectral guilt behind Stark's repeated effort to put "a suit of armor around the world"—an impossible guilt itself traceable to his original 2008 recognition of what his weapons were actually doing and subsequent abandonment of their manufacturing—redeems itself in his sacrifice. A new subject tired of his self-boycotting efforts at protecting the Earth, Tony Stark's guilt, in other words, is redeemed in a subjectivizing leap in which the very temporal folds previously traversed show to have led to an ultimate appropriation of (his) time and death. Yet even if we follow the moral at the end of *Iron Man 3* that it is the man that makes the suit, it is still *as* Iron Man that Stark exhausts his symbolic determinations, goes to the deadly real of his desire, and brings forth a genuine ethical act. It's still the undecidable knot tying man and suit within diachronic identity what destroys itself to defeat Thanos and change subsequent, not only biological, but *symbolic* life. So the question arises: is this heroic (*qua* sacrificial) and sovereign (*qua* debt-redeeming) approach to subjective transformation the only thing we can expect from the temporal challenge to death implicit in their topological unity? Like the

Avengers daring to conceive the time heist, can we raise the bet and make of the very dice of time and death *cosmic*? Moving away from Stark's all-too-Christ-like sacrifice and towards a Dionysian (time) machine, it is perhaps in Steve Rogers' joyful consumption of repetition through the circular consummation of his fate that something different lies.

Kinetic Impersonal Death

At its worst, Lacan's Hegel-inspired thanatology serves to defy Heideggerian autonomy while ultimately repeating its problems in its avoidance of the dangerous consequences that may derive from the Moebian logic of psychoanalytic death. At its best, the latter indeed leads to a theory and clinic of impersonal subjectivity oriented towards the paradoxical subjectivation of the para-ontological and iterative waste of a "dialectical exhaustion of being," while still remaining too tied to Freud and Hegel to consider its non-, anti-, and over-human dimension as it is revealed not by the dying proper to the signifier, but by the one proper to its *failure* —see, for example, Lacan's cautious musings on the lamella as a myth for life-giving death by the end of the eleventh seminar. At worst, in sum, residual autonomy insists in spite of radical heteronomy, while at best, radical heteronomy still fails to break the Moebian strip free from the subjective form. And finally, rounding off this analysis, although Blanchot acknowledges the eternally returning death that (the) writing at the edge of language opens, he considers its overhuman significance a metaphysical confusion sometimes amendable by Hegelian speculative dialectics, sometimes by Heideggerian historized ontology.

Which leads us to Gilles Deleuze. Following the Nietzschean notion of a morphology of becoming in order to sidestep the apories of post-Kantian phenomenology while also following Hume, Spinoza, Sartre, and Bergson in pursuing it to its most rigorous, almost self-abolishing version (transcendental empiricism), Deleuze indeed conceived of death and time in an internal—and no longer merely external yet fundamental—relation. Desire does not "desire" death, as a pre-Lacanian, Freudian formulation of the death drive might suggest. Instead, and in what amounts to a properly post-Lacanian insight, *death itself desires in a Moebian temporal structure that Nietzsche discovered and named eternal return.* Meaning that not only the personal death but also the anthropomorphism with which these remarks started were destined to be pulverized.

Deleuze's Nietzsche-influenced thought searches for a philosophy of phenomena-productive, sub-representational intensities, fluxes, and singularities. Indeed, several of his works celebrate Blanchot's finding —"Death as event, inseparable from the past and future into which it is divided, never present, an impersonal death"—while further exploring its Nietzschean significance and the revaluation it means for the entire problematic of death, time, and desire. In *Difference and Repetition*, for example, Thanatos names eternal return as the third of a series of passive temporal syntheses in which the habitual-mnemonic tautology formed by the actual present and the virtual past is shattered by difference as the time of the future, iterative death thus appearing as "a pure form— the empty form of time." Similarly, in *The Logic of Sense*, desexualized and neutral libido constitutes thought as an impersonal and metaphysical surface of pure sense, a "speculative" death drive that in an undecidable torsion binds resonating series in "the advent of Univocity—that is, the Event which communicates the univocity of being to language." These gestures follow an evident Nietzschean thrust, meaning that the twisted faces of the Lacanian spectrality of phantasmatic reality—the sameness impossibly demanded by the drive and the difference disappointedly offered by desire—become a joyous double affirmation as the very motor of becoming: the dice throw affirms chance, purely differential becoming as a million impersonal, intensive, eternally returning little deaths, while the affirmation of its landing wills it as necessary, and thus identity, precisely, as that which does not return.

The two sides of this single conceptual surface become clearer in the way *Anti-Oedipus* returns to the eternal return of difference as a *selective* principle in Deleuze's 1962 book *Nietzsche and Philosophy*. In their reformulation of *Difference and Repetition*'s three passive syntheses of time, Deleuze and former Lacanian analyst Félix Guattari ascribe their conception of the death drive to unproductive halts interrupting the anarchic, affective connections of the machinic production of the real. As zero-intensities, these failures threaten organization by carrying a *model* of death —a full and sterile body without organs that is also the recording surface for organizational forms themselves—, which means that in this specific sense, iterative death as pure empty time does indeed "desire." But if intensive becomings presuppose zero-intensity, they are also a site of change: "The *experience* of death is the most common of occurrences in the unconscious, precisely because it occurs . . . in every passage or becoming, in every intensity as passage or becoming" (my italics). And here, differential selection conjoins the impersonal and productive force of death in a third synthesis of consumption-consummation in which, perpetually pulverized by the ring of recurrence, a residual, fortuitous, and nomadic subject wills it all as necessary in the most rigorous form of what Klossowski called a "renewed version of metempsychosis." Deleuze and Guattari explain this schizologic: "It is not a matter of identifying with various historical personages, but rather identifying the names of history with zones of intensity on the body without organs; and each time Nietzsche-as-subject exclaims: 'They're *me*! So it's *me*!'".

A multiverse within immanence: that desiring production as onto-hetero-genesis evokes the dice throw of the wave-function collapse calls precisely to the relation that interests us, that of becoming as a transcendental field of eternally returning death not only to the quantum multiverses through which the Avengers loop inevitable death against itself, but to the field of undecidability *between* them. Up until now, it is Doctor Strange who is getting closer to the madness of exploring the multiverse, and we can wonder how much the Marvel Cinematic Universe could push its possibilities towards what a "Nietzschean Cinematic Universe" would promise in "eternal confirmation and seal"—let us also add that, on its part, the Klossowskian notion of a conspiracy of eternal return is aimed at the logical yet impossible advent of the overhuman.

There can be no model, then, but if pure time is death selecting its own return, there is a basic normative distinction in the fact that the innocent irresponsibility of non-linear causation lies so far beyond heroic, sovereign, still all-too-human subjective destitution.

Which means that the inevitability closer to being engraved in the very fabric of reality does not belong to Thanos or Iron Man and their personal deaths, but to Steve Rogers, Peggy Carter, and their cosmic dance.[1]

---

[1] This is for Stephanie.

VI

Character

28

How Captain Rogers Became a Good Man

REBECCA SHEARER

> Whatever happens tomorrow you must promise me one thing. That you will stay who you are. Not a perfect soldier, but a good man.
>
> —DR. ERSKINE

This is the instruction Dr. Erskine gives Steve Rogers before he undergoes the process that turns him into Captain America. The super-soldier that Erskine envisioned was never meant to be the perfect soldier that the Army was hoping for. He was meant to be a good man. Captain America's arc in the eight Marvel Cine-matic Universe movies he appears in, traces his search for what it means to be a "good man" in a superhuman way.

The super serum is meant to enhance every part of Steve Rogers, and bring each cell to its absolute extreme, muscle bone, and brain cells. This way he'll reach peak physical ability and the peak of whatever his character is capable of being. Neither of these happens immediately, with the mental elements taking the longest to develop because of their complexity. Captain America is strong right away, but that doesn't mean he doesn't learn fighting skills as he goes along, becoming more effective.

Likewise, he starts as the good man he always was, but he has a black-and-white sense of duty, which is a part of moral absolutism, which is the expectation for a good soldier because a soldier is expected to follow orders without question. However, in the real world, the best choice is not always clear, and being a good person often means living in a grey area and the painful contradictions that come from balancing love and duty. The reality of this grey area is what Captain America has to wade through as he grows toward being a truly good man.

Even though Erskine recognizes that at heart Steve Rogers is closer to a good man than a bad man, he recognizes that the idea of being a truly good man is as aspirational as being a perfect soldier at this pre-serum point in Rogers development. These concepts are presented as the two directions that Steve Rogers can take as he becomes Captain America. Since he is good at heart, the serum doesn't make him evil like Red Skull. He's also not like Bucky, who seems to be morally neutral or average so that when he's given the serum, it doesn't make him better or worse. It's the brainwashing that makes him bad, and the influence of Steve that makes him good again. The serum is only physical for him because he isn't overwhelmingly good or bad. He's normal, like the rest of us.

Because Steve Rogers is naturally more of a good person than average, the options for who he will become after the serum is injected isn't a good person or a bad person, but a good person or a perfect soldier. It's the difference between moral absolutism and moral consequentialism. This idea can be confused with the idea that the outcome is the *only* thing that matters, but that's more chaos than any kind of actual morality. Most of us can understand how that kind of morality doesn't work. Life is complicated, and moral questions have complicated answers.

With each Marvel Cinematic Universe film that he appears in, Captain America moves further along the spectrum from the "perfect soldier" he was told to be towards the good man he was designed to be. In *Avengers: Endgame* Steve Rogers completes his transformation into the optimally good man, and this is proven when he is able to summon Mjölnir. Cap is worthy of Thor's hammer, and the pain the comes from moral uncertainty has made him worthy.

Steve Rogers Reporting for Duty

By *Endgame,* no one seems to give much thought to where and how Steve Rogers started his journey as Captain America. But without the context of where he started, where he ended up is less meaningful, and less interesting to us as viewers. Characters who are stagnant are boring. We especially like characters that start like us (or worse) and end up spectacular. It gives us a conscious or unconscious hope that we can also be amazing. Not necessarily in a superhuman way, but in an impressive for a normal person way.

Steve Rogers in *Captain America: The First Avenger* has a worse than average life. He's tiny, sick, and all his family have died. His best and maybe only friend, Bucky Barnes, is about to leave for war. No matter how badly Steve wants to join the Army and feel useful, they just won't let him. We can all relate, to some extent, to feeling insufficient, rejected, and having experienced loss. We can all relate to Steve at the beginning of his hero's journey.

Rogers and Aristotle

According to Aristotle's ideas of virtue (what makes you a good person), the different virtues are all determined by how you respond to negative influences on your life. Aristotle believed that no one is born with any fully formed virtue and that all virtue has to be learned. But some people are born with a natural tendency towards a virtue, just as some people are born naturally athletic or naturally musical.

Dr. Erskine is immediately able to see that Steve Rogers already possesses the virtues of courage and justice. He's willing to sacrifice his well-being (courage) and stand up for himself and others (justice). This assures the team that Rogers won't turn out like Red Skull and makes Dr. Erskine hopefully that Rogers can develop all of the virtues. Once you've developed a few virtues, the others are often a lot easier.

The problem with Steve Rogers is that he's almost too pure. Sure, he's experienced pain and loss, but he hasn't experienced the moral stress and paradox that leads to fully realized virtue. Aristotle also suggested that each virtue rests in the middle of two vices. That means that virtues are by nature living in the grey area between extremes, and the extremes themselves are therefore undesirable. To Aristotle, the very idea of binaries was problematic. Simplifying anything as starkly as good versus evil is dangerous because we all know how much nuance is in between.

Some of the virtues and their vices are:

- **Courage: can be defined as bravery and valor, or standing up to something that causes fear. Sits in between cowardice and rashness.**

- **Restraint: can be defined as self-control and discretion. Sits in the middle of insensibility and excessive indulgence.**

- **Charity: can be defined as generosity and bigheartedness. Sits in the middle of stinginess and wastefulness.**

- **Humility: can be defined as the modest opinion of one's self. Sits in between shame and pride**

- Confidence: can be defined as assurance and belief in one's self. Sits in between self-loathing and arrogance

- Honor: can be defined as respectfulness, while showing a sense of reverence and admiration. Sits in the middle of disregard and idolatry.

- Wisdom: can be defined as level-headedness while practicing discernment and displaying equanimity. Sits in between foolishness and being judgmental.

- Friendliness: can be defined as being entertaining and sociable. Sits between promiscuous and reclusive.

- Truthfulness: can be defined as straightforwardness, frankness, and candor. Sits in the middle of dishonesty and being boastful.

- Wit: can be defined as a tasteful sense of humor. Sits in the middle of boorishness and buffoonery.

- Friendship: can be defined as camaraderie and the ability to provide strong companionship. Sits in the middle of quarrelsomeness and using people.

- Justice: can be defined as fairness and impartiality. It sits between exploitation and injustice.

- Love: can be defined as feelings of warm personal attachment or deep affection, as for a parent, child, or friend. It sits between selfishness and hatred.

- Loyalty: can be defined as faithfulness to commitments or obligations. Sits between treachery and abandonment.

- Self-sacrifice: can be defined as accepting personal inconvenience or pain for the sake of someone else avoiding inconvenience or pain. Sits in the middle of selfishness and altruistism.

Being a good person is a hard thing to do. It's even harder when you're stuck in a black and white world that can fall apart as soon as you can't control something. Moral grey areas happen when you can't control what's going on around you but still have to make a choice. When Steve Rogers dives on a grenade, it's a black and white choice within the sense of courage and justice that he feels. When he sneaks away with Peggy and Howard to find Bucky, he is making a more nuanced choice. However, since Captain America hasn't developed his other virtues yet, he most likely wouldn't have done the same thing without believing that is was the right thing to do and fits within his sense of virtue. If Bucky had been alone or already brainwashed, he may not have gone at this point. The extent of the rescue made breaking the rules okay.

Captain America the Follower

Once Cap joins the twenty-first century in *The Avengers,* the rules start to change. At the beginning of the mission, Cap struggles to believe that the people in command, "the good guys", might actually be doing something bad.

To be fair, Cap has jumped forward in time and doesn't have a lot to anchor himself with, to stabilize what must be a mind-boggling experience. If you try to imagine what it would be like to wake up seventy-five years in the future, you probably can't do it, because it's that crazy. Life on Earth will change so much in that time period that it's impossible to imagine what kind of technology will exist, and how the ideology and morality of our society will change. This is what Cap is experiencing. He left a world with a clear evil and a clear good for a world with a million enemies and a million victims, and a million ways to look at every problem. A world overrun by a monster is easier to navigate than a world that appears to be prosperous on the surface while hiding subtle problems and pains.

In the world Cap has just left, it was essential to make choices for the greater good and follow the plan. The safety of the world was at stake. The virtues mentioned above have simple interpretations in this context. But context is everything. How do you deal with a threat you barely understand? How do you deal with the reality that your authority figures are just as deadly as your enemies?

Perfect Soldier versus Winter Soldier

Captain America: Winter Soldier starts with a simple premise of good versus evil, represented by perfect solder versys winter soldier. Captain America is just doing his job and fighting a bad guy. There's no real moral dilemma because the right choice lines up with Cap's understanding that his role in a world with moral absolutes is to obey the authorities above him. He doesn't quite see himself as an authority over himself or others yet.

As soon as Bucky comes into the picture, it becomes an entirely different moral question. Up until this point, Cap has ultimately seemed to believe that justice, courage, and obedience were the ultimate virtues that he needed to process as a superhuman force for good in the world. However, if you look closely at the list of virtues from before, you'll notice that obedience isn't actually a virtue, while love, friendship, loyalty, and self-sacrifice are. As already mentioned, each virtue fits in with all of the others to create a virtuous life. Obedience would get in the way of several other virtues, and therefore it can't be a virtue. Letting go of the idea that obedience in any form is necessary for virtue allows all of the other virtues to become stronger.

Cap cannot sacrifice his love of Bucky for the idea of obeying orders. That sense of friendship, loyalty, and self-sacrifice are suddenly the most important thing. This is Cap's first real rebellion. However, as we see in *Age of Ultron,* Steve Rogers as Captain America is not yet worthy to wield Mjolnir. Why? Because he hasn't reached the fullness of the virtues, because pain hasn't pushed him that far yet. No one truly grows when things in their life are going great. If anything, they usually get worse because you stop being proactive.

Once Steve Rogers is released from the ice, he has to figure out what is even good and bad in his life. It's confusing but ultimately isn't deeply painful. Even the loss of Peggy isn't deeply painful because they had a short relationship beforehand. The only thing that can cause enough pain for Cap to mature in into the virtuous leader that Dr. Erskine intended him to be is the life-long friendship with Bucky.

The pain of having to go against what he previously believed to be right to attempt to save and care for Bucky strengthens the relationship Cap has with all of the virtues, which allows him to begin to move away from moral absolutism into moral consequentialism.

Captain America the Outlaw

When Captain America becomes a full-fledged outlaw, he is actually demonstrating the most moral strength. He's making choices based on the morality of their consequences instead of how they fit within the established rules. Rules will never dictate morality, but morality and virtue should always dictate personal actions. To be fair, Tony Stark did sincerely believe that he was doing the right thing. But some of those convictions came from the excess of virtue that turns into vice. He was fueled by his own guilt and insecurities and that changed his perception of the correct moral choices.

Captain America made his choices much closer to virtuous middles. He demonstrates justice, courage, self-sacrifice, loyalty, love, truthfulness, and friendship, to name a few. Cap's objective, ultimately is to keep the bad guy from doing the bad thing. The benefit of improving the life of his friend is a starting motivator, but not so much of a motivator that he wouldn't stick to his moral code. The process of having to choose the types of choices he makes, and the tension of having to do so, refines his sense of virtue and morality. He is refined by fire, so to speak.

Civil War also provides Cap with his first opportunity to be a leader, and help determine the morally correct choice for himself and those who follow him. Having to be the one who makes those choices also refines his sense of virtue. When you're a follower you always have the option to make the easy choice to let someone else tell you what's right or wrong, but a leader has to make the hard choices and become a better or worse person in the process.

In *Infinity War,* Captain America proves himself a bold leader who's willing to break the rules to do the right thing. He's also able to stay calm and guide others to do the same, which demonstrates the virtues of temperance and wisdom. We don't know for sure what Cap was doing as an outlaw, but since he didn't become a villain, we can assume that he was working for the greater good, even outside of the guidance of an authority. He was separated from the only people he had the opportunity to grow close to during his time in the twenty-first century. He had the opportunity to grow bitter and hateful but instead is willing to step in and help as soon as he's needed again. He doesn't let his personal disagreements, his potential vice of pride, keep him from making choices that have good moral consequences.

Endgame Leader

Steve Rogers, alias Captain America, runs the risk throughout his character arc of becoming the same kind of moral absolutist as Thanos. Meaning, if he had chosen to be a perfect soldier rather than a good man, he might have agreed with Thanos, because there is some black and white moral absolutist value to the idea. However, we know that the collateral damage far outways the "good" of trying to save the resources of the universe and the expense of its inhabitants. Though Thor is set off as an emotional foil to Thanos, Cap is the ideological parallel. Pre–*Winter Soldier* Cap may have even been willing to hear Thanos out because Thanos's binary mindset wasn't really that much different than naive Captain America trying to figure out how to wield power in a world that doesn't make much sense.

Captain America plays the role of a gracious leader in *Endgame*. He is open to everyone's ideas but is willing to take control and do what he feels is wise. The failure of the Avengers in *Infinity War* has clearly affected him and changed him. While the failure led Thor to deep depression, Cap worked on moving on. It wasn't the first time his world had been flipped upside down, and the aftermath of the Snap is sort of like his story coming full circle. He has already experienced loss that he doesn't understand, while also experiencing the unexpected and complicated return of some of what was lost. He has an unprecedented hope for restoration. This helps others move on and eventually pushes the team forward when all seems lost.

Captain America in *Endgame* seems to have very little in common with the Steve Rogers we meet in *The First Avenger.* He has learned how to follow his own sense of virtue and do the right thing even if he was alone in doing so. His conflicts with the other avengers for Bucky's sake has taught him that doing the right thing is what's most important. Being a good man is more important than being an obedient man because power can shift so quickly that it's hard to tell which side is right.

Cap's progression through rebellion and towards moral con-sequentialism turns him into a virtue-filled good man. He's finally worthy of wielding Mjölnir in the final battle for the uni-verse. He was not worthy before because he was not truly mak-ing his own moral choices, and he wasn't embracing the grey areas and complications that make life meaningful. Making the hard choices and risking repercussions from authority have made him a more complex character and a strong leader.

Had Captain America not overcome pain and leaned into hard choices, he could not have become worthy as the epitome of human morality. As a good man, he was worthy.

29

I Am Iron Man

EARL A. P. VALDEZ AND JEMIMA MARIE MENDOZA

When we first meet Tony Stark in the Marvel Cinematic Universe, he is the embodiment of excess, luxury, and even violence—a crisp glass of what looks to be expensive whiskey on hand, discussing his carnal escapades with unnamed soldiers in the middle of a war zone. He has just finished delivering a stunning exhibition of his company's deadliest weapon yet. His arms outstretched, as if he's God, as the bombs explode into the mountains behind him.

When we say goodbye to Tony Stark, he's still in a war zone. But gone is the charming, confident arrogance, and we haven't seen him drink a drop of alcohol in a very long time. Instead of strangers, he's surrounded by family and friends. There is no witty banter; in fact, he's incapable of speech. He lies dying, the Infinity Gauntlet smoldering on his right arm. He has saved the universe, but at the cost of his own life.

The contrast between his introduction and his death is undoubtedly striking. The man once called the Merchant of Death becomes the ultimate protector of life. With a simple Snap, Tony ends a fifteen-year journey that began with a question echoing inside a small, cold cave—"Is this the last act of defiance of the great Tony Stark?"—that defines the rest of his life. It leads him to that very moment of self-sacrifice, his actual last act of defiance, and his most selfless one: his life for the universe.

For the decade and a half that spans the Marvel Cinematic Universe timeline from *Iron Man* to *Avengers: Endgame*, Tony Stark was at its center. His evolution from the playboy in California to the family man in Upstate New York follows a trajectory of decisions and actions that sets up that final confrontation against the Mad Titan Thanos, and ultimately ends with a heart-wrenching funeral that shows what Tony left behind: a legacy he had no choice but to die for.

Not What We Know but What We Do

This all started in a cave, with a bunch of scraps, and the singular decision to live. That decision began to shape Tony Stark's identity as Iron Man, Avenger, friend, mentor, husband, and father for the rest of his life. It laid down the path for others to follow. Therefore, to understand Tony Stark is to see the significance of his actions, not merely as an expression of his identity, but also the dynamic force that changed it and lead to his growth.

The French philosopher Maurice Blondel (1861–1949) insisted on the primacy of *action* in the human person's search for meaning and fulfillment. Blondel's attention to human action, over and above reason and thought as the primary characteristic of the human being, is a reaction against the rise of scientific positivism in secular France. Born and raised Roman Catholic and his philosophy deeply informed by faith, he questioned the primacy of clear and certain knowledge, delivered by empirical science and the emerging social sciences deliver.

According to Blondel, the scientific emphasis on knowledge as the primary defining character of the human being treats human existence as a mere *object* for study and analysis, disregarding the interior life of the human being—which includes desires, hopes, and dispositions toward living. Blondel considered science as meaningful but not exhaustive. The sciences are "flat projections on a plane surface," that do not account for the dynamism within the human consciousness.

It is this conviction that propelled him to write his 1893 dissertation on human action. He begins with what is more obvious in the human being, namely the desire to go outside and beyond his own self, not merely to satisfy his basic material needs, but also the "higher," spiritual needs consisting of knowledge, meaning, and fulfillment. He sees that the way for the human being to satisfy these desires is through the drive of the human will to know, to act, and to respond. He sees that even the capacity to know is something is brought about by a person's own will, for while information may come to him through his perception and understanding, they only become knowledge when he *wills* to accept it and take it in as such. Even knowing must first be willed before it can truly be considered as such. Otherwise, there are simply sense perceptions and information that hover around and provide no meaning to the human being.

He then composed what he calls "the science of practice," in which he laid down the dynamics of human action—precisely as a living *subject*—and what it means when one brings up the question on the meaning of human existence. Blondel draws several insights on the nature of human action, which he primarily sees as the "synthesis of the self" that hopes to reach out to the world as a whole, thus a synthesis between self as subject and the world as an object. Central among these insights is the fact that individual, willed actions, all build together and support a certain ultimate end that the human being wills for, and therefore acts for. As Blondel puts it, the *willed will* of individual actions contribute and build up the *willing will* closer to this ultimate end.

The human being goes outside of himself or herself through action, and it is only through action that they discover the ultimate meaning and purpose of their life and pursues it through whatever means they are capable of. Central to Blondel's insight of action is the fact that

> When we act without knowing entirely why (and it is always so), when the reasons we give ourselves are neither the only ones nor the truest ones, it is no doubt because in this immediate approximative explanation of our behavior there always subsists, alongside some clear ideas, a vague sense wherein are summed up our natural inclinations, the hereditary habits, the slowly constructed desires, the entire organism and the entire universe; but it is especially because the known motive dominating all prior energies, exploits them for ulterior ends that always surpasses experience and even foresight.

The Road to Infinite Responsibility

What we essentially derive from Tony Stark's journey in the Infinity Saga is the realization of Blondel's study of the nature of human action and fulfillment. The character's evolution begins at a point of lavish possession and selfishness, and encounters a turning point when he is faced with the reality of what he has done. All of his actions moving forward stem from that moment of total and unequivocal awareness.

Iron Man is devoted entirely to this turning point, and sets the stage for the next fifteen years of Tony's life. His capture by a terrorist organization in Afghanistan subjects him to not just the physical torture of captivity, but also the internal torment of accepting the consequences of his actions, and trying to wrap his head around its implications for his individual self. His cell-mate and fellow engineer, Ho Yinsen, articulates Tony's distress out loud, so he cannot escape from them. "What you just saw . . . that is your legacy, Stark. Your life's work in the hands of those murderers. Is that how you want to go out? Is this the last act of defiance of the great Tony Stark? Or are you going to do something about it?" he demands from Tony as Tony slowly unravels.

Once he is back in his world, Tony makes his raison d'être clear: "I had become part of a system that is comfortable with zero accountability. . . . I had my eyes opened. I came to realize that I had more to offer this world than just making things that blow up." This is precisely why Iron Man was born—not solely because Tony had to escape, but because he had found his true purpose. Later in the movie, he tells Pepper Potts:

> There is nothing except this. There is no art opening, there is no ben-efit, there is nothing to sign. There is the next mission, and nothing else. . . . I shouldn't be alive unless it was for a reason. I'm not crazy, Pepper. I just finally know what I have to do. And I know in my heart that it's right.

It's easy to be distracted by the pomp and circumstance sur-rounding Iron Man. Despite finding his purpose, Tony doesn't really do much to shake off his pre-Afghanistan image. But that is nothing but smoke and mirrors—after he haughtily brags to Captain America that he is a "genius, billionaire, play-boy, philanthropist" in *The Avengers,* he doesn't hesitate to carry a nuclear warhead bound for New York into a wormhole, even if that means he doesn't get to come back home. He may be smart enough to find ways to "cut the wire," but he will not wait to lay down on the wire and let others walk over him.

That first act of self-sacrifice in *The Avengers* is triggering for Tony. For the rest of his time in the Marvel Cinematic Universe, he becomes haunted by the idea that one day, he might be unable to save those who need saving. In *Iron Man 3,* he attempts to deal with this trauma through the creation of more Iron Man suits. This spills over into *Avengers: Age of Ultron,* where he tries, but fails, to "build a suit of armor around the world"—an endeavor precipitated by a possible future that Scarlet Witch shows to him in a vision: that of a cold world, where everyone that he cares about is dead in front of him. Because of that failure, he is determined to ensure that it never happens again. The conflict in *Captain America: Civil War* revolves around Tony's ultimate goal of protecting humanity. He believes that by keeping the Avengers together even at great personal cost, the planet will have the best chance of defending itself from existential threats. And if that means having to accede some of their freedoms, then that is the price they have to pay.

Despite his best efforts to prevent his worst nightmare from happening, Tony is not able to stop Thanos from wiping out half the universe in *Avengers: Infinity War.* What is most painful and cruel is that he watches his mentee turn to dust in his arms, millions of light-years away from home, with almost no hope of return. And when he does finally return to Earth, he is hurting, defeated, and absolutely spent. In his failure, he retreats to a quiet life, with his superhero alter ego taking a back seat as he raises his family.

But when he is called to world-saving business once again in *Avengers: Endgame*, he can't ignore it. Tony tells Pepper, now his wife and the mother of his child, "Something tells me I should put it in lockbox and drop it in the bottom of the lake, go to bed." Pepper looks at him sadly, and asks in a gentle, yet resigned tone, "But will you be able to rest?" She knows that there's absolutely no way that Tony will reject the call to undo the suffering that Thanos had caused. He will not be able to find fulfillment or meaning if he repudiates his purpose.

Throughout his journey from the suffocating cave in Afghanistan, to the infinite expanse of space, to the final battle on Earth, Tony Stark carried the infinite responsibility of the other, which became the primary essence of his actions. He was driven by that radical love to keep humanity safe, wherein every single choice he made, every object he created, every plan he concocted, existed to serve that love. It may have seemed that his will to act upon radical love was above reason, but his actions themselves create the very reason for the ultimate act of radical love.

Tony's final snap is the fullness of fifteen years of actions combined. It goes beyond himself not just because he saves the other, but also because the act carries a responsibility to the future, wherein those he left behind faces an unknown horizon. Tony's sacrifice alone brings with it the gift of living in this new world with the fullness of courage and hope, despite the anguish of losing a great hero, mentor, friend, husband, and father. Because Tony will always put others above himself, he would not have chosen otherwise.

When Ho Yinsen sacrifices himself so that Tony can escape the cave in Afghanistan, he tells Tony, "Don't waste it. Don't waste your life." For a decade and a half, Tony keeps those words close to his chest as he makes decision after decision that are beyond his individual self and consistent with his what he knows in his heart to be right. As his final choice, the snap is when he finally surrenders in service of the other. That is the infinite legacy of Tony Stark's pure act of radical love, and the ultimate achievement of his existence.

30
Socratic Superheroism

CHAD WILLIAM TIMM

Humanity is destroying the planet. Our dependence on fossil fuels drives catastrophic climate change and our inability to empathize with those different from us leads to persecution, violence, and conflict.

If we could just find someone brave enough and heroic enough to stand up and save us from ourselves! We need bold action and brave leaders for life in our universe to survive! Wait, isn't that exactly what Thanos attempts to do in *Infinity War* and *Endgame*? Doesn't Thanos try to save humanity from itself by taking drastic measures to preserve the planet? Does that make Thanos a hero?

The line between superhero and supervillain in the Marvel universe is often blurry. One minute the Winter Soldier tries to kill Black Panther and the next minute T'Challa presents the Captain's best buddy with a new vibranium bionic arm. Loki flip flops like a pancake between villain and hero. In one movie Nebula is fighting the Guardians of the Galaxy and the next she is working with them to stop Thanos. Since there seems to be some confusion as to what it means to be a hero, instead of looking at current Marvel characters for insight let's go back in time 2,400 years and look at the life of Socrates (469–399 B.C.E.), the first ever philosopher-hero.

I Am Incapable of Error

Instead of wielding Mjolnir like the mighty Thor or manipulating chaos magic like Scarlet Witch, heroism for Socrates meant living a "good" life, one devoted to wrestling with important philosophical questions like 'What is courage?' and 'How can we be virtuous?'

He set out to live this kind of life because the priestess Pythia from the Oracle at Delphi named Socrates to be the wisest person in Athens. Shocked by the Oracle's statement, Socrates said "Whatever does the god mean? . . . I am very conscious that I am not wise at all." Because he believed that all he knew was that he knew nothing, Socrates set out to understand what the Oracle meant by claiming him to be wise. He decided to spend every day hanging out in the Athenian marketplace questioning the poets, politicians, artisans, and anyone else who had a reputation for being wise. His method of questioning became known as . . . wait for it . . . the Socratic Method! Socrates's best student, Plato, wrote down several exchanges or dialogues where Socrates used this method, and they often started something like this hypothetical dialogue with Thanos's daughter and Gamora's sister, Nebula:

> SOCRATES: Nebula, my friend! Where have you been and where are you going?
>
> NEBULA: I was with my father, Thanos, the son of A'lars of Chronos, and I am going for a walk because I have much on my mind.
>
> SOCRATES: What have you been talking to Thanos about that has you so deep in thought? Oh, I know: Thanos must have been entertaining you with a feast of eloquence.
>
> NEBULA: In fact, Socrates, you're just the right person to hear the speech that Thanos gave, since, in a roundabout way, it was about the limits of knowledge.
>
> SOCRATES: Wonderful! Please, Nebula, you must recite Thanos's speech as I am eager to hear it.
>
> NEBULA: I will do my best, Socrates. Thanos's speech began with "I now hold omnipotence. What should I do with such almighty power? The answer to that is actually quite simple: Anything I want. I am incapable of error."

Remember when Socrates responded to the Oracle's prophecy by questioning whether it could be true? In this way Socrates demonstrated the first quality of Socratic Heroism, which is questioning all assumptions and only keeping those that you arrive at through reason and logic. Does Thanos ever second-guess or doubt himself? Never! He decides what he wants to do and then seeks to impose his will on all those around him, destroying those who stand in his way. Socrates, on the other hand, believed in taking ideas that society considers "true" and questioning them in order to see just how true they are.

When Thanos, in the comic book *Infinity Gauntlet*, tells Mephisto "I am incapable of error," he asserts that he has unlimited power and cannot be wrong. Socrates would challenge this assumption with a series of questions, and more than likely conclude, just as he did when questioning a prominent Athenian who claimed to be wise, that:

> For my part, I thought to myself as I left, "I'm wiser than that person. For it's likely that neither of us knows anything fine and good, but he thinks he knows something he doesn't know, whereas I, since I don't in fact know, don't think that I do either."

You see, Socrates recognized there is much he doesn't know and that the first step in learning anything is recognizing how much there is to learn! The willingness to admit the limits of your knowledge is the second quality of Socratic Heroism. Think of it as intellectual humility. If you go into a conversation or discussion openly admitting you don't have all the answers, then you're less likely to be closed-minded by thinking you already know everything you need to know.

This is Socrates's position while Thanos, on the other hand, is the definition of arrogance and closed-mindedness. When Thanos, in *Avengers: Infinity Wars* tells Loki, Thor, and the Hulk "Destiny still arrives all the same. And now it is here. Or should I say, I am!" he is being intellectually vain, not humble!

Reality Can Be Whatever I Want

NEBULA: By Zeus, Socrates, I agree with you. I think that is reasonable. But what's the purpose of questioning all assumptions and being intellectually humble? Where will that get you against the power of Thanos? Look at me! My father replaced a piece of me with a machine each time Gamora defeated me in training. He is ruthless!

SOCRATES: Oh Nebula, you rascal! Do you not know what the priests and priestesses say about divine matters? What they say is this: the soul is immortal; at times it comes to an end, which they call dying, at times it is reborn, but it is never destroyed and one must therefore live one's life as piously as possible.

NEBULA: But Socrates, after acquiring the reality stone Thanos told Gamora "Reality is often disappointing. That is, it was. Now reality can be whatever I want." What do you say to this?

When Thanos claims "Reality is whatever I want," he asserts that for him, truth is relative. In this context the truth is more than "Tell the truth, you think beer-belly Thor's dad-bod is hot, don't you?" When philosophers discuss truth, they are usually referring to the quality of a belief or set of propositions. A belief is true if it corresponds to the way things actually are. For Thanos, Thor's beer-belly dad-bod is hot if he says so.

Instead of believing that the truth is relative, or whatever you want it to be, the philosopher-hero Socrates claimed that while the physical, material world is constantly changing and in flux, there are unchanging objective and universal truths that exist in the heavens. Instead of Natasha Romanov's beauty being in the eye of the beholder, Socrates believed that an objective truth of beauty exists and Natasha's beauty just reminds us of this. Hold on to your Gameboy Groot, because this is going to get crazy. Socrates believed that the soul is immortal, and that at one time all our souls traveled throughout the heavens and saw the objective truth of everything before falling to the Earth and inhabiting our bodies. At one time our souls, for example, witnessed the true form of beauty. According to Socrates, when we open our eyes at birth everything we see in the material world is just an imperfect and temporary copy of the truth in the heavens. When we look at Thor or Natasha and see beauty, it's our soul remembering the truth of beauty it once witnessed but has forgotten because the material world tricks and deceives us.

The reason Socrates believed we should live the examined life of the philosopher, questioning all assumptions and being intellectually humble, is because in the process of questioning assumptions and recognizing the limits of our knowledge we can save our souls. This means the more we ponder the beauty of Gamora, Captain America, or Okoye the faster our soul remembers the truth of beauty! Yes! I can get behind this idea, can't you? Socrates' believed this so strongly that he felt living any other way wasn't living at all, asserting that

> it's the greatest good for a man to discuss virtue every day, and the other things you've heard me discussing and examining myself and others about, on the grounds that the unexamined life isn't worth living for a human being.

"The unexamined life isn't worth living" are perhaps the most important words ever spoken in philosophy because they challenge us not just to live, but to live by actively engaging in a life of questioning.

The End Is Near

SOCRATES: Speak now, Nebula. When a man reaches my age he doesn't have the time to mince words. What is on your mind?

NEBULA: I'm looking for words, old man . . . What's the purpose of living an examined life when Thanos threatens us all? Thanos plans to kill half of all living creatures on Earth in order to save the planet and maintain what he calls a balance. I am a warrior and I will not rest until his dying screams fill my ears.

SOCRATES: Dear Nebula, your zeal is invaluable, if a right one: but if wrong, the greater the zeal the greater the evil; and therefore we ought to consider whether these things shall be done or not.

While living an examined life certainly improves the soul of the individual philosopher, Socrates had a bigger goal in mind. Socrates loved his home city of Athens and repeatedly referred to his desire to improve it. He believed that by living the life of the philosopher and challenging fellow Athenians to examine their own lives he could improve his society. Think of it this way: if everyone challenges assumptions and recognizes that they don't have all the answers while working to improve our souls, we can all live in a philosopher-hero paradise!

Wait, then how is this different from what Thanos wants? When Gamora says "The entire time I knew Thanos, he only ever had one goal: To bring balance to the Universe by wiping out half of all life," doesn't this reflect a similar desire to improve society? While Thanos believes that the only way to save society and bring balance is by eliminating half of all life and Socrates wants everyone to be philosopher heroes, isn't the objective of improving society exactly the same? Thanos's argument is that sometimes you have to sacrifice the few to save the many. His position, however, it not the same as Socrates at all!

Don't get it twisted, Socrates didn't believe in just living, but in living a just and honorable life through seeking wisdom and virtue, and in doing so making sure your soul is in the best possible condition. In fact, Socrates said "One shouldn't do injustice in return for injustice, as the majority of people think—seeing that one should never do injustice." For Socrates, doing injustice meant doing wrong, and he claimed that a person should never intentionally do wrong when we he continued, saying "So one must neither do injustice in return nor wrong any man, no matter what one has suffered at his hands." Combined with challenging assumptions and being intellectually humble, the desire to improve one's society and not harm it represents the third element of Socratic Heroism.

Thanos's claim of wanting to bring balance to the Universe rings hollow anyway, because in *Avengers: Endgame* he laments "I thought that by eliminating half of life the other half would thrive . . . But you have shown me that's impossible." In *Endgame*, Thanos no longer pretends to want to save the many in the Universe by sacrificing the few and instead is hell bent on getting revenge and destroying all life. This is further evidence that he doesn't question his own assumptions, he doesn't recognize the limits of his wisdom, and instead of aiming to help society his goal is to destroy it. He continues "I will shred this universe down to its last atom and then, with the stones you've collected for me, create a new one teeming with life that knows not what it's lost . . . but only what it has been given." So far on the Socratic Hero Scorecard, Thanos is 0 for 3.

The Courage to Act

NEBULA: Socrates, old man, you are quite convincing. So convincing that you have me considering running off to become a Guardian of the Galaxy.

SOCRATES: By Zeus, Nebula, that is wonderful to hear. You would make quite a Guardian!

NEBULA: I'm not sure, Socrates. I still believe the courageous thing to do is to hunt my father like a dog and tear him limb from limb.

SOCRATES: Courage? What do you know of courage, my Nebula? What must one do in order to be deemed courageous?

When Socrates set out to understand what the Oracle meant by naming him the wisest in the land he questioned prominent members of society and found they weren't wise at all. Watching Socrates question and ultimately mic drop these phony wise men became quite the social event for up and coming Athenians who followed him around and took copious notes. Like a fourth-century B.C.E. social media influencer his popularity among the young increased to the point that he posed a threat to city leaders who didn't like being called out for their ignorance. Socrates's commitment to the life of a philosopher eventually got him into trouble, accused of corrupting the minds of the youth, and teaching about false gods. The fellow Athenians he held in such high regard found him guilty and sentenced him to death. Who would have thought the life of a philosopher could be so dangerous! Socrates never backed down, telling the jury in his trial that "If you put me to death, you won't easily find another like me." You see, Socrates saw himself as a gadfly, a pesky and persistent voice buzzing around your head annoying you and provoking you into examining your life. He said:

> It's as just such a gadfly, it seems to me, that the god has attached me to the city—one that awakens, persuades, and reproaches each and every one of you and never stops alighting, everywhere on you the whole day.

Isn't Thanos a gadfly too, although a much bigger and uglier version? Socrates challenged his fellow citizens to live the life of the philosopher and to provoke and push them to examine their lives. Doesn't the threat posed by Thanos similarly provoke us to reconsider how we are abusing each other? His claims that humanity ruined our one and only planet by depleting its resources and therefore must be punished is, at first glance, gadfly-like. But that's the *Infinity Wars* Thanos, not the *Endgame* Thanos. The *Endgame* Thanos just wants to murder, destroy, and seek revenge. There's no courage in that, unless we let Thanos decide that courage can be whatever he wants it to be and as wannabe Socratic Heroes we can't let that happen!

Like everything else for Socrates, nothing is "relative," so there must be an objective truth to courage, a true form of courage only found in the heavens. Frustratingly, as in his dialogues about beauty, virtue, and wisdom, Socrates resisted giving definitions and instead asked questions of people who claim to possess these qualities to determine exactly they mean. By examining and questioning those who claimed to be courageous Socrates hoped to help his soul remember the truth.

The best way to understand what courage meant to Socrates is for us to consider how he lived his life. He asked questions with an open mind in the hopes of helping, not hurting, his society and he continued to do this even when his own life was at risk. He remained steadfast to what is right even in the face of death. This is courage to Socrates, and it makes up the final quality of Socratic Heroism. Thanos may be able to use the Infinity Stones to bend physical time and space to his will, but he can't change truth in the heavens. Thanos' actions are not right because they intentionally cause harm, which means he isn't courageous and instead finishes 0 for 4 when it comes to Socratic Heroism.

One Strange Doctor

NEBULA: You are convincing, old man and not as weak and feeble as you look.

SOCRATES: What a wonderful compliment, I thank you. But you speak of weakness, what do you know of weakness Nebula?

NEBULA: Forget it! I don't have time for any more of your questions. Now I have a question and I want a real answer, not another answer in the form of a question. Who among the Avengers is most like a Socratic Hero? I would like to study them and see what this looks like.

SOCRATES: The Avenger I have in mind is a master of the mystic arts.

Being a Socratic Hero isn't for the faint of heart, and the member of the Marvel Universe that comes closest in my mind is my favorite member of the Marvel Socratic Universe, the Master of the Mystic Arts, Doctor Stephen Strange.

Doctor Strange is a perfect example of what happens when you commit to living an examined life. Prior to his debilitating automobile accident that ended his career as a world-class surgeon, Stephen Strange personified arrogance, closed mindedness, and selfishness. The exact opposite of a Socratic Hero, this Stephen Strange didn't have society's best interest in mind, only his own. Not until he traveled to Kamar Taj to meet the Ancient One did Stephen Strange realize the limits of this physical, material world and devote his life to protecting the Universe from dark forces.

Is he intellectually humble? Doctor Strange's encounter at Kamar Taj humbled him intellectually. The Ancient One motivated him to stop trying to master the physical world as a man of science, when she told him "We're just another tiny momentary speck in the middle of an indifferent universe" and then pushed Strange's astral form out of his physical form, "a place where the soul exists outside the body." This experience began Stephen Strange's journey to become Doctor Strange. His newly found intellectual humility, along with a willingness to now challenge assumptions that he once took for granted, set him down a path that ultimately led to his helping save the Universe from the madman Thanos.

Does he question assumptions? In *Infinity Wars*, Doctor Strange questions the compelling desire to keep the Time Stone hidden from Thanos, instead giving up the stone which allows the life-destroying Snap to happen. The obvious decision would be to keep the Time Stone from Thanos, but Doctor

Strange challenges this assumption and then shows the intellectual humility to let go of his own ego, recognize how much he doesn't know, and trust that only Iron Man can stop Thanos.

So far Doctor Strange questions assumptions and is intellectually humble, making him 2 for 2 for Socratic Heroism. What about the moral courage to be steadfast for what is right even in the face of danger? Are you kidding? Doctor Strange gives Thanos the Time Stone and watches him snap his fingers, then disintegrates into ashy nothingness. If that's not courage I don't know what is. But, you might say, giving the Time Stone to Thanos killed half the life on Earth and Socrates said we can't intentionally cause harm.

This would be a fair criticism of Doctor Strange had he not been correct. Viewing 14,000,605 futures convinced him that the only way to defeat Thanos would be to give him the Time Stone and count on Iron Man to make the ultimate sacrifice, rewriting the timeline, bringing everyone back, and defeating Thanos in Endgame. Who is your favorite Marvel character? Do they meet the standard for heroism set by Super Socrates?

Wanted: Socratic Heroes

Although there's no Thanos to threaten us with annihilation and extinction, we're doing a pretty good job ourselves of threatening each other and our planet. But you don't need the Eye of Agamotto or a vibranium shield to be a Socratic Hero.

Being humble, admitting you don't know everything, and working to improve your society doesn't require superpowers or super gadgets. But you will need some courage to remain steadfast for what is right. Challenging your friends' assumptions while being a gadfly might frustrate them because people don't generally like being forced to think.

Do you have what it takes to live an examined life and inspire those around you to do the same? I hope so. All our souls might depend on it.

31

Does the Hulk Have a Soul?

Dru Graham and Adam Barkman

The Marvel Cinematic Universe has done a phenomenal job of having the science of everything "make sense." The writers and producers have used just enough believability and realism to satisfy the mechanics and the physicists of the world, while at the same time not losing the wonder of the superhero world. However, can the same be said of this Universe's underlining philosophy—especially its metaphysics?

To get on the track of the question, Does Hulk have a soul?, we can begin by asking, What is a mind? Dictionary definitions of 'mind' are often confusing and contradictory. To keep it simple, we'll define the mind as the conscious, self-aware "I" that perceives, wills, and feels.

Next up is the question, What is the soul? Well, a typical understanding of the soul—going back to Plato, Homer, and beyond—is that the soul is the "entire immaterial you"—your ghost, if you like. It's not so much that a person "has" a soul, as that a person "is" a soul. While many people make a distinction between the mind and the soul—with mind being the pure "thinking part" of the soul—we will use them interchangeably here as the conscious, immaterial, self-aware "I" that perceives, wills, and feels.

If the mind and soul, then, are necessarily connected (or if they're the same thing), then it seems that Hulk is or has a soul only if he also is or has a mind and vice versa. If the mind is reducible to physical component parts, then, by definition, the body is necessary for the mind and soul to exist, making the mind extinguishable by death.

In philosophical debates down the centuries, there are three different views on what the mind is and how it relates to the physical or material world. These are Substance Dualism, Physicalism, and Idealism.

Substance Dualism

Substance dualism holds that the brain is a physical object that has physical properties and the mind or soul is a mental object that has mental properties. Mind and matter are two different "substances"—fundamentally different kinds of things. So a substance dualist claims that there are two basic kinds of things in the universe, the physical and the non-physical. A substance dualist will place things like the brain, an iPhone, shoes, or Thor's hammer in the "physical" category, while they will place the mind, God, or ghosts in the "non-physical" category.

The First reason why a substance dualist would say Hulk has a mind is called the "hard problem of consciousness." The hard problem of consciousness arises from the difficulty in explaining the relationship between brain processes and mental states. The experience of pain seems to be a very different kind of thing from the physical process in the body that corresponds to pain.

Philosophers would call such "experiences of pain" qualia. Qualia are subjective experiences. Examples are the way the color of an apple appears to our visual sense, a feeling of pain or of pleasure, and the feel of the texture of this page. To explain why this is called a "hard problem," let's use the example of the experience of color. Imagine that there are two completely identical copies of Bruce Banner down to the molecular level. We'll affectionately call them BB1 and BB2. It is possible to imagine that when BB1 looks at a red apple, he experiences a red apple. However, when BB2 looks at that same apple, he *experiences* a green apple, but has always called that subjective experience of the color green "red."

Although both BBs will call the apple red, BB2 is experiencing the apple in a way that BB1 would call "green." The only way for BB1 to fully know if he were experiencing the same color as BB2 is to somehow look inside BB2's mind. If BB1 were able to somehow do this, when looking at that same apple, he might say, "The color of that apple is what *I* would call *green!*" This example shows that the experience of an object seems to be *over and above* the physical nature of that object. What reasonably follows is that the mind has different characteristics than the body has. Therefore, the mind must not only exist, but be of a different *substance* than the body—we arrive at substance dualism.

The second reason why a substance dualist claims that the Hulk has a soul is called the modal argument, put forward by Alvin Plantinga and other philosophers.

1. **If me and my body are identical than whatever is true of me is true of my body**

2. It is possible to conceive of me existing without my body

3. Therefore, there is something true of me that is not true of my body

4. Therefore, I am not my body

This argument has its roots in Leibniz's Law which states that two things are numerically identical only if they have exactly the same properties. For example the reason that Peter Parker is identical to Spider-Man is that Peter Parker and Spider-Man have exactly the same properties. Everything that is true of Peter Parker is also true of Spider-Man because Peter Parker *is* Spider-Man. So, although Peter Parker and Spider-Man have different names, they have *absolutely* the same properties, making them numerically identical (according to Leibniz's Law).

If it's true that mental states have different properties than brain states, then it follows that there is something true of mind that is not true of body. Therefore, Leibniz's Law tells us that our minds and bodies are not identical, meaning that they are two different kinds of substances. It seems to follow that we can say that the Hulk has a mind or a soul.

Now that we've seen why substance dualists would say that the Hulk has a soul, let's look at the main *problem* with substance dualism. This is the problem of how the two differing substances interact with each other. If the mind and the body are two different substances, how is it possible for one to influence the other? Although substance dualism provides a coherent argument for the existence of the mind, it only raises new questions as to how they interact. Not only does dualism not explain how they can interact with each other, dualism suggests that they *cannot* interact with each other.

However, many studies in neuroscience have shown that increased mental effort and training can change the neurological structure of the brain. A recent study on Cognitive Behavioral Therapy and spider phobia by Vincent Panquette suggests "that a psychotherapeutic approach, such as Cognitive Behavioral Therapy, has the potential to modify the dysfunctional neural circuitry associated with anxiety disorders. They further indicate that the changes made at the mind level, within a psychotherapeutic context, are able to functionally 'rewire' the brain" ("Change the Mind and You Change the Brain"). Sam Kean has also explained that a change to the brain, such as brain damage, can affect someone's mental state.

Physicalism

The second philosophical theory that speaks to the question of the mind is physicalism, which states that all mental states are really physical. To quote early Stephen Strange, "I do not believe in fairy-tales about chakras or energy or the power of belief. There is no such thing as spirit. We are made of matter and nothing more."

While substance dualism divides the things in the world into two different kinds of things, physicalism is a "monist" position, meaning that it asserts that there is only one type of substance. Everything, therefore, is *reducible* to matter. Reducible meaning that they can all be explained by smaller, more fundamental physical processes (from psychology to neurology to biochemistry to molecular chemistry to atomic physics to quantum mechanics). So, a physicalist rejects the notion that the mind is a radically different substance from the brain.

The first reason why a physicalist would say the Hulk does not have a mind distinct from his brain is because if he did, it would violate the principle of causal closure. Causal closure states that every physical occurrence has a sufficient physical cause. For example, let's imagine that the Hulk lifts his arm because he wants to. The Hulk *wanting* to raise his hand is a mental event, and the actual *raising* of his hand is a physical event. Therefore, if the raising of the Hulk's hand is a physical event, it must follow that the *wanting* to raise his hand is also physical.

The second reason why a physicalist would say the Hulk does not have a mind is because if he did, it would violate the principle of conservation of energy. The principle of conservation of energy states that energy can be neither created nor destroyed. This position is grounded in the fact that if the mind were to assert itself and impact the physical world (acting upon the desire to raise one's hand), then it would change this "mental energy" into physical energy. This means that physical energy is being created, and thus, violates this well-established principle of physics.

What causal closure does not permit is the impact of the non-physical on the physical (it may be possible that there exists a non-physical reality, but this reality cannot affect the physical world). However, if this were the case, then objective truths must also not be able to affect the physical world. By objective truths we mean *truths that exist whether or not they are discovered*. For example, $1 + 1 = 2$. The discovery of $1 + 1 = 2$ had a massive impact on the human species. It changed the way that they thought about and interacted with the world. Therefore, if it is universally true that $1 + 1 = 2$, then this means that this truth exists in a non-physical reality. The discovery of this truth has changed human society, and human beings themselves. Thus, causal closure is justly violated. Peter Sjöstedt-H, in his essay "Why I Am Not a Physicalist," put it this way:

> On the one side, if the laws of logic are to be considered objective—that is, they are true for all—then they must exist in a non-temporal, non-physical third realm that has causal influence upon the physical, thereby annulling the causal closure principle and, in turn, physicalism. On the other side, if the laws of logic are considered to be not objective, then physicalism cannot claim to be objectively logical. Either way, physicalism falters.

The second problem with physicalism is the principle of the conservation of energy. Although we could argue that the mind simply redirects physical energy, we don't believe that this answer is sufficient in and of itself. A violation of the principle of conservation of energy requires more scientific backing. Sean Michael Carroll, a theoretical physicist, says in his essay "Space Emerging from Quantum Mechanics," that energy is only conserved if "The background on which particles and forces evolve, as well as the dynamical rules governing their motions, are fixed, not changing with time." In short, energy is only conserved if space and time are static and unchanging.

Einstein's theory of relativity states that space and time are, in fact, dynamic and can change over time. Therefore, when a particle moves through space, if that space is changing (which it is) then the total energy of those particles is not conserved. The critique, then, would not be that the mind warps space-time to interact with the world, but more simply that the principle of the conservation of energy is not universally constant. Therefore, we should not argue as if it were.

A third problem with physicalism is the visual binding problem which states that there is no part of the brain that combines objects and colors into one "quale" or subjective experience. For example, let's bring back our old friend Bruce Banner. BB looks at a red apple on his desk and experiences a "red apple." However, the brain processes "red" and "looks like an apple" into separate regions of the brain. Nowhere in the brain are these two things brought together to form what would become the experience of a "red apple."

We're not saying that this part of the brain has not yet been found. Researchers noted that although the entire visual system was mapped, there is no part of the brain that unifies the "red" and the "looks like an apple" into one subjective experience. According to Jerome Feldman, "What we do know is that there is no place in the brain where there could be a direct neural encoding of the illusory detailed scene. . . . enough is known about the structure and function of the visual system to rule out any detailed neural representation that embodies the subjective experience."

Idealism

The final philosophy that deals with the problem of the mind is idealism, which says that things that exist are mind-like in nature. Idealism rejects dualism, asserting that there is only mind and the mind's experience of reality. This is not to say that nothing exists outside of the experience of reality, but what does exist outside of our experience is mind-like in nature. To explain this, what the idealist will point to is the holographic principle in quantum mechanics. The holographic principle states that all of reality is actually a 3D hologram of 2D information. The "information" describes the arrangement of particles that we "observe" as 3D reality. According to Sean Caroll again:

> Mathematically, wave functions are elements of a mathematical structure called Hilbert Space. That means they are vectors—we can add quantum states together (the origin of Superpositions in quantum mechanics) and calculate the angle ('dot product') between them. . . . The word 'space' in 'Hilbert space' doesn't mean the good old three-dimensional space we walk through every day, or even the four-dimensional spacetime of relativity. It's just math-speak for 'a collection of things,' in this case 'possible quantum states of the universe.'

In short, the entire universe can be explained with 1's and 0's like a computer. In fact, all of space-time can be literally described as a virtual reality video game.

The first reason why an idealist would say that the Hulk has a mind is called the master argument. Here is George Berkeley's argument:

1. **If things exist outside of our minds or independent of a subject, it ought to be conceivable that they exist outside of our minds or without being observed by a subject.**

2. **For example, think of an infinity stone. I can, in my mind, picture an infinity stone that nobody is looking at or conceiving.**

3. **However, simply by virtue of conceiving of such an unconceived infinity stone, it is a conceived object. Thus, it is inconceivable that there exists an infinity stone independent of minds.**

The key to this argument is understanding the difference between possible and conceivable. When a philosopher says, "It is impossible for a human to jump twenty feet," what they mean is that, given the way the world works, it is impossible for a human to jump twenty feet. However, if circumstances were different (for example, if we were on the moon) it might be possible for a human to jump twenty feet. The word *inconceivable* is reserved for much stronger assertions. It is inconceivable, for example, for 2 + 2 to equal 5. One might call these things logically impossible. So, if there is a reality outside of our minds, it should be logically possible (conceivable) that it can exist without being seen by someone.

The second reason an idealist would say that the Hulk has a mind is the scientific evidence against a fixed physical reality. This is something that arises from the "quantum enigma" of quantum mechanics. This states that by your free choice you could demonstrate either of two contradictory physical realities. You can, for example, demonstrate an object to be someplace. But you could have chosen to demonstrate the opposite: that it was not in that place. Observation created the object's position. Quantum theory has all properties created by their observation.

In short, physical reality is dependent on there being a conscious observer to create an object's position. This principle was put to the test and confirmed by Alain Aspect in 2007. If someone is not looking at something, the object as we would experience it does not exist. This evidence provides a strong case for there being no fixed physical reality and that everything is made of "information." This information is what an idealist would call "mind." Stranger yet, when objects pop into existence, the underlying information "uploads" a back history of what would have been the case if they had always been there. It seems possible, then, that the world is information that the mind experiences.

Of course, there are some objections, particularly the problem of unconsciousness. If idealism is true, then all that exists is consciousness. However, we know of unconscious processes. If there are unconscious processes, then there is at least one thing that is not conscious. This means that idealism must be false. In short, if there only exist things that are of the same substance as conscious minds, then it would be impossible for anything to be unconscious.

This problem can be addressed by differentiating between two types of consciousness. These are what Bernardo Kastrup would call "consciousness proper" and "self-reflexive consciousness." Consciousness proper is experience itself; while self-reflexive consciousness is the *knowledge* of the experience that comes with experience itself. It is possible for someone to experience something without knowledge of it. One prime example of this is sleeping. When you sleep, you experience a lack of knowledge of those experiences, but that does not mean you did not experience those things. When we make this distinction, the problem of unconsciousness falls short in refuting idealism.

The Hulk's Soul

On the whole, then, we think that idealism can explain the nature of the mind best, and so is the best candidate to help us understand the nature of Banner's mind and the Hulk's soul. If the brain is not in a separate world, then interaction between Banner's "body" and "mind" is not a matter of substance dualism. Moreover, idealism explains how the Hulk's manifestation changes the shared "body" of Bruce Banner and the Hulk. This is the result of what we experience as reality being 2D information. If the mind is truly information, then we would expect that mental information to be represented in a 3D form. That is in our "bodies." In Idealism, your body can be described as a 3D representation of your mental information. When your mind believes that it is depressed, this changes the information, and thus, changes the body. This method of conceptualizing the world is exactly what is described in the movie *Doctor Strange*.

When explaining magic to Doctor Strange, the Ancient One says, "The language of the mystic arts is as old as civilization. The sorcerers of antiquity called the use of this language spells. But if that word offends your modern sensibilities, you can call it a program. The source code that shapes reality." It is this "source code" that separates idealism from substance dualism. While substance dualism and idealism will agree—or can be made to agree—on almost everything, what separates the two is what each claim is "base" reality. An idealist asserts that everything is "mind" or "information." It is this information that makes up everything.

So, it seems very likely that Hulk is a mind or soul, but this mind or soul is the same as Banner's—the difference between the two them, then, is just the 3D "body" projection that the same mind/soul puts forth. Or, at least, so we could argue.

Bibliography

Arendt, Hannah. 1968 [1951]. *The Origins of Totalitarianism*. Houghton Mifflin Harcourt.

Ansart, Olivier. 2010. Embracing Death: Pure Will in *Hagakure*. *Early Modern Japan: An Interdisciplinary Journal* 18.

Aristotle. 1975. *Categories and De Interpretatione*. Oxford University Press.

———. 2016. *Metaphysics*. Hackett.

Barnstone, W. 1993. *The Poetics of Translation*. Yale University Press.

Bennett, B. 2018. *Sacred Languages of the World*. Wiley.

Bentham, Jeremy. 1988. *The Principles of Morals and Legislation*. Prometheus.

Blanchot, M. 1995. *The Writing of the Disaster*. University of Nebraska Press.

Boethius, Ancius, 1999. *The Consolation of Philosophy*. Penguin.

Bostrom, Nick. 2011. Infinite Ethics. *Analysis and Metaphysics* 10.

Burkert, W. 1996. *Creation of the Sacred*. Harvard University Press.

Butler, Judith. 2006. *Precarious Life: The Powers of Mourning and Violence*. Verso.

———. 2016. *The Frames of War: When Is Life Grievable?* Verso.

Callender, C., ed. 2010. *The Oxford Handbook of Time*. Oxford University Press.

Camus, Albert. 2018. *The Myth of Sisyphus*. Vintage.

Carroll, Sean M. 2020. *Something Deeply Hidden: Quantum Worlds and the Emergence of Spacetime*. Dutton.

Deleuze, Gilles. 1990. *The Logic of Sense*. Athlone.

———. 1994. *Difference and Repetition*. Continuum.

Deleuze, Gilles, and Felix Guattari. 1983. *Anti-Oedipus: Capitalism and Schizophrenia*. University of Minnesota Press.

Deutsch, David. 2012. *The Beginning of Infinity: Explanations that Transform the World*. Penguin.

Deutsch David, and Michael Lockwood. 1994. The Quantum Physics of Time Travel. *Scientific American* 270:3.

Dostoevsky, Fyodor. 1990. *The Brothers Karamazov*. North Point Press.

Duggan, Gerry. 2018. *Infinity Countdown*. Marvel.

Davies P. 2002. How to Build a Time Machine. *Scientific American* 287:3.

Descartes, René. 1999. *Discourse on Method and Meditations on First Philosophy*. Hackett.

Earman J., C. Wüthrich, and J. Manchak. 2016. Time Machines. *Stanford Encyclopedia of Philosophy*.

Eco, Umberto. 1972. Review: The Myth of Superman. *Diacritics* 2:1 (Spring).

Eisenberg, Eric. 2013. Joss Whedon Explains Why He's Limiting Ultron's Powers in the Avengers Sequel. *Cinemablend*.

Ewald, William, and Wilfried Sieg, eds. 2013. *David Hilbert's Lectures on the Foundations of Arithmetic and Logic, 1917–1933*. Springer.

Feige, K., producer, and J. Gunn, director. 2014. *Guardians of the Galaxy*. Marvel Studios.

Feige, K., producer, and J. Whedon, director. 2012. *Avengers*. Marvel Studios.

Feige, K., producer, J. Russo, and A. Russo, directors. 2018. *Avengers: Infinity War*. Marvel Studios.

Feige, K., producer, J. Russo, and A. Russo, directors. 2019. *Avengers: Endgame*. Marvel Studios.

Feldman Jerome. 2013. The Neural Binding Problem(s). *Cognitive Neurodynamics* 7:1.

Freud, Sigmund. 1990. *Jokes and Their Relation to the Unconscious*. Norton.

———. 2010. *Civilization and Its Discontents*. Norton.

Fry, Charles, ed. 2018. *The Word of the Cross: Martin Luther's Heidelberg Disputation*. 1517 Publishing.

Gruner, Charles R. 2017. *The Game of Humor: A Comprehensive Theory of Why We Laugh*. Routledge.

Hardin, Garrett. 1968. The Tragedy of the Commons. *Science* 162:3859.

Heidegger, Martin. 1962. *Being and Time*. Blackwell.

———. 1997. *Filosofía, Ciencia, y Técnica*. Editorial Universitaria (Chile).

———. 2008. *Basic Writings*. HarperCollins.

Hilbert, David. 2013. Über das Unendliche. In Wilfried and Sieg 2013.

Hobbes, Thomas. 1994. *Leviathan*. Hackett.

Homer. 1997. *Iliad*. Hackett.

Horkheimer, Max. 2013. *Eclipse of Reason*. Bloomsbury.

Jackson, Frank. 1991. Decision-Theoretic Consequentialism and the Nearest and Dearest Objection. *Ethics* 101.

Kant, Immanuel. 1979 [1798]. *The Conflict of the Faculties*. University of Nebraska Press.

———. 1993. *Grounding for the Metaphysics of Morals*. Hackett.

Kastrup, Bernardo. 2017. On the Plausibility of Idealism: Refuting Criticisms. *Sciendo*.

Kean, Sam. 2014. Phineas Gage: Neuroscience's Most Famous Patient. *Slate*.

Kierkegaard, Søren. 1941 [1846]. *Concluding Unscientific Postscript*. Princeton University Press.

———. 2003 [1843]. *Fear and Trembling*. Penguin.

Klossowski, P. 1997. *Nietzsche and the Vicious Circle*. University of Chicago Press.

Lacan, Jacques. 1981. *The Four Fundamental Concepts of Psychoanalysis (1964–1965): The Seminar of Jacques Lacan Book XI*. Norton.

———. 2006. *Écrits: The First Complete Edition in English*. Norton.

———. 2008. *The Ethics of Psychoanalysis (1959–1960): The Seminar of Jacques Lacan Book VII*. Routledge.

Lanthimos, Y., director. 2017. *The Killing of a Sacred Deer*. Curzon Artificial Eye.

Lee, Stan. 2019. *Marvel Encyclopedia: New Edition*. DK.

Levinas, Emmanuel. 2000. *God, Death, and Time*. Stanford University Press.

Lewis, David. 1976. The Paradoxes of Time Travel. *American Philosophical Quarterly* 13:2 (April).

Lipton, Peter 1991. *Inference to the Best Explanation*. Routledge.

Locke, John. 1996. *An Essay concerning Human Understanding*. Hackett.

Lose, David. 1999. The Ambidextrous God: Luther on Faith and Politics. *Word and World* XIX:3.

Malthus, Thomas Robert. 2015 [1798]. *An Essay on the Principle of Population and Other Writings*. Penguin.

McKay, Claude. 2018. *Harlem Shadows: The Poems of Claude McKay*. Martino.

Mencken, H.L. 1922. *Prejudices: Second Series*. Knopf.

Merleau-Ponty, Maurice. 2013. *Phenomenology of Perception*. Routledge.

Mill, John Stuart. 2002. *Utilitarianism*. Hackett.

———. 2015. *On Liberty, Utilitarianism, and Other Essays*. Oxford University Press.

Machiavelli, Niccolò. 2009. *Discourses on Livy*. Oxford University Press.

———. 2010. *The Prince*. Hackett.

Nietzsche, Friedrich. 1969. *On the Genealogy of Morals*. Vintage.

————. 2009. *Thus Spoke Zarathustra: A Book for Everyone and Nobody*. Oxford University Press.

Nitobe, Inazo. 2014 [1900]. *Bushido: The Soul of Japan*. Kodansha.

Nubiola, Jaime. 2005. Abduction or the Logic of Surprise. *Semiotica*.

Parfit, Derek. 1984. *Reasons and Persons*. Oxford University Press.

Pascal, Blaise. 2008. *Pensées and Other Writings*. Oxford University Press.

Peirce, Charles Sanders. 1878. Deduction, Induction, and Hypothesis. *Popular Science Monthly*.

————. 2014. *Illustrations of the Logic of Science*. Open Court.

Pilgrim, Will Corona. 2018. *Avengers: Infinity War Prelude Issue #1*. Marvel.

————. 2018. *Avengers: Infinity War Prelude Issue #2*. Marvel.

Plato. 1989. *Symposium*. Hackett.

————. 2002. *Five Dialogues: Euthyphro, Apology, Crito, Meno, Phaedo*. Hackett.

Radin, Paul. 1987. *The Trickster: A Study in American Indian Mythology*. Schocken.

Russo, Joe, and Anthony Russo, directors. 2018. *Avengers: Infinity War*. Marvel Studios.

Russo, Joe, and Anthony Russo, directors. 2019. *Avengers: Endgame*. Marvel Studios.

Sartre, Jean-Paul. 1992 [1943]. *Being and Nothingness: An Essay on Phenomenological Ontology*. Simon and Schuster.

————. 2007. Existentialism Is a Humanism. Yale University Press.

Schachner, Nathaniel. 1933. Ancestral Voices. *Astounding Stories* (December).

Schmitt, Carl. 1986. *Political Romanticism*. MIT Press.

————. 2008. *Political Theology: Four Chapters on the Concept of Sovereignty*. University of Chicago Press.

Schopenhauer, Arthur. 1966. *The World as Will and Representation*. Volume 2. Dover.

Smeenk, C., and C. Wüthrich. 2010. Time Travel and Time Machines. In Callender 2010.

Soler, F. 1997. Prologo. In Heidegger 1997.

Starlin, Jim. 1982. *Warlock*. Marvel.

————. 2019. *The End*. Marvel.

————. 2018. *Silver Surfer: Rebirth of Thanos*. Marvel.

————. 2019. *The Infinity Gauntlet*. Marvel.

Starlin, Jim, and Stan Lee. 2013. *The Avengers Annual* 7. Marvel.

Starlin, Jim, and Tom Raney. 1993. *The Warlock Chronicles*. Marvel.

SuperMegaMonkey. 1985–2020. Marvel Comics Chronology <http://www.supermegamonkey.net/chronocomic/entries/marvel_two-in-one_50.shtml>.

Thomas, Roy. 2007. *Warlock*. Marvel.

Troyer, John, ed. 2003. *The Classical Utilitarians: Bentham and Mill*. Hackett.

Williams, D.C. 1951. The Myth of Passage. *Journal of Philosophy* 58:15.

————. 2018. *The Elements and Patterns of Being: Essays in Metaphysics*. Oxford University Press.

Wittgenstein, Ludwig. 2009. *Philosophical Investigations*. Wiley-Blackwell.

Yudkowsky, Eliezer. Pascal's Mugging: Tiny Probabilities of Vast Utilities. *Lesswrong*. <https://www.lesswrong.com/posts/a5JAiTdytou3Jg749/pascal-s-mugging-tiny-probabilities-of-vast-utilities>.

Guardians of Philosophy

JOHN ALTMANN is an independent scholar in philosophy who writes primarily on philosophy of disability and who has worked closely with the Avengers in fighting ableism across the globe including Thanos's pro-eugenics mindset with his belief in The Snap.

ADAM BARKMAN is Professor of Philosophy at Redeemer University. He is the author or editor of a dozen books, most recently *A Critical Companion to Robert Zemeckis* (2020). While he wouldn't mind having a beer with Fanboy Thor, the Worthy Thor is why we care about this stuff in the first place.

RAY BOSSERT is a senior learning designer at University of Maryland Global Campus. He holds a doctorate in early modern English literature from University of Maryland College Park. His Avengers code name is Captain Tsundoku. (Shout out to all of his Geek Lit students from F&M and NDMU: GeekLit4eva!)

BENJAMIN CARPENTER is a doctoral research student at the University of East Anglia, UK—the arts center of which once served as the Avengers' home base. They did not allow him onto the set. His research pursues the idea of the self, and how it gets used in contemporary identity politics.

TALIA DINSTEIN is a junior at Byram Hills High School and loves to spend her (non-existent) free time watching and rewatching Marvel movies. She gives credit to her father, Orrie Dinstein, for providing advice on how to Thanos-snap away half of her original eighteen-page draft, and to her teacher, Mr. Andriello for introducing her to this opportunity and offering insight along the way.

AMBER S. DONOVAN is an aspiring philosopher currently studying at Durham University. She spends most of her time reading, writing, and thinking about how to be a good person and enjoys testing these ideas on fictional characters. So, when her Facebook feed was spammed with "Thanos did nothing wrong" memes she naturally spent way too much time thinking about why exactly he did. If she had the Infinity Gauntlet she'd give everyone perfect moral vision.

CHARLENE ELSBY is the Philosophy Program Director and Assistant Professor of Philosophy at Purdue University Fort Wayne, specializing in Aristotle and realist phenomenology. She is the author of *Asses, Arrows, and Undead Cats: An Introduction to Philosophy through Paradox*. Like Captain Marvel, Charlene Elsby has been known to singlehandedly destroy the spaceships of intergalactic warlords.

DUNCAN GALE is in the Endgame of Phase Three of his PhD in Philosophy of Religion at Claremont Graduate University. He's also an adjunct professor of philosophy at Chaffey College in Rancho Cucamonga, California. He continues to hold out hope for the possibility of time travel so that he can watch all twenty-three Marvel Cinematic Universe movies in a single day.

ANGEL LUIS GONZALEZ (who writes as Angel L.G.) is an independent scholar and author of *Despite Wisdom* and *Despite Paradise*. Ironically, while working on his next book, *Despite Luck*, his laptop was mysteriously pierced by an arrow with a note attached that was signed "Ronin."

DRU GRAHAM is a graduate student in philosophy at McMaster University. He is interested in perspectives rarely explored in all fields of inquiry, especially metaphysics and social philosophy, and so is a kindred spirit to those who think Batman the real villain and white privilege's time is up with Sam Wilson Captain America.

JAMES HART is a PhD student at the University of Reading, studying the structure of ethics. If he could have one superpower it would be to gain knowledge by osmosis, that way he could learn just by being surrounded by smarter people. Plus, the less concentrated he is, the better it would work!

SUSAN HEMPINSTALL is a consultant with the Department of National Defense at HQ in Ottawa, Canada. While acquiring her PhD at the University of Ottawa (Philosophy of Mind and Artificial Intelligence), she was employed maintaining the University's mainframe student information system where she took particular pleasure identifying and removing system level bottlenecks. At her present posting she enjoys unraveling snags in the universal fabric of pay systems, but prefers to consider her efforts to be more in line with the Doctor of the UK media universe as opposed to the Marvel one.

During his childhood years in the mystical little village Halsua, Finland, JARNO HIETALAHTI received a strange new power of universal humanism. He has harnessed this power for the ultimate good; to serve the ever-growing field of philosophy of humor. His recent years at the University of Jyväskylä have not gone in vain; Dr. Hietalahti now understands how humane humor is possible. The next step will be to understand the possibilities of superhuman humor!

LEONARD KAHN is Associate Professor and Chair of the Department of Philosophy at Loyola University New Orleans. His teaching and research are primarily in moral theory and applied ethics. He has edited or co-edited three books: *Mill on Justice*; *Consequentialism and Environmental Ethics*; and *Mill's 'On Liberty'*. He has published articles in *Philosophical Studies*; *Ethical Theory and Moral Practice*; *The Journal of Moral Philosophy*; *Ethics, Policy, and Environment*; *Essays in Philosophy*, and *Theoretical and Applied Ethics*, as well as chapters in several philosophy books.

JOHN V. KARAVITIS took *Groot* as an elective in college. It took a lot of self-discipline, seeing as how it's an incredibly abstruse, confusing, enigmatic, incomprehensible, mystifying, perplexing, and unfathomable—dare I say *alien*—tongue. But John, being a cunning linguist, took to it like a fish to water. Here, I'll give you a brief example. John once told me: "I am John V. Karavitis! I am John V. Karavitis! I am John V. Karavitis! I am John V. Karavitis! I am John V. Karavitis!" (Oops! I should have left out that last sentence! Hope the editors don't speak *Groot!*)

J. KEEPING is an associate professor at York University in Toronto, Canada. He grew up on Marvel Comics and later moved on to reading and writing science fiction. He has published scholarly articles too numerous to count (assuming you get bored and give up at six or seven) on topics ranging from Nietzsche's will to power to the phenomenology of animal consciousness.

DIEGO PÉREZ LASSERRE is Researcher at the Law School, Universidad San Sebastián, Valdivia, Chile.

KING-HO LEUNG, a son of Hong Kong, is Research Fellow in Philosophical Theology at the University of St. Andrews, and previously Lecturer in Philosophy and Theology at the University of Chester.

JONATHAN LYONHART is a writer, philosopher and ordained minister. He has a wide range of interests that he publishes about, including phenomenology, film studies, early modern philosophy, and the philosophy of time and space. He and his wife Madison live in the UK together with their twin boys, Søren and Augustine.

TUOMAS W. MANNINEN is a Senior Lecturer at Arizona State University, West Campus, where he teaches courses in critical thinking, philosophy of mind, political philosophy, and other assorted topics. He has realized that with philosophy, as with time-travel, either it's all a joke, or none of it is. Like Natasha, he likes to cut his PB&J diagonally—and maybe even for the same reason. He lives in Phoenix, Arizona, with his wife, Bertha, and two daughters, Michelle and Julia.

MARCO MARCHESIN is a doctoral research student at the University of East Anglia, UK. His research is interested in the philosophy of Wittgenstein and his ideas on logic and meaning. In his free time, Marco tries to solve the paradox of the old Cap in the bench at the end of *Avengers: Endgame*. No success so far.

T.J. MCSHERRY is completing his BA in Philosophy at American Military University while he serves on active duty. His primary areas of interest include ethics, aesthetics, and the philosophy of theater/drama. T.J. has haphazardly stumbled with relative success into most of his life choices, and the Marvel character he most relates to is the mouse who unwittingly pushes a button to bring back Ant-Man from the Quantum Realm—without whom the Snap would not be undone.

ADAM T. MORTON, a son of Minnesota, is a PhD candidate at the University of Nottingham. Like Steve Rogers and Tony Stark, Adam and King-Ho have put aside their differences on Luther to work for the greater good. While King-Ho is trying not to end up like fat Thor after the fall of his hometown, Adam is still in mourning for Ant-Man's taco.

PHILIP M. MOUCH reads comics and teaches philosophy at Minnesota State University Moorhead.

EDWARDO PÉREZ trained in Kamar Taj with the Axe of Angarruumus and the Vaulting Boots of Valtoor (sorry Mordo, for stealing your shoes). Edwardo imparts his rhetorical wisdom as a professor of English, writing essays and blogs, studying popular culture, and contemplating the philosophy of the multiverse and other dimensions. In his spare time, Edwardo apprentices with Eitri in Niðavellir, learning how to forge his own version of Dragonfang.

RODRIGO FARÍAS RIVAS was bitten by a radioactive copy of *The Anti-Christ* at age fifteen. His origin story then led him to major in philosophy and clinical psychology in his home country of Chile, and his current gritty reboot has him finishing a PhD in philosophy in Chile and the Netherlands. He has written about Wittgenstein, Heidegger, Lacan, Foucault, and Deleuze, but his true calling is making a superhero movie in which an overhuman philology professor ends up defeating a giant CGI representation of Western nihilism in the streets of nineteenth-century Turin.

REBECCA SHEARER, your friendly neighborhood moral philosopher, is an independent scholar studying how pop culture influences the moral decisions of those who consume it. She writes by night and keeps her crime-fighting identity a secret by working at a marketing agency by day.

TOM STEIN is an in-house patent agent for NOKIA Oy in Ottawa, Canada. While acquiring his BASc (Systems Design Engineering, University of Waterloo) there was a particular class assignment involving translating MIT's *"Limits to Growth"* model into Waterloo's modelling language—and as part of the assignment, making the future have a happy ending. The difficulties were edifying. In terms of the Marvel Universe, Tom is most sympathetic with JARVIS—as patent agents know, engineers hate documentation—and it's pretty clear who has to document Tony Stark's cutting-edge designs as he fiddles in his millionaire's workshop.

CHAD WILLIAM TIMM is an Associate Professor of Teacher Education at Simpson College in Indianola, Iowa. He's spent the last ten years teaching philosophy of education courses and helping future teachers become Socratic heroes. His students often refer to him as Doctor Strange and while he hopes they are referring to the similarities with his favorite Marvel Avenger, he's inclined to believe they just think he's weird.

KATELYN BOTSFORD TUCKER holds a Master of Arts in Teaching from Sacred Heart University and a Master of Arts in American Studies from Fairfield University. She is a writer and middle-school social studies teacher. She reminds students daily that with great power comes great responsibility and, on occasion, to stop playing Galaga. She resides in Connecticut with her husband, two children, and pet flerken.

EARL A.P. VALDEZ writes different essays and journal articles particularly on French phenomenology and the history of Catholic Christian theology, having published works particularly on Blaise

Pascal, St. Thomas Aquinas, and the French Catholic thinker Jean-Luc Marion. He also does research on twentieth-century Catholic theology, especially the Second Vatican Council and the years that led up to it. He did his master's degrees on Philosophy and Theology, and once dreamed of being in the ten most intelligent people in the world, in the ranks of Amadeus Cho and Reed Richards. This dream was largely unfulfilled, but he still finds that this life as a scholar and cleric, one among fourteen million possible outcomes, has been meaningful so far.

HAYDEN WEISS is a high-school sophomore in attendance at Byram Hills High School in Armonk, New York. He's a dedicated member of the debate team and has a passion for pop culture. As someone who has seen every Marvel movie ever released, the opportunity to write a paper on the pinnacle of the Marvel cinematic universe was an awesome one. Ever since he was old enough to understand the idea of a superhero, it has been a staple of his interests and though he wasn't old enough to watch the original *Iron Man* as it was released, he's seen each Marvel Cinematic Universe movie many times over.

PHILIP WILSON is Lecturer in Philosophy at the University of East Anglia. His publications include *Literary Translation: Re-drawing the Boundaries* (with Jean Boase-Beier and Antoinette Fawcett); *The Bright Rose*; *Translation after Wittgenstein*; and *The Routledge Handbook of Translation and Philosophy* (with Piers Rawling). He first encountered the Avengers in the pages of *Terrific* comic in the Sixties and is very happy that they continue to assemble

RHYS WOODWARDS graduated from Kings College London in 2020, with a keen interest in Philosophy of Mind, Perception, Modal Metaphysics and the philosophy of Nietzsche. He's looking for funding for postgraduate studies so if there's anyone out there . . . Just like Scott Lang, Rhys always looks confused and like he's got no idea what he's doing here. He's insistent that he's got the body of Thor (in *Endgame*) and Bruce Banner's brains (in *Ragnarok*).